DESIGNERS

Marie Wallin • Martin Storey • Lisa Richardson
Kaffe Fassett • Brandon Mably • Sarah Hatton
Amanda Crawford • Julia Frank • Josh Bennett
Ruth Green • Vibe Ulrik • Galina Carroll

INCLUDES 34 DESIGNS

& 3 EXCLUSIVE
R O W @ N
FREE PATTERNS

R O W A N

EDITOR'S LETTER

Gosh it's been a long winter and its not quite over yet. However at this time of year when we release the summer edition of the Rowan Magazine it feels like summer is just around the corner. When you first flick through Magazine 53 you will be bedazzled by the bright colours and sunshine of the warm days to come.

My favourite story has to be 'Glorious' which was shot on the beautiful island of Santorini, you can almost feel the sun on your skin. The colourful natural backdrops are echoed in the simple and ornate floral, pretty lace and crochet stitches. The flavour is of the 1950's and 1960's with neat little knits in multicoloured yarns and floral Jacquards coming together perfectly with the season's full or flippy skirts. Playful, fun and supremely feminine I love this story, it is so uplifting. The icing on the cake for me is the local villagers that add a different dimension and turn the whole look of the shoot into a film set. In many ways it takes me back to my childhood of Mediterranean holidays in a caravan when life was so much simpler.

If flowers are not your thing and you prefer a more geometric design to knit then 'Ikon' will be the story for you. Inspired by technology you have pixilated digital patterning contrasting against the bold graphics of the Modernist age. This is a collection of clean, sophisticated but fun women's and men's knits. Colour blocking is still strong from last season in clear and bright colours mixed amongst white and black. Silhouettes are elegant with long, lean shapes with graphic details. Retro influence of the 1960's inspires this 'New Mod' look. Geometric inserts, stripes, contrasting trims update simple summer styles with an emphasis on youthful fun and easy to wear style.

Since this season is heavily patterned it is an excellent opportunity to take up colour knitting if you have not done so already. Learn how to Fairisle and intarsia through our new on-line tutorials, just go onto the KnitRowan website and become a Row@n member and all the tutorial and other content is absolutely free.

Enjoy whatever challenge you take on this season and as always happy knitting.

Kate Buller
Rowan Brand Manager

ON THE COVER
Santorini by Marie Wallin
Photographer Peter Christian Christensen
Art Direction & Styling Marie Wallin
Hair & Make-up Frances Prescott (One Make Up)
Model Sandra Berube (Leni's Model Management)

Rowan Brand Manager Kate Buller
Rowan Head Designer Marie Wallin
Design & Publications Manager David MacLeod
Marketing and Publications Co-ordinator Lyndsay Kaye
Graphic Designer Web and Print Karl Hallam
Rowan Graphic Designer Paul Calvert
Graphic Designer and Web Assistant James Knapton
Rowan Designer & Pattern Editor Lisa Richardson
Rowan Assistant Designer Gemma Atkinson
Yarn & Photoshoot Co-ordinator Ann Hinchliffe
Garment Co-ordinator Vicky Sedgwick
Knitting Co-ordinator Andrea McHugh
Garment finishing Lisa Parnaby & Pauline Ellis

Rowan Magazine Design Layout Simon Wagstaff

Commercial Director Emma Mychajlowskyj
Marketing Manager Emma Irving

With special thanks to the following handknitters:
Ann Newton, Marjorie Pickering, Audrey Kidd,
Yvonne Rawlinson, Val Deeks, Andrea McHugh, Linda Watson,
Ros Miller, Janet Oakey, Jenny Shore, Ann Banks, Wendy Stevens,
Linda Szemiako, Angela Cheyne, Clare Landi, Pauline Ellis,
Cindy Noble, Honey Ingram, Carol Bayless, Joyce Limon,
Sally Bentley, Jyoti More, Lisa Parnaby, Diane Armstrong,
Dorothy Dawson, Paula Dukes, Helen Betts, Sarah Dennis,
Lisa Winter, Jean Pulcella, Margaret Morris, Sophia Reed,
Judith Chamberlain and Janet Mann.

First published in Great Britain in 2012 by Coats Crafts UK.
Green Lane Mill, Holmfirth, West Yorkshire, England, HD9 2DX
E-mail: mail@knitrowan.com

British Library Cataloguing in Publication Data
Rowan Yarns.
Rowan Knitting & Crochet Magazine Number 53
ISSN 2045-340X

Copyright Coats Crafts UK 2012
Printed in the UK
Reprographics by Gloss Solutions

CONTENTS

Visit our website **www.knitrowan.com** to download your **FREE R O W@N** exclusive patterns.

ROWAN

glorious

.....is inspired by the joy and happiness
induced by the summer sun and an
abundance of flowers. Pretty lace stitches
and flowers of all shapes and sizes are at
the heart of this playful, fun and very
feminine collection.

SANTORINI
Purelife Revive & Wool Cotton
Marie Wallin
🧶104

x

z

7

SYMI WRAP
Fine Lace & Kidsilk Haze
Vibe Ulrik
🧶 89

Kos
Siena 4ply
Marie Wallin
98

ARTEMIS
Purelife Revive & Kidsilk Haze
Lisa Richardson
90

SAMOS
Fine Lace
Vibe Ulrik
🧶 102

KEFALONIA
Wool Cotton 4ply & Kidsilk Haze
Marie Wallin
🧶 95

Photographer: Peter Christian Christensen. **Styling:** Marie Wallin. **Hair & Make Up:** Frances Prescott (One Make Up). **Art Direction:** Marie Wallin. **Model:** Sandra Berube (Leni's Model Management). **Production:** Key productions – Many thanks to Yorgos Galaziis. **Location:** Photographed on the island of Santorini.

HALKIDIKI
Fine Lace & Kidsilk Haze
Marie Wallin
111

Vibe Ulrik

Words by Dr Margy Cockburn

There we were, walking together along London's Southbank, on the opening week of the 2012 Olympics, chatting about how designer Vibe Ulrik finds her inspiration. My eyes were popping as we wove our way through the throngs of face-painted, flag-waving, sports fans and pink and purple-garbed stewards sharing semaphore signals and maps of London to keep the crowd moving. We'd just passed a steel band, a unicyclist, a waving stone statue, an uncanny Michael Jackson look-alike and were somewhere between a Peruvian man impossibly balancing his partner on a thin wooden stick and a Viking complete with fur waistcoat and horned helmet, when Vibe stopped me and whispered "There!". I expected at least a fire-eating, Flamenco dancer but her interest had been captured by a lady wearing a white waffle-stitch dress.

"That's the sort of thing I notice. I am always on the lookout for inspiration and I am fascinated by texture and touch. I always keep an eye out for good models as well. In fact, I sometimes feel a bit as if I am stalking people," she adds in a soft voice that perfectly matches her cool beauty. Spotting a particularly striking five-year-old was part of the story of how Vibe came to be a guest designer in this issue. But a bit of a rewind is needed for the full story.

Vibe was brought up in Denmark. Her mother was a fashion designer with a studio attached to the house, so from an early age, Vibe developed a visual acuity and an awareness of the importance of quality and detail. But it was her Grandmother who honed her knitting skills.

"My sister and I spent a lot of time with our Grandma and she used to get us both to knit, probably to keep us quiet, but it wasn't really

03

04

something I spent a lot of time doing. I rather drifted along and when the time came to choose something to do at College, I opted to go and stay with some relatives in California, to do a year's photography course."

For a variety of reasons, the return to Copenhagen at the end of the course was not a happy one so Vibe decided a change was needed and flew to London where she got a job with the iconic lifestyle store The Conran Shop, and loved every minute of it. She overheard friends talking about Kingston University being a good college for design and on a bit of whim, applied to do a fashion design course.

"I was completely clueless really. I remember waiting for the interview and looking at the other candidates clutching large story boards and suitcases full of garments. I had made precisely two things and then photographed them with an old bike against a brick wall: a jacket in some loosely woven linen I'd found in Berwick Street market and a skirt without a zip that you could call 'unstructured' but was actually like that because I had no idea how to put a zip in."

It was a good decision. Vibe made lots of friends, started putting Granny's training to good use, and was set on her path. After graduating (and some months tumbling through the usual frustrating cycle of not being offered a job …because you haven't the experience… because no one will offer you a job!) she took an internship with Nicole Farhi - a time of reading lots of books to perfect different stitch techniques and designing swatch selections. Then came the meeting with the arresting five-year old which offered a way to perfectly meld Vibe's two passions – design and photography. Vibe plucked up the courage to ask the mother if she would

allow her daughter to model some knitwear, obtained the same permission from the mother of another beautiful, half-Spanish, half-Japanese, three-year old (whom she also just happened upon) and despite communication being a tad difficult, the photo shoot went well and voila, Vibe had the basis for a book.

"I sent out the synopsis to a range of publishers and got lots of polite refusals but, eighteen months later, still no positive interest. I was feeling completely disillusioned and was about to give up and do something less painful, like an office job, when Collins and Brown offered me a contract. I sent some of my designs to Rowan - I have always loved their whole design and aesthetic – they gave me some yarns to use and … here I am."

The hardback: *'Labour of Love – Over 20 Knitting Patterns for Treasured Girls'* got rave reviews and unleashed a collective sigh of longing: "I just wish the patterns would fit me....." Rowan is delighted to oblige and in your hands, you are holding Vibe's first published patterns for grown-ups – a short-sleeved jumper in Frost Flower lace and a summer shawl. Enjoy!

01. Vibe Ulrik
02. Symi Wrap from Glorious.
03 & 04. Samos from Glorious.

ikon

...is inspired by strong Modernist graphic patterning with a 1960's retro feel, creating a clean, sophisticated and fun collection of women's and men's knits.

HIP
Panama, Siena 4ply & Kidsilk Haze
Lisa Richardson
🧶 110

VIDAL
Creative Linen
Josh Bennett
141

40

PIERRE
Handknit Cotton
Marie Wallin
🧶 125

MOD
Handknit Cotton
Ruth Green
🧶 126

BONNIE
Creative Linen
Marie Wallin
🧶 94

LAMBRETTA
Summerspun & Wool Cotton
Brandon Mably
🧶 120

OSSIE
Cotton Glacé
Marie Wallin
🧶 115

51

Photographer: Peter Christian Christensen. **Styling:** Marie Wallin. **Hair & Make Up:** Frances Prescott (One Make Up). **Art Direction:** Marie Wallin. **Set Design:** Veronique Zanettin (www.veroniquezanettin.com). **Models:** Heidi Rock (Premier Model Management), Ralph Ward (Select Model Management).

Sonia Delaunay: and Modernism in Fashion

Words by Dr Kate Davies

01

Today, modern art and fashion seem familiarly hand-in-glove. Patricia Field uses the work of Keith Haring to define her version of New York style; Yayoi Kusama collaborates with Louis Vuitton to create novel polka-dotted accessories; Phillip Lim appropriates the art of Roy Lichtenstein to lend his latest collection graphic edge. This contemporary fashion / art symbiosis is at its most obvious -- perhaps at its most simple -- in Lisa Perry's recent work. Perry is a fashionable art collector as much as a fashion designer, and in her Madison Avenue store -- its bright space-age interior echoing the set-design of Kubrick's 2001 -- you'll find sharp, neatly-cut shift dresses decorated with the work of De Kooning or Ellsworth Kelly. Perry treats the dress as a blank canvas upon which the work of her favourite artists might be showcased. Her work is frequently lauded as "new-mod" or "futuristic" for its minimal lines, its optimism, its bold use of colour, and, of course, for its explicit grandstanding of the works of modern art that she most admires. But Perry's modernist dress of the future also has a past.

Rewind to 1911. A woman sits in a Paris apartment, stitching a quilt for her son. She selects disparate scraps of cloth, placing blocks and stripes and chevrons of coloured fabric in jarring, daring juxtaposition. The high-contrast result is bold and pleasing to her. She looks around at her apartment, its dark and fussy decoration, its heavy, ornate furniture. Something must be done. Little by little, she embarks upon the radical re-design of the spaces in which she lives. The walls are simply rendered, the furniture is replaced by minimal, modern pieces, and the rooms are gradually transformed into a series of blank planes that seem to wait to be enlivened. The woman continues to cut and stitch, to paint and to embroider. A set of curtains here, a pair of cushions there. Upon the wall, she daubs and hangs a canvas of interlocking discs lit up with incandescence. Turning to her own garb, she adopts loose, unstructured clothing, counteracting her garments' economy of line with bold, swirling, surface colour. The woman's world is now awash with dynamic hues and her lived environment -- clothes, furnishings, paintings,

01. YSL Mondrian Dress.

02. Dancer wearing a Delaunay costume from 'La P'tit Parigot' (1929). Image reproduced with courtesy of the Library of Congress.

03. 'Jeff Koons Monkey Train Dress by Lisa Perry. © Lisa Perry LLC.

04. Sonia Delaunay design from 'Sonia Delaunay: Ses Peintures, Ses Objets, Ses Tissus Simultanes' (1923-5). Image reproduced with courtesy of the Fashion Institute of Technology Special Collections.

05. Women 'on the move'. American actress, Myrna Loy in flying goggles. Image reproduced with courtesy of the Library of Congress.

decorative objects - have all become part of the same wild collage. This woman is Sonia Delaunay, whose distinctive aesthetic and many talents made her central to the development of modernist fashion design.

Born in Ukraine, and educated in St Petersburg, Sonia Terk's background was privileged, and her education wide-ranging. She excelled in mathematics, needlework and painting, debuting her talents in the latter with a solo show in Paris in 1908. It was in Paris that she met Robert Delaunay -- one of the early Cubist group of artists interested in transforming contemporary theories of colour. While Robert's canvases explored new ways of making colour itself the subject of art, Sonia brought her own sense of colour to life in a perhaps far bolder and more extensive way, moving beyond fine art to household textiles, theatre, poetry, film, print, interior design, commercial illustration and, of course, fashion.

Delaunay's early approach to colour was exemplified in La Prose du Transsiberien, a 1913 collaboration with Swiss poet, Blaise Cendrars. Over the unfolding pages of this spectacular book-object, (published at some considerable expense by Cendrars himself) text and colour were brought together in a unique relationship. Cendrars' words, and Delaunay's colours intermingle, collide, wrap around each other. Delaunay was not merely illustrating Cendrars' text, nor was she developing what might be regarded as a simple dialogue between text and image. Rather, her contribution to La Prose du Transsiberien was to enable colour to become a creative participant in the poetry itself. Delaunay's rhythmic swirls and splotches produce alternate dissonance and harmony, dynamism and movement, traveling across and around, up and down the page, as Cendrars' narrator takes an uneasy journey through the conflict and chaos of revolutionary Russia. In the final section, text and image are jointly illuminated with energy as the narrator arrives in Paris, with its bustling streets, new technologies, and iconic constructs -- most notably the Eiffel Tower, which announces itself joyously in Delaunay's brilliant blocks of colour. Each printed copy of La Prose du Transsiberien was contained in a wrapper declaring itself to be "the first simultaneous book," neither text nor artwork, but an object that demanded to be seen and read at the same time. Cendrars and Delaunay had together painted a picture of words, and written a poetry of colour.

"Simultaneous" was a word that Delaunay applied to much of her work -- paintings, illustrations, printed textiles, and embroideries. The word "simultaneous" referred primarily to her particular take on hue (in which contrasts co-exist, lending images and fabrics movement and multiplicity), but extended beyond this to describe her collaborative and often multidisciplinary methods of working. Delaunay's exuberant idea of the "simultaneous" meant that she might regard the making of a dress, a dance, a poem, a painting, a hat, a melody, a film, a building or a bookbinding -- as part of the same energetic creative process. While other artists of her generation struggled with disciplinary boundaries, she happily ignored the distinctions that were assumed to exist between fine and applied art, or indeed between art, craft, and commercial design. Certainly, her distinctive brio as artist and designer derives from her confident handling of so many different media. "For me" she wrote: "there was no gap between my painting and what is called my decorative work ... I never considered the minor arts to be artistically frustrating: on the contrary, it was an extension of my art, it showed me new ways while using the same method."

After the dark days of the First World War (which the Delaunays spent in exile in Portugal and Spain), Paris began to reinvent itself anew as the quintessential modernist city. The world seemed to suddenly spring to life with energy and rhythm: electricity, mass production, jazz. Delaunay's work chimed with the moment, its new sense of optimism, its dynamism, its bright variety and contrast. She began a series of

productive collaborations with like-minded artists in a wide range of fields. She was commissioned by Sergei Diaghilev to create costumes for the Ballets Russes, produced robes poemes with Tristan Tszara, and worked with film makers Rene le Somptier and Marcel L Herbier on costume and set design. Delaunay developed a particular interest in dance, becoming fascinated by the relationship between the body and the textiles that clothed it. For someone who regarded "colour as the skin of the world" it seemed obvious that dress might become a sort of mobile, dynamic tattoo. Delaunay's friend Blaise Cendrars, celebrated the effect of her clothing in his famous poem On her Dress she has a Body, and Delaunay herself regarded the wearing of "simultaneous" clothing as a sort of physical performance. She and Robert sported her brilliant simultaneous outfits at Parisian balls and cultural events, attracting considerable attention from their contemporaries. This idea of dress as performative, wearable art, resonated with many modernist movements, including the constructivists, surrealists, and of course the futurists (who made clothing central to their manifestos).

Delaunay began to receive commissions, and swiftly rose to prominence as a commercial textile designer. She was just as confident in the world of fashion as she was in that of fine art, declaring herself incredibly frustrated with the trends that had dominated the 1910s, condemning the hobble skirt ("the skirt is not adapted to walking, but walking to the skirt, which is nonsense") and what she saw as the pointless "multiplied refinements" of Art Nouveau. Like Chanel, she favoured a total economy of line and garments in which form clearly followed function. "Dress," wrote Delaunay, "must be adapted to the necessities of daily life, to the movements which it dictates." Her modern customers were clearly in agreement. In Paris, Baudelaire's male flaneur had transformed into the female flapper: women were cutting their hair, wearing dresses they could dance in, and adopting the mode garçonne. Delaunay was keen to design modern clothes for modern women, clothes with a purpose and function to the fore. Her simultaneous fashions were meant to move with the body that moved in them. She designed hats to drive in; skirts to dance in; swimsuits to swim in; thick coats and wraps in which to swathe the body during a brisk Winter's walk. Her bold garments, in which the female body was animated by the colours and rhythms of the modern city, had found their moment, and were the surprise hit of the 1925 Paris exposition.

"How natural it will be," Robert Delaunay enthused of Sonia's newly popular designs: "to see a woman get out of a sleek new car, her appearance answering to the modernised interior of her home, which is also shaking off its old, dusty cornices to rediscover simple, pure lines. [Sonia Delaunay's simultaneous fashions] are responsive to the painting, to the architecture of modern life, to the bodies of cars, to the beautiful and original forms of airplanes -- in short, to the aspirations of this active, modern age which has forged a style intimately related to its incredibly fast and intense life. [Sonia Delaunay] creates fabrics that are oriented to an era yet to come."

Delaunay suddenly found her talents in great demand, and was celebrated everywhere by fashion writers and cultural commentators as the designer of the "dress of the future."

What was it about Delaunay's simultaneous fashions that made them feel so modern, so very future-oriented, in the 1920s? First, of course, is her particular use of colour. At a first glance, her palettes seem to be almost abandoned, alive with multiple, wild hues, but on closer examination one sees that they are in fact almost minimalist -- generally limited to three or four shades plus neutrals. She tends to use vivid contrasts, and a little tonal shading, in signature arrangements of chevrons and swirling discs. In Delaunay's "simultaneous" outfits, it is these chevrons and zig-zags -- sometimes printed, sometimes rendered in

06. Women 'on the move'. Image reproduced with courtesy of the Library of Congress.

07, 09 & 10. Sonia Delaunay design from 'Sonia Delaunay: Ses Peintures, Ses Objets, Ses Tissus Simultanes' (1923-5). Image reproduced with courtesy of the Fashion Institute of Technology Special Collections.

08. An actor wearing a Delaunay dressing gown from 'La P'tit Parigot' (1929). Image reproduced with courtesy of the Library of Congress.

dense, embroidered satin stitch -- that are key to creating the undulating, almost prismatic effect of movement from her carefully-chosen palettes. Her shapes have rhythm, but they are also freed by a lack of strict regularity (Delaunay often became irritated with those who suggested her designs were geometric as she felt this reduced their vitality and individuality to a sort of painting-by-numbers.)

But Delaunay's simultaneous fashions were also modern, and modernist, in their use of fabric as a plane. Among her contemporaries in couture, her designs were perhaps definitively planar, two-dimensional, in their treatment of material. While other designers (Fortuny; Vionnet) were exploring innovative three-dimensional sculptural techniques of pleating and cutting, Delaunay saw her simply-shaped designs as flat surfaces waiting to be animated by rhythm and colour. (She later described herself as "incapable of sculpting"). The straight-up-and-down shift dress was, then, her ideal blank canvas, and its simple, unobtrusive lines perfectly suited to being transformed by her into a walking work of art. In this sense, her work has much in common with the Bauhaus treatment of planes and surfaces (indeed Walter Gropius was a friend of Delaunay's, and a great admirer of her interiors).

Delaunay had her own vision for fashion's new direction. Designers should not be tempted, she wrote, to take "inspiration derived from the past" but must instead "grapple with the subject as if everything begins anew each day." The work of artists would achieve popular currency, and be properly valued; collaborations with technologists would make beautiful, quality design accessible, affordable and wearable by all, and through improved mass production, fashion would at last "democratise itself, and this democratisation can only be beneficial since it will raise the general standards of the industry." "The future of fashion is very clear to me," she wrote with characteristic confidence.

Delaunay was speaking, of course, with the familiar optimism of the 1920s. Her perspective (as much as her bold aesthetic) is recognisably modernist in its faith in new technology, its wonder at the potential of mass production, and its belief in a better future. Things appeared rather less bright and hopeful over the next few decades, as the world was shaken by economic collapse, horrific war, and its grim aftermath. Delaunay closed the fashion end of her business, continued to paint, and worked closely with the Amsterdam firm, Metz & Co, producing innovative surface designs for textiles. She began to explore the potential of the square, and professed admiration for the work of Piet Mondrian.

Not until the 1960s did Western culture feel an optimism, an energy, a hope for the future comparable with that of the milieu Delaunay had inhabited forty years previously. And how did fashion mark this moment? With a straight up-and-down shift dress whose simple lines were enlivened with a bright and striking work of modern art.

By the late 1950s, mod girls, frustrated with the era's fashions, began to stitch up their own simple shift dresses -- dresses in which they could dance to the rhythms of jazz and soul. Designers such as Andre Courreges took their cue from the street -- raising hems, and radically simplifying the line with the elimination of bust and waist in a manner obviously reminiscent of the 1920s. The season following the first appearance of Courreges' angular mini dresses, Yves Saint Laurent debuted a collection whose show-stopping garment was a shift dress boldy emblazoned with a painting he identified as Piet Mondrian's number 81. Yves Saint Laurent famously declared himself as "a failed painter," but like much of his work, this dress was certainly suggestive of aesthetic innovation rather than deficiency. Situated at the intersections of art, fashion, and popular culture, it spoke powerfully to the moment. By 1965, largely

11. Women 'on the move'. Image reproduced with courtesy of the Library of Congress.

12 & 14. YSL Mondrian Dresses.

13. Marcel Breuer - Tubular Steel Chair, 1928. Image reproduced with courtesy of Hofmobiliendepot.

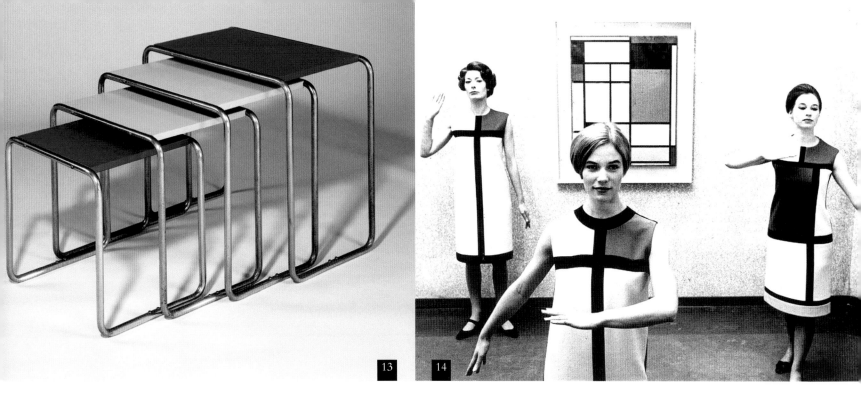

13 14

because of photographic reproductions, the work of Mondrian was so instantly recognisable that it had become iconic. In a canny move, YSL, in effect appropriated that iconic status for his dress which, when it appeared on the cover of Vogue in 1965, created an international sensation. It was hailed by Harper's Bazaar as "the dress of tomorrow" and within weeks, printers and cutters were hard at work creating copycat Mondrian shift dresses for everyone, at every price point. The YSL originals cost around £1800, and were fashioned from high-quality wool jersey. Each coloured block and line was painstakingly cut and individually stitched to create a bold streamlined patchwork. But by 1966, cotton or rayon dresses featuring a Mondrian-esque design printed directly onto the fabric were circulating on the streets of London for between £37 and £60. Then, in a shift that anticipates some of the complexities of the art-fashion nexus today, the popular currency of the YSL dress began to reflect back on the commercial value of the work that had inspired it. As iconic fashion borrowed from iconic art, so art capitalised on fashion as Mondrian's work began to circulate for astronomical sums on the US art market.

In a way, YSL's Mondrian dress achieved Sonia Delaunay's modernist vision of the popularisation of art, and the democratisation of fashion (though Delaunay would have probably preferred it if this had been accomplished through high-end mass production techniques rather than copies of ever-diminishing quality). The Mondrian dress also carried clear echoes of Delaunay's work in its sharp cut, its simple lines, its striking use of colour, and, of course, in the treatment of the garment as canvas. In an interview of 1968, Delaunay dismissed YSL's Mondrian dress as "society entertainment, circus, promotion," but also grumpily conceded its evident debt to her work "clever people have made hundreds of millions from my idea." So was Sonia Delaunay, 1920s designer of the colourful, radical "dress of the future," the first mod? We might certainly remember her vim and originality when contemplating the rather more obvious -- some might even say calculated -- work of contemporary designers like Lisa Perry.

Further Reading:
Shari Benstock, Women of the Left Bank (1986)
Jacques Demase, Sonia Delaunay: Fashion and Fabrics (1976)
Adam Geczy and Vicki Karaminas, eds, Fashion and Art (2012)
Matilda McQuaid and Susan Brown, eds, Colour Moves: Art and Fashion by Sonia Delaunay (2011)
Christopher Wilk, ed., Modernism: Designing a New World (2006).

essentials

is a collection of the key shapes and
textures on trend, designed into more
simple, easy to wear styles that will
complement the season's ESSENTIAL
looks. Using a bright summer colour
palette, ranging from spring greens and
blues to soft neutrals, this is the 'must have'
collection of the season.

THE SEMI-SHEER KNIT

MARSHMALLOW
Kidsilk Haze & Handknit Cotton
Julia Frank
 140

AMARETTO
Panama
Lisa Richardson
🧶 130

BANOFFI

Panama & Siena 4ply

Lisa Richardson

 134

THE
SLASH NECK
CROP

PRALINE
Summerspun
Lisa Richardson
139

RUM & RAISIN
Panama
Amanda Crawford
131

BUBBLEGUM
Panama
Marie Wallin
135

THE
BOXY
LACE
KNIT

COOKIES & CREAM
Creative Linen
Ruth Green
137

HONEYCOMB
Handknit Cotton
Ruth Green
🧶 132

THE
SHAPED
SWEATER

CAPPUCCINO
Panama
Sarah Hatton
136

THE
TEXTURED
CROP

PISTACHIO
Summerspun
Julia Frank

138

TUTTI FRUTTI
Summerspun
Marie Wallin
144

Photographer: Peter Christian Christensen. **Styling:** Marie Wallin. **Hair & Make Up:** Frances Prescott (One Make Up). **Art Direction:** Marie Wallin. **Model:** Caroline Kristiansen (First Model Management).

Love.....
.....cotton

words by Marie Wallin

COTTON is a soft and fluffy fibre that grows forming a protective structure around the cotton seed. The cotton plant is from the *Gossypium* genus and is a shrub native to tropical and subtropical regions around the world. Cotton is one of the world's leading agricultural crops; it is plentiful and economically produced, making cotton products relatively inexpensive to produce. Every part of the cotton plant can be used. The long cotton fibres are spun into yarn or thread and used to make a wide variety of textile products. The short fibres are used by the paper making industries as well as being used in produce 'lint' products such cotton wool and bandages. Cotton seed is widely used as a supplement in dairy feed and is also processed into oil.

HISTORY Cotton was first cultivated approximately 7000 years ago. The earliest cotton fabrics have been found in a cave in Mexico and date from 5800BC. In the Indus valley of Pakistan, cotton was being grown, spun and woven into cloth by 3000BC. At about the same time, natives of Egypt's Nile valley were making and wearing cotton clothing. Arab merchants brought cotton cloth to Europe around 800AD. When Christopher Columbus discovered America in 1492, he found cotton growing in the Bahamas. By 1500, cotton was known throughout the world. The first cultivated cotton grown in America was believed to be planted in Florida in 1556 and in Virginia in 1607. Cotton was first spun by machinery in England in 1730 and the industrial revolution and the invention of the cotton gin paved the way for cotton being one of the most important fibres in the world.

TODAY Cotton is grown in many warm areas of the world which enjoy a climate with at least 200 frost free days annually. The most important cotton growing countries are the USA, China, India, Pakistan and Australia. China produces about 30% of the world's cotton crop, mostly in the eastern part of the country. In the US, cotton is grown in the southern states, the largest producer being Texas.

GROWING Cotton needs a hot and sunny climate to grow. The soil needs to be well drained and rich in nitrogen and the plants require a lot of water during the growing season. In some areas cotton is grown on irrigated land and in most cases the land is treated with chemical fertilisers to improve the soil and increase the nitrogen content. In the spring, cotton seeds are planted in rows invariably by machine or by hand. Three weeks after germination the flower buds begin to form. The flowers are white which turn red before falling from the plant. The flowers produce a green fruit called a boll which contains the seed. White fibres of different lengths grow inside the boll around the seed. Cotton is harvested when the boll matures and bursts revealing the white fibres about 150 to 200 days after planting. Cotton plants are susceptible to pest and weed infestations. Farmers growing conventional cotton use

01

pesticides and herbicides to help combat these problems; even so, about 15% of the world's cotton production is still lost to disease spread by pests. Most cotton is harvested by machine; organic cotton and cotton grown in under-developed countries is harvested by hand.

PROCESSING The first process in turning cotton fibre into cloth is cotton ginning. The gin machine separates the seed from the fibre and during this process the cotton fibre is also cleaned of any dirt, leaves, stems and burs. The cotton fibre is then combed, cleaned, dried and pressed into bales. Cotton buyers or merchants buy the raw cotton which is then sold to textile mills. Here the cotton is spun into yarn and thread for the weaving and knitting industries.

QUALITY Cotton fibre varies in length depending on the variety of cotton grown. The longer the staple length of the fibre, the softer the handle of the fabric produced and therefore higher the quality. Physically the individual cotton fibres consist of a single long tubular cell. Its length is about 1200 to 1500 times that of its width. Length of cotton fibre varies from 16mm to 52mm. The longer the staple length of the cotton fibre, the finer it is. The four types of cotton most commonly grown are: Indian cotton (16mm – 25mm), American cotton (20mm – 30mm), Sea Island cotton (38mm – 52mm) and Egyptian cotton (30mm – 38mm). The best quality cotton is Sea Island cotton.

COTTON FACTS

- Cotton is the most widely produced non edible crop.

- Cotton can grow to a height of 2 metres.

- Consumption of cotton has increased by 2% annually since the mid 1900's.

- Cotton fibre can be made into soft, breathable fabrics such as, velvet, corduroy, jersey, flannel and denim and also knitted to produce machine and hand made garments.

- The short fibres of the cotton boll are used to produce cotton wool, cotton buds, bandages as well as being used in making paper.

- Cotton seed produces oil for cooking which is cholesterol free and high in poly-unsaturated fats.

- Cotton seed oil is also found in soap, margarine, cosmetics and rubber and plastic products.

- Cotton is hypoallergenic.

- Cotton is very easy to dye.

- Cotton is a good conductor of heat, regulating the body's temperature.

- The growth of organic cotton production has increased recently but still only accounts for 0.76% of global cotton production.

Further information:
www.ccgga.org
www.textileclass.com
www.cotton.org
www.cottoncrc.org.au

01. A cotton plant ready for harvesting, the boll has matured and burst revealing the white fibres of cotton.

02. A typical cotton field.

03. A postage stamp from St. Christopher Nevis Anguilla, celebrating the island's Sea Island Cotton.
Picture credit: Solodov Alexey/Shutterstock.com

Scottish Heritage Knits

05

Not long after he had finished the designs for his new book, *Scottish Heritage Knits*, Martin took himself off on a Shetland Island knitting holiday (led by Rowan design consultant Jane Crowfoot). You might think this sounds like 'coals to Newcastle' but such is his love for these islands and their long history of both traditional colourwork and lace patterns, that he wanted nothing more than to steep himself in them while recharging his creative batteries. It worked brilliantly, he says, and he learned plenty – including the surprising discovery that many knitting ladies not in the first flush of youth are nonetheless an absolute whizz with their I-pads, downloading patterns from the internet or checking out knitting blogs like there's no tomorrow!

The collection of 24 designs in his new book, while paying homage to the great traditions of colour work and cables from the Scottish islands, also has a contemporary twist, in part as a result of Martin's great talent at finding unusual and exciting colour combinations (his US publishers, Interweave, say they just love his "quirky colours", particularly when he turned up on the stand at one of the US knitting shows wearing his trademark red trousers and a purple scarf!

His ability to mix unexpectedly contrasting patterns together using colour as the common link is second to none. One beautiful sweater in this book mixes a traditional Argyll pattern in pinks, mauves and greens with a little diamond pattern border in red and yellow for the cuffs and hem to singular effect. It sounds like it shouldn't work, but it absolutely does. In this new book, he has put together a great range of designs both for garments and accessories, plus a couple of heirloom blankets.

Martin chose to use the Rowan Fine Tweed for many of the Fair Isle patterns in this book, partly because the slight fleck in the yarn softens off the shades to just the right degree but also because the 4ply pure wool yarn is just the right weight for this kind of colour work. It prevents the knitted

fabric, with the stranded yarn at the back, from becoming too stiff and bulky.

For those who want a break from mixing colours, he has included a few special cable designs, including a really pretty cowl-necked tunic, a cropped cardigan and a supersize poncho.

ISBN: 978-1-907544-38-5
Price: £15.99

08
09

01. Portree Sweater.
02. Aberdeen Argyle Sweater.
03. Shetland Cushion.
04. Tay tartan & Aberdeen.
Argyle Gloves.
05. Dundee Spot Socks.
06. Peebles Stole.
07. Shetland Knee Rug.
08. Thistle Cardigan.
09. Tweed Hat.

travel journal

words by Marie Wallin

SANTORINI
Glorious location

The beautiful and idyllic island of Santorini was the perfect setting for our GLORIOUS collection. The pretty white villages clinging to the volcanic steep hills, together with the friendliness of the islanders and the breathtaking sunsets makes Santorini a very special place to visit.

Santorini is actually a group of islands consisting of Thera, Thirasia, Aspronisi, Palea and Nea Kameni and is located in the most southern part of the Cyclades in the Aegean Sea. Thera – the main island has a population of 13,600 people living in 13 villages.

The present day crescent shape of the island is a consequence of volcanic activity, feeding the myth of the lost civilisation of Atlantis. Santorini is in fact what remains of a massive volcanic explosion 3600 years ago, which created the impressive geological feature, the 'Caldera'. This giant central lagoon is 12Km by 7Km in size and is surrounded by 300m high steep cliffs on three sides. Subsequent mild volcanic activity has created the two small islands of Palea and Nea Kameni within the Caldera.

We photographed GLORIOUS mainly between two villages on the island – the beautiful villages of Megalohori and Oia.

Megalohori is a small village which sits on a hill facing to the east of Santorini. As you approach the centre of the village the roads become narrower and narrower, revealing the village's pretty alleyways. The village has a lovely mix of white and cream coloured traditional Cycladic houses with a smattering of a few churches. The alleyways lead down to a beautiful square which gives host to a few friendly tavernas.

Oia, pronounced 'Ia', is the most famous of all the villages of Santorini. It is known throughout the world for its beauty, the quiet life and the fantastic sunsets. The village is situated on top of an impressive cliff which affords tremendous views across the Caldera. It is a traditional village with charming white washed houses arranged along narrow lanes, blue domed churches and lots of small tourist shops, cafes and tavernas.

Oia also has a small port. Ammoudi is the harbour area and can be reached by a set of 300 steps leading down from the main village. If you're not feeling energetic enough to walk back up, a friendly donkey will oblige!

We also photographed the 'All Seasons Chunky Collection' brochure on the island. The harbour area of Ammoudi was the lovely setting for part of the brochure with the rest of the collection being photographed on the stunning beach at Vlychada. This long stretch of dark grey sand is surrounded by the most unusual rock formations which give the area a moonscape appearance. Luckily for us, the only taverna at the beach kindly stayed open for us as we were photographing well after dark!

The whole trip went very smoothly and this was largely due to the organisation and help given by Yorgos Galaziis and his team at Key Productions. Thank you Yorgos and thank you for the great Moussaka recipe!

The Rowan crew stayed at:
Anemomilos Hotel Apartments,
Oia, 84702,
Santorini
www.anemomilos.com

Exclusive download patterns available to our R O W @ N members only.
For more information go to **www.knitrowan.com**

R O W @ N
EXCLUSIVE
FREE DOWNLOAD

VANILLA
Siena 4ply
Sarah Dallas

R O W @ N

Become part of our online family with the free club called R O W @ N

Registration is completely free, and allows exclusive access to:

- Members area and Design Room
- Free pattern downloads
- Forums
- News and eNewsletters
- Events
- Calendar
- Video tutorials
- Technical help

and much, much more...

To register go to **www.knitrowan.com** and select R O W @ N

R O W A N

S U B S C R I P T I O N

If you want to receive your Rowan magazines delivered direct to your door, Rowan Subscription is the club for you.

You will receive the following great benefits:

- 2 x Rowan Knitting and Crochet Magazines
- 2 x Rowan Subscription Newsletters
- Members exclusive pattern collection
- Exclusive members only gift
- 10% discount on Rowan UK weekend workshops
- 5% discount on all participating UK workshops
- Manage your account online
- Purchase back issues of our magazines

All this for; UK £25.00, Europe £32.00, North America £32.00, Rest of World £41.00.

To subscribe or renew simply call today on 0333 200 6466, or go to **www.knitrowan.com** and select Rowan Subscription.

what's new

A whole season's worth of knitting books, magazines and exhibitions covering all aspects of knitting and textile design.

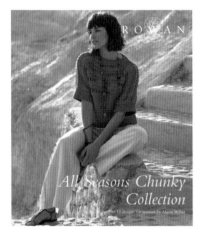

Rowan All Seasons Chunky Collection

The beautiful Greek island of Santorini is the perfect setting for this lovely collection of 12 easy to knit and easy to wear relaxed designs by Marie Wallin using the new addition to the All Seasons Cotton range – *All Seasons Chunky*.

Rowan All Seasons Chunky Collection is available from Rowan stockists from 1st February 2013.

Order Code: ZB136

Visit **www.knitrowan.com** to view the collection online.

Rowan Softknit Collection

With 16 timeless designs for both women and men by Martin Storey, this lovely brochure showcases one of our new yarns for the season, *Softknit Cotton*.

Rowan Softknit Collection is available from Rowan stockists from 1st February 2013.

Order code: ZB129

Visit **www.knitrowan.com** to view the collection online.

Rowan Simple Shapes Cotton Glacé

A modern classic mini collection of 8 simple knits by Martin Storey, using our popular *Cotton Glacé* yarn.

Rowan Simple Shapes Cotton Glacé is available from Rowan stockists from 1st February 2013.

Order code: ZB131

Visit **www.knitrowan.com** to view the collection online.

Rowan Simple Shapes
Handknit Cotton Collection

A relaxed stylish mini collection of 8 simple knits by Martin Storey, using our popular *Handknit Cotton* yarn.
Rowan Simple Shapes Handknit Cotton is available from Rowan stockists from 1st February 2013.

Order code: ZB128

Visit **www.knitrowan.com** to view the collection online.

Rowan Summer Textures

Using inspiration from tribal folk art, Lisa Richardson and Sarah Hatton have designed a lovely collection of 16 knit and crochet designs using our *Savannah, Summer Tweed and All Seasons Cotton* yarns.
Rowan Summer Textures is available from Rowan stockists from 1st February 2013.

Order code: ZB130

Visit **www.knitrowan.com** to view the collection online.

David Bowie Album cover shoot for Aladdin Sane, 1973. Photograph by Brian Duffy. Design by Brian Duffy and Celia Philo. Make Up by Pierre La Roche. © Duffy Archive.

David Bowie is

23rd March – 28th July 2013

The V&A has been given unprecedented access to the David Bowie Archive to curate the first international retrospective of the extraordinary career of David Bowie. **David Bowie is** will feature more than 300 objects that include handwritten lyrics, original costumes, fashion, photography, film, music videos, set designs and Bowie's own instruments.

The Victoria and Albert Museum, London

Admission charges will apply. Timed tickets will be in operation and advanced booking is strongly recommended.

www.vam.ac.uk

Kaffe Fassett – A Life in Colour

22nd March – 29th June 2013

Kaffe Fassett – A Life in Colour is a celebration of the work of one of the great practitioners of contemporary craft. This exhibition, the first in London since Kaffe Fassett's record-breaking show at the Victoria and Albert Museum in 1988, features over 100 works including designs for Bill Gibb, Missoni, printed patchwork fabrics, glorious quilts and inspired needlepoint.

The autobiography **'Kaffe Fassett Dreaming in Colour'**, accompanies the exhibition, published by Stewart, Tabori & Chang, £25.00.

The Fashion and Textile Museum, London

Admission charges will apply.

www.ftmlondon.org

ROWAN SIZING GUIDE

When you knit and wear a Rowan design we want you to look and feel fabulous. This all starts with the size and fit of the design you choose. To help you to achieve a great knitting experience we have looked at the sizing of our womens and menswear patterns. This has resulted in the introduction of our new sizing guide which includes the following exciting features:

Our sizing now conforms to standard clothing sizes. Therefore if you buy a standard size 12 in clothing, then our medium patterns will fit you perfectly.

The menswear designs are now available to knit in menswear sizes XSmall through to 2XL ie. 38" to 50" chest.

Dimensions in the charts below are body measurements, not garment dimensions, therefore please refer to the measuring guide to help you to determine which is the best size for you to knit.

STANDARD WOMENS SIZING GUIDE

The sizing within this chart is also based on the larger size within the range, ie. M will be based on size 14.

UK SIZE	S	M	L	XL	XXL	
DUAL SIZE	8/10	12/14	16/18	20/22	24/26	
To fit bust	32 – 34	36 – 38	40 – 42	44 – 46	48 – 50	inches
	81 – 86	91 - 97	102 – 107	112 – 117	122 – 127	cm
To fit waist	24 – 26	28 – 30	32 – 34	36 – 38	40 – 42	inches
	61 – 66	71 – 76	81 – 86	91 – 97	102 – 107	cm
To fit hips	34 – 36	38 – 40	42 – 44	46 – 48	50 – 52	inches
	86 – 91	97 – 102	107 – 112	117 – 122	127 – 132	cm

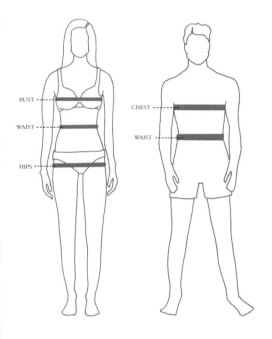

STANDARD MENS SIZING GUIDE

UK SIZE	XXS	XS	S	M	L	XL	XXL	2XL	
EUR Size	46	48	50	52	54	56	58	60	
To fit chest	36	38	40	42	44	46	48	50	inches
	91	97	102	107	112	117	122	127	cm
To fit waist	28	30	32	34	36	38	40	42	inches
	71	76	81	86	91	97	102	107	cm

SIZING & SIZE DIAGRAM NOTE

The instructions are given for the smallest size. Where they vary, work the figures in brackets for the larger sizes. **One set of figures refers to all sizes.** Included with most patterns in this magazine is a **'size diagram'** - see image on the right, of the finished garment and its dimensions. The measurement shown at the bottom of each **'size diagram'** shows the garment width 2.5cm below the armhole shaping. To help you choose the size of garment to knit please refer to the sizing guide. Generally in the majority of designs the welt width (at the cast on edge of the garment) is the same width as the chest. However, some designs are 'A-Line' in shape or have a flared edge and in these cases the welt width will be wider than the chest width.

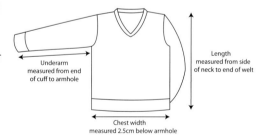

MEASURING GUIDE

For maximum comfort and to ensure the correct fit when choosing a size to knit, please follow the tips below when checking your size.

Measure yourself close to your body, over your underwear and don't pull the tape measure too tight!

Bust/chest – measure around the fullest part of the bust/chest and across the shoulder blades.

Waist – measure around the natural waistline, just above the hip bone.

Hips – measure around the fullest part of the bottom.

If you don't wish to measure yourself, note the size of a favourite jumper that you like the fit of. Our sizes are now comparable to the clothing sizes from the major high street retailers, so if your favourite jumper is a size Medium or size 12, then our size Medium should be approximately the same fit.

To be extra sure, measure your favourite jumper and then compare these measurements with the Rowan size diagram given at the end of the individual instructions.

Finally, once you have decided which size is best for you, please ensure that you achieve the tension

required for the design you wish to knit.

Remember if your tension is too loose, your garment will be bigger than the pattern size and you may use more yarn. If your tension is too tight, your garment could be smaller than the pattern size and you will have yarn left over.

Furthermore if your tension is incorrect, the handle of your fabric will be too stiff or floppy and will not fit properly. It really does make sense to check your tension before starting every project.

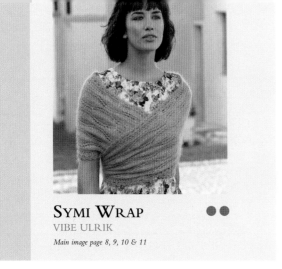

SYMI WRAP
VIBE ULRIK
Main image page 8, 9, 10 & 11

●●

YARN
Fine Lace and Kidsilk Haze
A FL Ochre 930   1   x 50gm
B KSH Ember 644   2   x 25gm

NEEDLES
1 pair 3mm (no 11) (US 2/3) needles
1 pair 4¹/2mm (no 7) (US 7) needles

TENSION
19 sts and 25 rows to 10 cm measured over lace patt using 4¹/2mm (US 7) needles and one strand each of Kidsilk Haze and Fine Lace held together.

FINISHED SIZE
Completed wrap measures approx 190 cm (75 ins) long and is 33 cm (13 ins) at widest point.

WRAP
Using 3mm (US 2/3) needles and one strand each of yarns A and B held together cast on 3 sts.
Row 1 (RS): K1, P1, K1.
Row 2: K3.
Row 3: K1, M1, P1, M1, K1. 5 sts.
Row 4: K1, (P1, K1) twice.
Row 5: K2, M1, P1, M1, K2. 7 sts.
Row 6: K1, (P2, K1) twice.
Row 7: K3, P1, K3.
Row 8: As row 6.
Row 9: K2, M1, K1, P1, K1, M1, K2. 9 sts.
Row 10: K1, (P1, K1) 4 times.
Row 11: K2, (P1, K1) twice, P1, K2.
Row 12: As row 10.
Row 13: K2, M1, (P1, K1) twice, P1, M1, K2. 11 sts.
Row 14: K1, P2, (K1, P1) twice, K1, P2, K1.
Row 15: K3, (P1, K1) twice, P1, K3.
Row 16: As row 14.
Row 17: K2, M1, (K1, P1) 3 times, K1, M1, K2. 13 sts.

Row 18: K1, (P1, K1) to end.
Row 19: K2, (P1, K1) to last st, K1.
Row 20: As row 18.
Last 20 rows set the sts and the increases – first and last st of every row worked as a K st, and centre sts in rib with inc sts worked 2 sts in from edges.
Keeping sts correct as set and taking inc sts into rib, cont as folls:
Work 2 rows.
Row 23: K2, M1, rib to last 2 sts, M1, K2.
15 sts.
Work 5 rows.
Row 29: As row 23. 17 sts.
Work 7 rows.
Row 37: As row 23. 19 sts.
Work 7 rows.
Row 45: As row 23. 21 sts.
(Work should meas approx 12 cm.)
Cont straight until work meas 28 cm **from last inc** (40 cm from cast-on edge), ending with **WS** facing for next row.
Next row (WS): Inc **twice** (by working into front, back and front again) in each of first 10 sts, inc **once** in next st, inc **twice** in each of last 10 sts. 62 sts.
Change to 4¹/2mm (US 7) needles.
Now work in lace patt as folls:
Counting in from both ends of last row, place marker after 7th st in from ends of row – 48 sts between markers.
Row 1 (RS): K4, yfwd, K2tog, K1, slip marker onto right needle, (sl 1, K1, psso, K3, yfwd, K2tog, yfwd, K2, yfwd, sl 1, K1, psso, yfwd, K3, K2tog) 3 times, slip marker onto right needle, K3, yfwd, K2tog, (yfwd) twice, K2.
Row 2: K2, (K1, P1) into double yfwd of previous row, K2, yfwd, K2tog, K1, slip marker onto right needle, P48, slip marker onto right needle, K3, yfwd, K2tog, (yfwd) twice, K2.
Row 3: K2, (K1, P1) into double yfwd of previous row, K2, yfwd, K2tog, K1, slip marker onto right needle, (sl 1, K1, psso, K2, yfwd, K2tog, yfwd, K4, yfwd, sl 1, K1, psso, yfwd, K2, K2tog) 3 times, slip marker onto right needle, K3, yfwd, K2tog, K4.
Row 4: Cast off 2 sts (one st on right needle), K3, yfwd, K2tog, K1, slip marker onto right needle, P48, slip marker onto right needle, K3, yfwd, K2tog, K4.
Row 5: Cast off 2 sts (one st on right needle), K3, yfwd, K2tog, K1, slip marker onto right needle, (sl 1, K1, psso, K1, yfwd, K2tog, yfwd, K6, yfwd, sl 1, K1, psso, yfwd, K1, K2tog) 3 times, slip marker onto right needle, K3, yfwd, K2tog, (yfwd) twice, K2.
Rows 2 to 5 form patt for edging sts beyond markers. (**Note:** Number of sts in edging varies.)

Keeping edging sts correct in patt as now set and slipping markers from left needle to right needle on every row, cont as folls:
Row 6 and every foll alt row: Patt to first marker, P to second marker, patt to end.
Row 7: Patt to first marker, (sl 1, K1, psso, yfwd, K2tog, yfwd, K8, yfwd, sl 1, K1, psso, yfwd, K2tog) 3 times, patt to end.
Row 9: Patt to first marker, (K1, yfwd, K2tog, yfwd, K3, K2tog, sl 1, K1, psso, K3, yfwd, sl 1, K1, psso, yfwd, K1) 3 times, patt to end.
Rows 11, 13 and 15: As row 9.
Row 17: Patt to first marker, (K2, yfwd, sl 1, K1, psso, yfwd, K2, K2tog, sl 1, K1, psso, K2, yfwd, K2tog, yfwd, K2) 3 times, patt to end.
Row 19: Patt to first marker, (K3, yfwd, sl 1, K1, psso, yfwd, K1, K2tog, sl 1, K1, psso, K1, yfwd, K2tog, yfwd, K3) 3 times, patt to end.
Row 21: Patt to first marker, (K4, yfwd, sl 1, K1, psso, yfwd, K2tog, sl 1, K1, psso, yfwd, K2tog, yfwd, K4) 3 times, patt to end.
Row 23: Patt to first marker, (sl 1, K1, psso, K3, yfwd, sl 1, K1, psso, yfwd, K2, yfwd, K2tog, yfwd, K3, K2tog) 3 times, patt to end.
Rows 25 and 27: As row 23.
Row 28: As row 6.
These 28 rows form patt for centre sts between markers.
Cont as now set until work meas approx 109 cm **from beg of lace patt**, ending after lace patt row 20 and with RS facing for next row.
Next row (RS): Patt to first marker (there are now 7 sts here), patt to second marker, K3, yfwd, K2tog, K2 (there are now 7 sts here).
62 sts.
Remove markers.
Next row: (P3tog) 10 times, P2tog, (P3tog) 10 times. 21 sts.
Change to 3mm (US 2/3) needles.
Next row (RS): K2, (P1, K1) to last st, K1.
Next row: K1, (P1, K1) to end.
These 2 rows set the sts as given for first end of wrap.
Cont as now set until work meas 28 cm **from dec row**, ending with RS facing for next row.
Next row (RS): K1, sl 1, K1, psso, rib to last 3 sts, K2tog, K1. 19 sts.
Working all decreases as set by last row, dec 1 st at each end of 8th and foll 8th row, then on 2 foll 6th rows, then on 3 foll 4th rows. 5 sts.
Work 1 row, ending with RS facing for next row.
Next row (RS): K1, sl 1, K2tog, psso, K1.
Next row: K1, P1, K1.
Cast off rem 3 sts.

MAKING UP
Press as described on the information page.

ARTEMIS

LISA RICHARDSON

Main image page 20 & 21

● ● ●

YARN

	S	M	L	XL	XXL	

To fit bust
81-86 91-97 102-107 112-117 122-127 cm
32-34 36-38 40-42 44-46 48-50 in

Purelife Revive and Kidsilk Haze

A Rev Diamond 477

11	12	13	14	16	x 50gm

B KSH Jelly 597

1	1	1	1	1	x 25gm

C KSH Fern 629

1	1	1	1	1	x 25gm

D KSH Brick 649

1	1	1	1	1	x 25gm

NEEDLES

1 pair 3¼mm (no 10) (US 3) needles
1 pair 4mm (no 8) (US 6) needles
3¼mm (no 10) (US 3) circular needle,
100 cm long
2.00mm (no 14) (US B1) crochet hook

BUTTONS – 7 x 1009 from Coats. Please see information page for contact details.

TENSION

27 sts and 27 rows to 10 cm measured over patt using 4mm (US 6) needles and yarn A (Purelife Revive).

SPECIAL ABBREVIATION

MK = P3tog leaving sts on left needle, yrn, P tog same 3 sts again and let all 3 sts slip off left needle.

CROCHET ABBREVIATIONS

ch = chain; **dc** = double crochet; **dtr4tog** = ★(yoh) twice, insert hook as indicated, yoh and draw loop through, (yoh and draw through 2 loops) twice, rep from ★ 3 times more, yoh and draw through all 5 loops on hook; **sp(s)** = space(s); **ss** = slip stitch; **tr** = treble; **tr3tog** = (yoh and insert hook as indicated, yoh and draw loop through, yoh and draw through 2 loops) 3 times, yoh and draw through all 4 loops on hook; **ttr3tog** = ★(yoh) 3 times, insert hook as indicated, yoh and draw loop through, (yoh and draw through 2 loops) 3 times, rep from ★ twice more, yoh and draw through all 4 loops; **yoh** = yarn over hook.

BACK

Using 4mm (US 6) needles and yarn A cast on 52 [64: 82: 100: 118] sts.

Now work in patt and shape back hem edge as folls:

Row 1 (RS): Knit.
Row 2: Cast on 6 sts, ★MK, rep from ★ to last st, P1.
Row 3: Cast on 6 sts, K to end.
Row 4: Cast on 6 sts, P2, ★MK, rep from ★ to last 2 sts, P2.
Row 5: Cast on 6 sts, K to end.
Row 6: Cast on 6 sts, P1, ★MK, rep from ★ to end. 82 [94: 112: 130: 148] sts.
These 6 rows form patt and beg hem shaping.
Keeping patt correct, cast on 6 sts at beg of next 7 rows, taking cast-on sts into patt and ending with **WS** facing for next row.
124 [136: 154: 172: 190] sts.
Work 17 rows, ending with RS facing for next row.

Shape darts
Counting in from both ends of last row, place markers after 21st [24th: 27th: 30th: 33rd] st, miss next 21 [24: 24: 27: 27] sts and place another marker - 4 markers in total and 40 [40: 52: 58: 70] sts at centre between second pair of markers.
Next row (dec) (RS): K2tog, (K to within 2 sts of marker, sl 1, K1, psso, slip marker onto right needle) twice, (K to marker, slip marker onto right needle, K2tog) twice, K to last 2 sts, K2tog. 118 [130: 148: 166: 184] sts.
Keeping patt correct within each section between markers, work 7 rows.
Rep last 8 rows once more, then first of these rows (the dec row) again.
106 [118: 136: 154: 172] sts.
Cont straight until back meas 23 [24: 25: 26: 27] cm **at centre of row**, ending with RS facing for next row.
Next row (inc) (RS): (K to marker, M1, slip marker onto right needle) twice, (K to marker, slip marker onto right needle, M1) twice, K to end. 110 [122: 140: 158: 176] sts.
Keeping patt correct within each section between markers, work 7 rows.
Rep last 8 rows once more, then first of these rows (the inc row) again.
118 [130: 148: 166: 184] sts.
Work 23 rows, ending with RS facing for next row. (Back should meas 38 [39: 40: 41: 42] cm **at centre of row**.)

Shape armholes
Keeping patt correct, cast off 5 [6: 7: 8: 9] sts at

beg of next 2 rows. 108 [118: 134: 150: 166] sts.
Dec 1 st at each end of next 5 [7: 9: 11: 13] rows, then on foll 3 [3: 5: 7: 9] alt rows.
92 [98: 106: 114: 122] sts.
Cont straight until armhole meas 20 [21: 22: 23: 24] cm, ending with RS facing for next row.

Shape back neck and shoulders
Next row (RS): Cast off 6 [6: 7: 8: 9] sts, patt until there are 21 [24: 26: 29: 31] sts on right needle and turn, leaving rem sts on a holder.
Work each side of neck separately.
Dec 1 st at neck edge of next 4 rows, ending with **WS** facing for next row, **and at same time** cast off 6 [6: 7: 8: 9] sts at beg of 2nd row, then 6 [7: 7: 8: 9] sts at beg of foll alt row.
Work 1 row.
Cast off rem 5 [7: 8: 9: 9] sts.
With RS facing, rejoin yarn to rem sts, cast off centre 38 [38: 40: 40: 42] sts, patt to end.
Complete to match first side, reversing shapings.

LEFT FRONT

Using 4mm (US 6) needles and yarn A cast on 7 sts.
Now work in patt and shape front hem edge as folls:

Row 1 (RS): Knit.
Row 2: Cast on 6 sts, ★MK, rep from ★ to last st, P1.
Row 3: Knit.
Row 4: Cast on 6 sts, P2, ★MK, rep from ★ to last 2 sts, P2.
Row 5: Knit.
Row 6: Cast on 6 sts, P1, ★MK, rep from ★ to end. 25 sts.
These 6 rows form patt and beg hem shaping.
Keeping patt correct, cast on 6 sts at beg of 2nd and foll alt row, then 25 [31: 40: 49: 58] sts at beg of foll alt row, taking cast-on sts into patt and ending with RS facing for next row.
62 [68: 77: 86: 95] sts.
Work 6 rows, ending with RS facing for next row.

Shape darts
Counting in from end (side seam edge) of last row, place marker after 21st [24th: 27th: 30th: 33rd] st, miss next 21 [24: 24: 27: 27] sts and place another marker - 2 markers in total and 20 [20: 26: 29: 35] sts at front opening edge of row after second marker.
Next row (dec) (RS): K2tog, (K to within 2 sts of marker, sl 1, K1, psso, slip marker onto

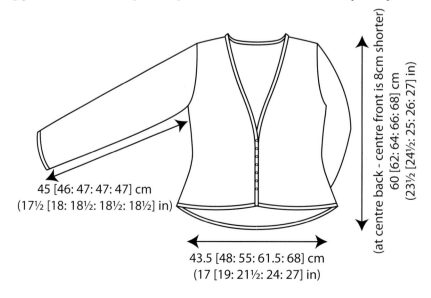

45 [46: 47: 47: 47] cm
(17½ [18: 18½: 18½: 18½] in)

43.5 [48: 55: 61.5: 68] cm
(17 [19: 21½: 24: 27] in)

(at centre back - centre front is 8cm shorter)
60 [62: 64: 66: 68] cm
(23½ [24½: 25: 26: 27] in)

right needle) twice, K to end.
59 [65: 74: 83: 92] sts.
Keeping patt correct within each section between markers, work 7 rows.
Rep last 8 rows once more, then first of these rows (the dec row) again. 53 [59: 68: 77: 86] sts.
Cont straight until side seam edge of left front matches side seam edge of back to first dart inc, ending with RS facing for next row.
Next row (inc) (RS): (K to marker, M1, slip marker onto right needle) twice, K to end.
55 [61: 70: 79: 88] sts.
Keeping patt correct within each section between markers, work 7 rows.
Rep last 8 rows once more, then first of these rows (the inc row) again. 59 [65: 74: 83: 92] sts.
Work 1 row, ending with RS facing for next row.
Shape front slope
Keeping patt correct, dec 1 st at end of next and foll 10 [9: 9: 8: 9] alt rows, then on 0 [0: 0: 1: 0] foll 4th row. 48 [55: 64: 73: 82] sts.
Work 1 [3: 3: 1: 3] rows, ending with RS facing for next row.
Shape armhole
Keeping patt correct, cast off 5 [6: 7: 8: 9] sts at beg and dec 0 [1: 1: 0: 1] st at end of next row.
43 [48: 56: 65: 72] sts.
Work 1 row.
Dec 1 st at armhole edge of next 5 [7: 9: 11: 13] rows, then on foll 3 [3: 5: 7: 9] alt rows
and at same time dec 1 st at front slope edge of next [3rd: 3rd: next: 3rd] and 2 [2: 4: 6: 7] foll 4th rows. 32 [35: 37: 40: 42] sts.
Dec 1 st at front slope edge **only** on 2nd [2nd: 4th: 4th: 4th] and 8 [8: 7: 6: 5] foll 4th rows.
23 [26: 29: 33: 36] sts.
Cont straight until left front matches back to beg of shoulder shaping, ending with RS facing for next row.
Shape shoulder
Cast off 6 [6: 7: 8: 9] sts at beg of next and foll alt row, then 6 [7: 7: 8: 9] sts at beg of foll alt row.
Work 1 row.
Cast off rem 5 [7: 8: 9: 9] sts.

RIGHT FRONT
Using 4mm (US 6) needles and yarn A cast on 7 sts.
Now work in patt and shape front hem edge as folls:
Row 1 (RS): Knit.
Row 2: *MK, rep from * to last st, P1.
Row 3: Cast on 6 sts, K to end.
Row 4: P2, *MK, rep from * to last 2 sts, P2.
Row 5: Cast on 6 sts, K to end. 19 sts.
Row 6: P1, *MK, rep from * to end.
These 6 rows form patt and beg hem shaping.
Keeping patt correct, cast on 6 sts at beg of next and foll 2 alt rows, then 25 [31: 40: 49: 58] sts at beg of foll alt row, taking cast-on sts into patt and ending with **WS** facing for next row.
62 [68: 77: 86: 95] sts.
Work 5 rows, ending with RS facing for next row.
Shape darts
Counting in from beg of last row, place marker after 21st [24th: 27th: 30th: 33rd] st, miss next 21 [24: 24: 27: 27] sts and place another marker - 2 markers in total and 20 [20: 26: 29: 35] sts at end of row after second marker.
Next row (dec) (RS): (K to marker, slip marker onto right needle, K2tog) twice, K to

last 2 sts, K2tog. 59 [65: 74: 83: 92] sts.
Complete to match left front, reversing shapings and working dart inc rows as "(K to marker, slip marker onto right needle, M1) twice, K to end".

SLEEVES
Using 3¼mm (US 3) needles and yarn A cast on 45 [47: 49: 49: 51] sts.
Row 1 (RS): K1, *P1, K1, rep from * to end.
Row 2: As row 1.
These 2 rows form moss st.
Work in moss st for 1 row more, ending with **WS** facing for next row.
Row 4 (WS): Moss st 4 [1: 2: 2: 3] sts, M1, (moss st 4 [5: 5: 5: 5] sts, M1) 9 times, moss st 5 [1: 2: 2: 3] sts. 55 [57: 59: 59: 61] sts.
Change to 4mm (US 6) needles.
Now work in patt as folls:
Row 1 (RS): Knit.
Row 2: P0 [1: 2: 2: 0], *MK, rep from * to last 1 [2: 0: 0: 1] sts, P1 [2: 0: 0: 1].
Row 3: (Inc in first st) 0 [0: 0: 1: 1] times, K to last 0 [0: 0: 1: 1] st, (inc in last st) 0 [0: 0: 1: 1] times. 55 [57: 59: 61: 63] sts.
Row 4: P2 [0: 1: 2: 0], *MK, rep from * to last 2 [0: 1: 2: 0] sts, P2 [0: 1: 2: 0].
Row 5: (Inc in first st) 1 [1: 1: 0: 0] times, K to last 1 [1: 1: 0: 0] st, (inc in last st) 1 [1: 1: 0: 0] times. 57 [59: 61: 61: 63] sts.
Row 6: P2 [0: 1: 1: 2], *MK, rep from * to last 1 [2: 0: 0: 1] sts, P1 [2: 0: 0: 1].
These 6 rows form patt and beg sleeve shaping.
Cont in patt, inc 1 st at each end of 5th [5th: 5th: next: next] and every foll 6th [6th: 6th: 4th: 4th] row to 77 [85: 93: 69: 77] sts, then on every foll 8th [8th: 8th: 6th: 6th] row until there are 87 [91: 95: 99: 103] sts, taking inc sts into patt.
Cont straight until sleeve meas 45 [46: 47: 47: 47] cm, ending with RS facing for next row.
Shape top
Keeping patt correct, cast off 5 [6: 7: 8: 9] sts at beg of next 2 rows. 77 [79: 81: 83: 85] sts.
Dec 1 st at each end of next 5 rows, then on every foll alt row until 45 sts rem, then on foll 9 rows, ending with RS facing for next row. 27 sts.
Cast off 4 sts at beg of next 2 rows.
Cast off rem 19 sts.

MAKING UP
Press as described on the information page.
Join both shoulder seams using back stitch, or mattress stitch if preferred. Join side seams.
Hem border
With RS facing, using 3¼mm (US 3) circular needle and yarn A, beg and ending at base of front opening edges, pick up and knit 56 [61: 70: 78: 86] sts from shaped left front hem edge, 111 [121: 139: 155: 171] sts from shaped back hem edge, then 56 [61: 70: 78: 86] sts from shaped right front hem edge.
223 [243: 279: 311: 343] sts.
Work in moss st as given for sleeves for 3 rows, ending with RS facing for next row.
Cast off in moss st.
Front band
With RS facing, using 3¼mm (US 3) circular needle and yarn A, beg and ending at cast-off edge of hem border, pick up and knit 69 [71:

73: 75: 77] sts up right front opening edge to beg of front slope shaping, 76 [78: 82: 84: 86] up right front slope, 39 [39: 41: 41: 43] sts from back, 76 [78: 82: 84: 86] down left front slope to beg of front slope shaping, then 69 [71: 73: 75: 77] sts down left front opening edge.
329 [337: 351: 359: 369] sts.
Work in moss st as given for sleeves for 1 row, ending with RS facing for next row.
Row 2 (RS): Moss st 12 [8: 10: 12: 8] sts, *work 2 tog, yrn (to make a buttonhole), moss st 7 [8: 8: 8: 9] sts, rep from * 5 times more, work 2 tog, yrn (to make 7th buttonhole), moss st to end.
Work in moss st for 1 row more, ending with RS facing for next row.
Cast off in moss st.
See information page for finishing instructions, setting in sleeves using the set-in method.
Four petal flowers (make 22)
Using 2.00mm (US B1) crochet hook and any colour of Kidsilk Haze, make 4 ch and join with a ss to form a ring.
Round 1: 1 ch (does NOT count as st), 8 dc into ring, ss to first dc. 8 sts.
Round 2: 1 ch (does NOT count as st), *1 dc into base ring enclosing sts of round 1, miss 1 dc, 3 ch, tr3tog into back loop **only** of next dc, 3 ch, rep from * 3 times more, ss to first dc, 10 ch, 1 ss into 2nd ch from hook, 1 ss into each of next 8 ch.
Fasten off.
Using all colours of Kidsilk Haze at random, make a further 21 four petal flowers.
Five petal flowers (make 22)
Using 2.00mm (US B1) crochet hook and any colour of Kidsilk Haze, make 7 ch and join with a ss to form a ring.
Round 1: 1 ch (does NOT count as st), 15 dc into ring, ss to first dc. 15 sts.
Break off this colour and join in next colour.
Roun0d 2: 1 ch (does NOT count as st), 1 dc into first dc, *3 ch, dtr4tog over next 2 dc inserting first 2 "legs" in next dc and last 2 "legs" in foll dc, 3 ch, 1 dc into next dc, rep from * to end, replacing dc at end of last rep with ss to first dc.
Fasten off.
Using all colours of Kidsilk Haze at random, make a further 21 five petal flowers.
Six petal flowers (make 22)
Using 2.00mm (US B1) crochet hook and any colour of Kidsilk Haze, make 4 ch and join with a ss to form a ring.
Round 1: 5 ch (counts as 1 tr and 2 ch), (1 tr into ring, 2 ch) 5 times, ss to 3rd of 5 ch at beg of round. 6 ch sps.
Break off this colour and join in next colour.
Round 2: 1 ch (does NOT count as st), 1 dc around 3 ch at beg of previous round inserting hook from front to back and from right to left, *4 ch, ttr3tog into next ch sp, 5 ch, 1 dc around stem of next tr inserting hook from front to back and from right to left, rep from * to end, replacing dc at end of last rep with ss to first dc.
Fasten off.
Using all colours of Kidsilk Haze at random, make a further 21 six petal flowers.
Using photograph as a guide, attach flowers to neck edge of garment.

HYDRA
MARTIN STOREY

Main image page 12 & 13

● ● ●

YARN

	S	M	L	XL	XXL	
To fit bust						
	81-86	91-97	102-107	112-117	122-127	cm
	32-34	36-38	40-42	44-46	48-50	in

Siena 4ply

A Tandoori 676						
	8	8	9	10	11	x 50gm
B Alpine 671						
	1	1	1	2	2	x 50gm
C Greengage 661						
	2	2	2	2	2	x 50gm
D Korma 677						
	1	1	2	2	2	x 50gm
E Mariner 672						
	1	1	1	1	2	x 50gm
F Cream 652						
	1	1	1	1	1	x 50gm

NEEDLES

1 pair 2¼mm (no 13) (US 1) needles
1 pair 3mm (no 11) (US 2/3) needles

TENSION

28 sts and 30 rows to 10 cm measured over patterned st st using 3mm (US 2/3) needles.

BACK

Using 2¼mm (US 1) needles and yarn A cast on 122 [134: 150: 166: 186] sts.
Row 1 (RS): K2, *P2, K2, rep from * to end.
Row 2: P2, *K2, P2, rep from * to end.
These 2 rows form rib.
Cont in rib, dec 1 st at each end of 21st and foll 6th row. 118 [130: 146: 162: 182] sts.
Work in rib for one row more, dec [inc: inc: dec: inc] 1 st at centre of row and ending with RS facing for next row.
117 [131: 147: 161: 183] sts.
Change to 3mm (US 2/3) needles.
Beg with a K row, work in st st for 2 rows, ending with RS facing for next row.
Beg and ending rows as indicated and using the **intarsia** technique as described on the information page, repeating the 36 st patt rep 3 [3: 4: 4: 5] times across each row and repeating the 76 row patt rep throughout, cont in patt from chart, which is worked entirely in st st beg with a K row, as folls:
Keeping patt correct, dec 1 st at each end of 5th and 2 foll 6th rows.
111 [125: 141: 155: 177] sts. (**Note**: Shaping is NOT shown on chart.)

Work 13 [13: 15: 15: 17] rows, ending with RS facing for next row.
Inc 1 st at each end of next and 4 foll 10th rows, taking inc sts into patt.
121 [135: 151: 165: 187] sts.
Cont straight until back meas 35 [36: 37: 38: 39] cm, ending with RS facing for next row.

Shape armholes

Keeping patt correct, cast off 6 [7: 8: 9: 10] sts at beg of next 2 rows.
109 [121: 135: 147: 167] sts.★★
Dec 1 st at each end of next 5 [7: 9: 9: 11] rows, then on foll 5 [6: 7: 8: 10] alt rows.
89 [95: 103: 113: 125] sts.
Cont straight until armhole meas 17 [18: 19: 20: 21] cm, ending with RS facing for next row.

Shape back neck and shoulders

Next row (RS): Patt 18 [21: 23: 28: 33] sts and turn, leaving rem sts on a holder.
Work each side of neck separately.
Dec 1 st at neck edge of next 4 rows, ending with **WS** facing for next row, **and at same time** cast off 5 [6: 6: 8: 10] sts at beg of 2nd and foll alt row.
Work 1 row.
Cast off rem 4 [5: 7: 8: 9] sts.
With RS facing, rejoin yarns to rem sts, cast off centre 53 [53: 57: 57: 59] sts, patt to end.
Complete to match first side, reversing shapings.

FRONT

Work as given for back to ★★.
Dec 1 st at each end of next 5 [7: 9: 9: 11] rows, then on foll 4 [5: 4: 6: 5] alt rows.
91 [97: 109: 117: 135] sts.
Work 1 row, ending with RS facing for next row.

Shape front neck

Next row (RS): Work 2 tog, patt 28 [31: 36: 40: 49] sts and turn, leaving rem sts on a holder.
29 [32: 37: 41: 50] sts.
Work each side of neck separately.
Keeping patt correct, dec 1 st at neck edge of next 8 rows, then on foll 4 [4: 5: 5: 6] alt rows, then on 3 foll 4th rows **and at same time** dec 0 [0: 1: 1: 1] st at armhole edge of 0 [0:

2nd: 2nd: 2nd] and foll 0 [0: 1: 0: 3] alt rows.
14 [17: 19: 24: 29] sts.
Cont straight until front matches back to beg of shoulder shaping, ending with RS facing for next row.

Shape shoulder

Cast off 5 [6: 6: 8: 10] sts at beg of next and foll alt row.
Work 1 row.
Cast off rem 4 [5: 7: 8: 9] sts.
With RS facing, rejoin yarns to rem sts, cast off centre 31 [31: 33: 33: 33] sts, patt to last 2 sts, work 2 tog.
Complete to match first side, reversing shapings.

SLEEVES

Using 2¼mm (US 1) needles and yarn A cast on 50 [54: 58: 58: 58] sts.
Work in rib as given for back for 22 rows, inc [dec: dec: dec: inc] 1 st at centre of last row and ending with RS facing for next row.
51 [53: 57: 57: 59] sts.
Change to 3mm (US 2/3) needles.
Beg with a K row, work in st st for 2 rows, ending with RS facing for next row.
Beg and ending rows as indicated and using the **intarsia** technique as described on the information page, repeating the 36 st patt rep once across each row and repeating the 76 row patt rep throughout, cont in patt from chart as folls:
Inc 1 st at each end of next and every foll 4th row to 81 [85: 87: 99: 107] sts, then on every foll 6th row until there are 95 [99: 103: 107: 111] sts, taking inc sts into patt.
Cont straight until sleeve meas 45 [46: 47: 47: 47] cm, ending with RS facing for next row.

Shape top

Keeping patt correct, cast off 6 [7: 8: 9: 10] sts at beg of next 2 rows. 83 [85: 87: 89: 91] sts.
Dec 1 st at each end of next 5 rows, then on every foll alt row until 55 sts rem, then on foll 9 rows, ending with RS facing for next row.
37 sts.
Cast off 4 sts at beg of next 4 rows.
Cast off rem 21 sts.

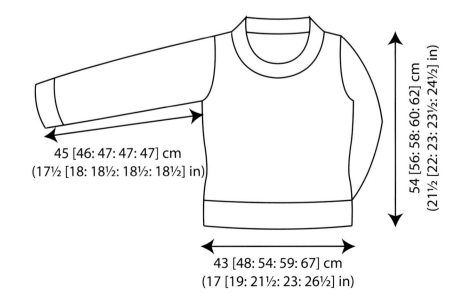

45 [46: 47: 47: 47] cm
(17½ [18: 18½: 18½: 18½] in)

54 [56: 58: 60: 62] cm
(21½ [22: 23: 23½: 24½] in)

43 [48: 54: 59: 67] cm
(17 [19: 21½: 23: 26½] in)

MAKING UP
Press as described on the information page.
Join right shoulder seam using back stitch, or
mattress stitch if preferred.
Neckband
With RS facing, using 2¼mm (US 1) needles
and yarn A, pick up and knit 49 [49: 50: 50: 53]
sts down left side of neck, 31 [31: 33: 33: 33] sts
from front, 49 [49: 50: 50: 53] sts up right side
of neck, then 61 [61: 65: 65: 67] sts from back.
190 [190: 198: 198: 206] sts.
Beg with row 2, work in rib as given for back
for 15 rows, ending with RS facing for next
row.
Cast off in rib.
See information page for finishing instructions,
setting in sleeves using the set-in method.

key

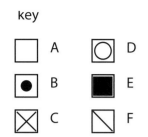

A   D

B   E

C   F

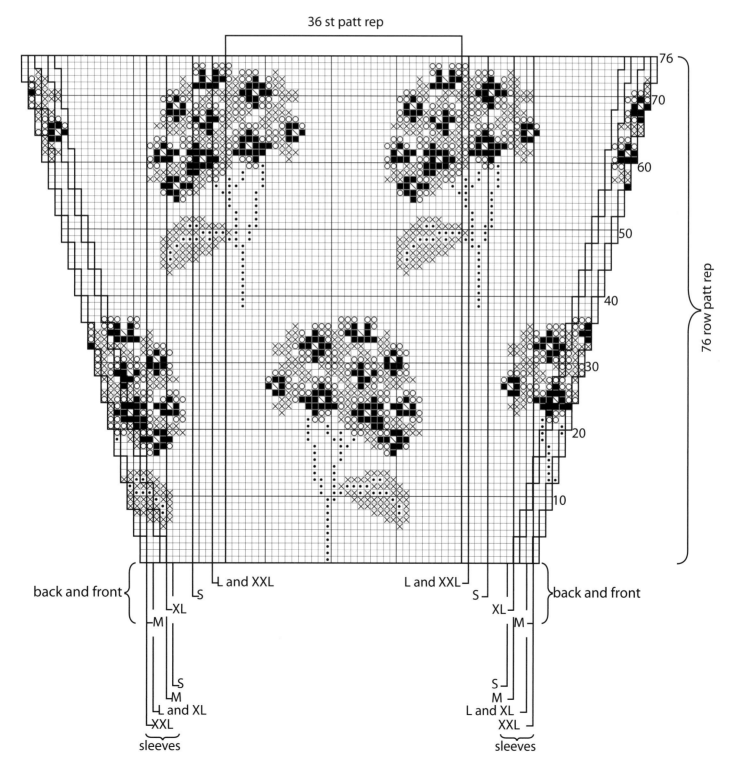

BONNIE
MARIE WALLIN
Main image page 44 & 45

YARN

	S	M	L	XL	XXL	
To fit bust						
	81-86	91-97	102-107	112-117	122-127	cm
	32-34	36-38	40-42	44-46	48-50	in

Creative Linen

A	Eggplant 638					
	2	3	3	3	4	x 100gm
B	Straw 622					
	1	2	2	2	2	x 100gm
C	Natural 621					
	1	1	1	2	2	x 100gm

NEEDLES

1 pair 3¾mm (no 9) (US 5) needles
1 pair 4½mm (no 7) (US 7) needles
3¾mm (no 9) (US 5) circular needle, 40 cm long

TENSION

21 sts and 28 rows to 10 cm measured over st st using 4½mm (US 7) needles.

BODY (worked in one piece, beg at lower edge of front)
Using 4½mm (US 7) needles and yarn A cast on 81 [91: 103: 117: 131] sts.
Beg with a K row, work in st st throughout as folls:
Work 1 row, ending with **WS** facing for next row.
Inc 1 st at each end of next 14 [14: 12: 12: 10] rows, then on foll 3 [3: 4: 4: 5] alt rows. 115 [125: 135: 149: 161] sts.
Work 1 row, ending with RS facing for next row.
Break off yarn A.
Using the **intarsia** technique as described on the information page, cont as folls:
Row 23 (RS): Using yarn B inc in first st, K68 [74: 81: 90: 97], using yarn C K45 [49: 52: 57: 62], inc in last st.
117 [127: 137: 151: 163] sts.
Row 24: Using yarn C P47 [51: 54: 59: 64], using yarn B P70 [76: 83: 92: 99].
These 2 rows set the sts.
Keeping colours correct as now set, cont as folls:
Inc 1 st at each end of next and foll 10 [9: 9: 8: 8] alt rows, then on 2 [3: 4: 5: 6] foll 4th rows. 143 [153: 165: 179: 193] sts.
Work 3 rows, ending with RS facing for next row.

Place markers at both ends of last row to denote base of armhole openings.
Work 24 [28: 30: 34: 36] rows, ending with RS facing for next row.
Break off yarns B and C and join in yarn A.
Work 18 rows, ending with RS facing for next row.
Shape neck
Next row (RS): K42 [47: 52: 59: 65] and turn, leaving rem sts on a holder.
Work each side of neck separately.
Work 3 rows, ending with RS facing for next row.
Break yarn and leave sts on a second holder.
With RS facing, rejoin yarn A to sts on first holder, cast off centre 59 [59: 61: 61: 63] sts, K to end. 42 [47: 52: 59: 65] sts.
Work 3 rows, ending with RS facing for next row.
Break yarn.
Join sections
With RS facing, rejoin yarn A and join sections as folls:
Next row (RS): K across 42 [47: 52: 59: 65] sts of first side of neck, turn and cast on 59 [59: 61: 61: 63] sts, turn and K across 42 [47: 52: 59: 65] sts of second side of neck.
143 [153: 165: 179: 193] sts.
Work 17 rows, ending with RS facing for next row.
Using the **intarsia** technique as described on the information page, cont as folls:
Next row (RS): Using yarn B K83 [89: 97: 106: 114], using yarn C K60 [64: 68: 73: 79].
Next row: Using yarn C P60 [64: 68: 73: 79], using yarn B P83 [89: 97: 106: 114].
These 2 rows set the sts.
Keeping colours correct as now set, cont as folls:
Work 22 [26: 28: 32: 34] rows, ending with RS facing for next row.
Place markers at both ends of last row to denote base of armhole openings.
Dec 1 st at each end of 5th and 2 [3: 4: 5: 6]

foll 4th rows, then on foll 10 [9: 9: 8: 8] alt rows. 117 [127: 137: 151: 163] sts.
Work 1 row, ending with RS facing for next row.
Break off yarns B and C and join in yarn A.
Dec 1 st at each end of next and foll 4 [4: 5: 5: 6] alt rows, then on foll 13 [13: 11: 11: 9] rows, ending with RS facing for next row.
Cast off rem 81 [91: 103: 117: 131] sts.

MAKING UP
Press as described on the information page.
Front hem border
With RS facing, using 3¾mm (US 5) needles and yarn A, pick up and knit 81 [91: 103: 117: 131] sts across front cast-on edge.
Row 1 (WS): P1, *K1, P1, rep from * to end.
Row 2: K1, *P1, K1, rep from * to end.
These 2 rows form rib.
Cont in rib until hem border meas 8 cm from pick-up row, ending with RS facing for next row.
Cast off in rib.
Back hem border
Work as given for front hem border, picking up sts across back cast-off edge.
Cuffs (both alike)
With RS facing, using 3¾mm (US 5) needles and yarn A, pick up and knit 67 [71: 75: 79: 83] sts evenly along row-end edge between markers.
Work in rib as given for front hem border until cuff meas 8 cm from pick-up row, ending with RS facing for next row.
Cast off in rib.
Neckband
With RS facing, using 3¾mm (US 5) circular needle and yarn A, pick up and knit 3 sts from left row-end edge of neck opening, 59 [59: 61: 61: 63] sts from front cast-off neck edge, 3 sts from right row-end edge of neck opening, then 59 [59: 61: 61: 63] sts from back cast-on neck edge. 124 [124: 128: 128: 132] sts.
Cast off purlwise (on **RS**).
See information page for finishing instructions.

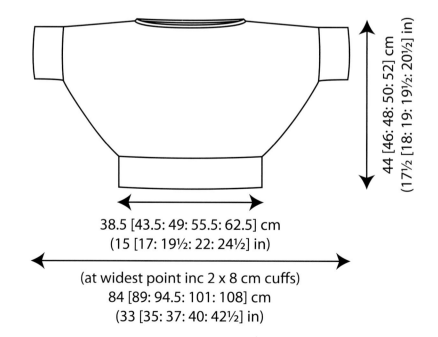

44 [46: 48: 50: 52] cm
(17½ [18: 19: 19½: 20½] in)

38.5 [43.5: 49: 55.5: 62.5] cm
(15 [17: 19½: 22: 24½] in)

(at widest point inc 2 x 8 cm cuffs)
84 [89: 94.5: 101: 108] cm
(33 [35: 37: 40: 42½] in)

Kefalonia
MARIE WALLIN

Main image page 26 & 27

● ● ●

YARN

	S	M	L	XL	XXL	
To fit bust						
	81-86	91-97	102-107	112-117	122-127	cm
	32-34	36-38	40-42	44-46	48-50	in

Wool Cotton 4ply and Kidsilk Haze

A 4ply String 481						
	7	8	9	10	11	x 50gm
B ★KSH Blushes 583						
	1	1	1	1	1	x 25gm
C ★KSH Jelly 597						
	1	1	1	2	2	x 25gm
D ★KSH Fudge 658						
	1	1	1	1	1	x 25gm
E 4ply Leaf 491						
	1	1	1	1	1	x 50gm
F ★KSH Brick 649						
	1	1	1	1	1	x 25gm
G ★KSH Candy Girl 606						
	1	1	1	1	1	x 25gm
H 4ply Old Rose 498						
	1	1	1	1	1	x 50gm
I ★KSH Marmalade 596						
	1	1	1	1	1	x 25gm
K ★KSH Ember 644						
	1	1	1	1	1	x 25gm

★Use Kidsilk Haze **DOUBLE** throughout

NEEDLES

1 pair 2¼mm (no 13) (US 1) needles
1 pair 2¾mm (no 12) (US 2) needles

TENSION

28 sts and 38 rows to 10 cm measured over patterned st st using 2¾mm (US 2) needles.

Pattern note: As body is worked in one piece to armholes, you may prefer to use a circular needle.

BODY (worked in one piece to armholes)
Using 2¼mm (US 1) needles and yarn A cast on 285 [313: 349: 381: 421] sts.
Work in g st for 2 rows, ending with RS facing for next row.
Change to 2¾mm (US 2) needles.
Now place charts as folls:
Row 1 (RS): K12, work next 94 sts as row 1 of chart **reading chart from right to left**, K73 [101: 137: 169: 209], work next 94 sts as row 1 of chart **reading chart from left to right** (to reverse design), K12.
Row 2: P12, work next 94 sts as row 2 of chart **reading chart from right to left** (to reverse design), P73 [101: 137: 169: 209], work next 94 sts as row 2 of chart **reading chart from left to right**, P12.
These 2 rows set the sts - 2 reps of chart with st st using yarn A between and at sides.
Cont as now set until chart row 16 has been completed, ending with RS facing for next row.
Counting in from both ends of last row, place markers after 12th and 126th [140th: 158th: 174th: 194th] sts. (4 markers in total, with 33 sts between markers at centre of row.)
Next row (dec) (RS): (K to within 2 sts of marker, K2tog, slip marker onto right needle, patt to next marker, slip marker onto right needle, sl 1, K1, psso) twice, K to end.
281 [309: 345: 377: 417] sts.
Work 15 rows.
Rep last 16 rows 8 times more, then first of these rows (the dec row) again.
245 [273: 309: 341: 381] sts.
Remove markers.
Cont straight until chart row 172 [174: 178: 182: 186] has been completed, ending with RS facing for next row. (Body should meas approx 46 [46: 47: 48: 49] cm.)

Divide for armholes

Next row (RS): Patt 61 [68: 77: 85: 95] sts and turn, leaving rem 184: 205: 232: 256: 286] sts on a holder. (**Note**: Armhole divisions are NOT shown on chart.)
Work on this set of sts only for right front.
Cont straight until chart row 212 [218: 222: 228: 228] has been completed, ending with RS facing for next row.

Sizes XL and XXL only

All 228 rows of chart have now been completed.
Complete work using yarn A **only**.
Work - [-: -: 2: 6] rows, ending with RS facing for next row.

All sizes

Shape front neck

Next row (RS): Break yarns. Slip first 13 sts onto another holder (for neckband), rejoin yarns and patt to end. 48 [55: 64: 72: 82] sts.

Keeping patt correct, dec 1 st at neck edge of next 10 rows, then on foll 4 alt rows, then on 1 [1: 2: 2: 3] foll 4th rows. 33 [40: 48: 56: 65] sts. (**Note**: For sizes S, M and L, when all 228 rows of chart have been completed, complete work in st st using yarn A **only**.)
Work 2 rows, ending with **WS** facing for next row.

Shape shoulder

Cast off 8 [10: 12: 14: 16] sts at beg of next and foll 2 alt rows.
Work 1 row.
Cast off rem 9 [10: 12: 14: 17] sts.

Shape back

Return to sts left on holder and rejoin yarns with RS facing, patt next 123 [137: 155: 171: 191] sts and turn, leaving rem 61 [68: 77: 85: 95] sts on holder.
Work on these sts only for back.
Work 61 [65: 69: 73: 77] rows, ending with RS facing for next row. (**Note**: Once all 228 rows of chart have been completed, complete work in st st using yarn A **only**.)

Shape back neck and shoulders

Next row (RS): Patt 39 [46: 54: 62: 71] sts and turn, leaving rem sts on a holder.
Work each side of neck separately.
Dec 1 st at neck edge of next 6 rows, ending with **WS** facing for next row, **and at same time** cast off 8 [10: 12: 14: 16] sts at beg of 2nd and foll 2 alt rows.
Work 1 row.
Cast off rem 9 [10: 12: 14: 17] sts.
With RS facing, slip centre 45 [45: 47: 47: 49] sts onto another holder (for neckband), rejoin yarns to rem sts, patt to end.
Complete to match first side, reversing shapings.

Shape left front

Return to sts left on first holder, rejoin yarns with RS facing and patt to end.
61 [68: 77: 85: 95] sts.
Work on these sts only for left front as folls:
Work to match right front, reversing shapings and working first row of neck shaping as folls:

Shape front neck

Next row (RS): Patt to last 13 sts and turn,

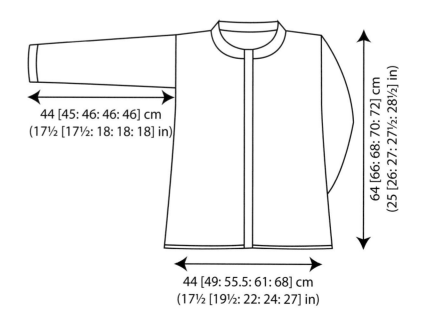

44 [45: 46: 46: 46] cm
(17½ [17½: 18: 18: 18] in)

64 [66: 68: 70: 72] cm
(25 [26: 27: 27½: 28½] in)

44 [49: 55.5: 61: 68] cm
(17½ [19½: 22: 24: 27] in)

leaving rem 13 sts on another holder (for neckband). 48 [55: 64: 72: 82] sts.

SLEEVES

Using 2¼mm (US 1) needles and yarn C cast on 57 [59: 61: 61: 63] sts.
Row 1 (RS): K1, *P1, K1, rep from * to end.
Row 2: P1, *K1, P1, rep from * to end.
These 2 rows form rib.
Keeping rib correct, now work in stripes as folls:
Rows 3 and 4: Using yarn C.
Rows 5 to 14: Using yarn A.
Rows 15 and 16: Using yarn C.
Break off yarn C and cont using yarn A only.
Change to 2¾mm (US 2) needles.
Beg with a K row, work in st st, shaping sides by inc 1 st at each end of 7th [5th: 5th: 5th: 3rd] and every foll 8th [6th: 6th: 6th: 4th] row to 83 [67: 81: 105: 73] sts, then on every foll 10th [8th: 8th: 8th: 6th] row until there are 89 [95: 101: 107: 113] sts.
Cont straight until sleeve meas 44 [45: 46: 46: 46] cm, ending with RS facing for next row. Cast off.

MAKING UP

Press as described on the information page. Join both shoulder seams using back stitch, or mattress stitch if preferred.

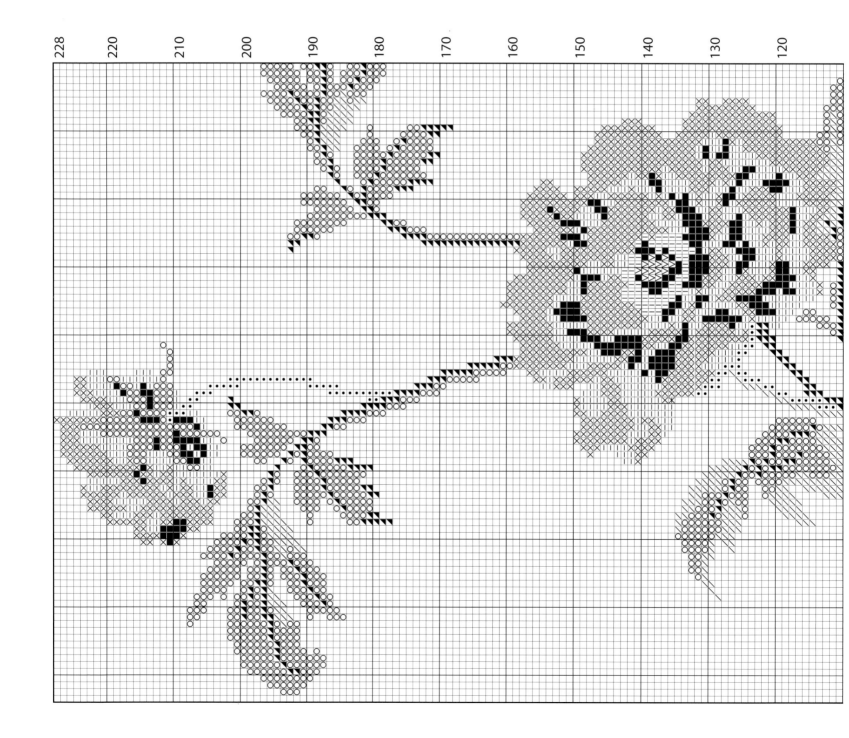

Neckband

With RS facing, using 2¼mm (US 1) needles and yarn C, K across 13 sts on right front holder, pick up and knit 25 [25: 29: 29: 33] sts up right side of front neck, and 7 sts down right side of back neck, K across 45 [45: 47: 47: 49] sts on back holder, pick up and knit 7 sts up left side of back neck, and 25 [25: 29: 29: 33] sts down left side of front neck, then K across 13 sts on left front holder.

135 [135: 145: 145: 155] sts.
★★Row 1 (WS): K1, ★P1, K1, rep from ★ to end.
Row 2: K2, ★P1, K1, rep from ★ to last st, K1.
These 2 rows form rib.
Keeping rib correct, now work in stripes as folls:
Rows 3 and 4: Using yarn C.
Rows 5 to 10: Using yarn A.
Row 11 (WS): Using yarn C.
Cast off in rib using yarn C.

Front bands (both alike)

With RS facing, using 2¼mm (US 1) needles and yarn C, pick up and knit 181 [187: 189: 195: 199] sts evenly along entire front opening edge, between cast-on edge and top of neckband.
Complete as given for neckband from ★★.
See information page for finishing instructions, setting in sleeves using the straight cast-off method.

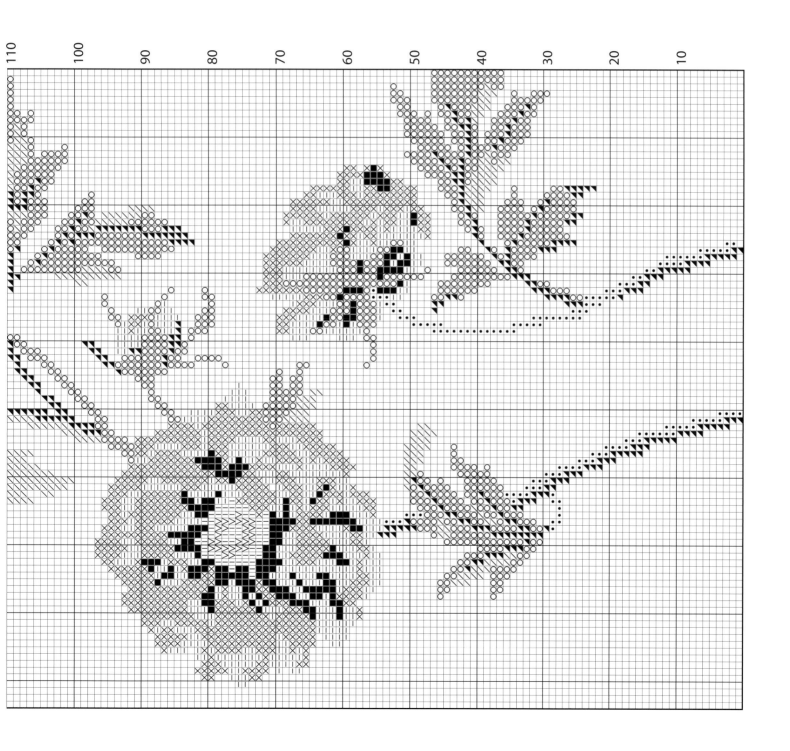

Kos

MARIE WALLIN

Main image page 14 & 15

● ● ●

YARN

	S	M	L	XL	XXL
To fit bust					

81-86 91-97 102-107 112-117 122-127 cm
32-34 36-38 40-42 44-46 48-50 in

Siena 4ply

8　9　9　10　11　x 50gm

(photographed in Lipstick 680)

CROCHET HOOK

3.00mm (no 11) (US C2) crochet hook

TENSION

21 sts to 10 cm and first 52 rows measure 42 cm measured over patt using 3.00mm (US C2) crochet hook.

CROCHET ABBREVIATIONS

ch = chain; **dc** = double crochet; **dtr** = double treble; **sp(s)** = space(s); **tr** = treble; **tr2tog** = (yoh and insert hook as indicated, yoh and draw loop through, yoh and draw through 2 loops) twice, yoh and draw through all 3 loops on hook; **tr3tog** = (yoh and insert hook as indicated, yoh and draw loop through, yoh and draw through 2 loops) 3 times, yoh and draw through all 4 loops on hook; **tr4tog** = (yoh and insert hook as indicated, yoh and draw loop through, yoh and draw through 2 loops) 4 times, yoh and draw through all 5 loops on hook; **ttr** = triple treble; **ttr4tog** = *(yoh) 3 times, insert hook as indicated, yoh and draw loop through, (yoh and draw through 2 loops) 3 times, rep from * 3 times more, yoh and draw through all 5 loops on hook; **yoh** = yarn over hook.

BACK

Using 3.00mm (US C2) crochet hook make 99 [107: 123: 131: 147] ch.
Now work in patt as folls:
Row 1 (WS): 1 dc into 2nd ch from hook, 1 dc into each ch to end, turn.
98 [106: 122: 130: 146] sts.
Row 2: 4 ch (counts as 1 tr and 1 ch), miss first 2 dc, *tr4tog into next dc**, 2 ch, miss 2 dc, rep from * to end, ending last rep at **, 1 ch, miss 1 dc, 1 tr into last dc, turn.
Row 3: 1 ch (does NOT count as st), 1 dc into first tr, 1 dc into next ch sp, *1 dc into next tr4tog**, 2 dc into next ch sp, rep from * to end, ending last rep at **, 1 dc into last ch sp, 1 dc into 3rd of 4 ch at beg of previous row, turn.

Rows 4 and 5: As rows 2 and 3.
Rows 6 and 7: As rows 2 and 3.
Row 8: 3 ch (counts as 1 tr), miss dc at base of 3 ch, 1 tr into each dc to end, turn.
Row 9: 3 ch (counts as 1 tr), miss tr at base of 3 ch, *1 tr into next tr, 3 ch, miss 2 tr, 1 dc into next tr, 3 ch, 1 dc into next tr, 3 ch, miss 2 tr, 1 tr into next tr, rep from * to last st, 1 tr into top of 3 ch at beg of previous row, turn.
Row 10: 3 ch (counts as 1 tr), miss tr at base of 3 ch, *1 tr into next tr, 1 ch, miss (3 ch and 1 dc), 4 tr into next ch sp, 1 ch, miss (1 dc and 3 ch), 1 tr into next tr, rep from * to last st, 1 tr into top of 3 ch at beg of previous row, turn.
Row 11: 3 ch (counts as 1 tr), miss tr at base of 3 ch, *1 tr into next tr, 2 ch, miss (1 ch and 1 tr), 1 tr into each of next 2 tr, 2 ch, miss (1 tr and 1 ch), 1 tr into next tr, rep from * to last st, 1 tr into top of 3 ch at beg of previous row, turn.
Row 12: 3 ch (counts as 1 tr), miss tr at base of 3 ch, 1 tr into next tr, *2 tr into next ch sp, 1 tr into each of next 2 tr, rep from * to end, working tr at end of last rep into top of 3 ch at beg of previous row, turn.
Row 13: 1 ch (does NOT count as st), 1 dc into each tr to end, working last dc into top of 3 ch at beg of previous row, turn.
Rows 14 and 15: As rows 2 and 3.
Rows 16 to 23: As rows 8 to 15.
Row 24: As row 8.
Row 25: 5 ch (counts as 1 dtr and 1 ch), miss tr at base of 5 ch, tr2tog into next tr, *3 ch, miss 3 tr, 1 dc into next tr, 3 ch, miss 3 tr**, (tr2tog, 3 ch and tr2tog) into next tr, rep from * to end, ending last rep at **, (tr2tog, 1 ch and 1 dtr) into top of 3 ch at beg of previous row, turn. 12 [13: 15: 16: 18] patt reps.
Row 26: 1 ch (does NOT count as st), 1 dc into first dtr, miss 1 ch, *2 ch, miss (1 tr2tog and 3 ch), 3 tr into next dc, 2 ch, miss (3 ch and 1 tr2tog), 1 dc into next ch sp, rep from * to end, working dc at end of last rep into 4th of 5 ch at beg of previous row, turn.
Row 27: 1 ch (does NOT count as st), 1 dc into first dc, *3 ch, miss (2 ch and 1 tr), (tr2tog, 3 ch and tr2tog) into next tr, 3 ch, miss (1 tr and 2 ch), 1 dc into next dc, rep from * to end, turn.

Row 28: 3 ch (counts as 1 tr), 1 tr into dc at base of 3 ch, *2 ch, miss (3 ch and 1 tr2tog), 1 dc into next ch sp, 2 ch, miss (1 tr2tog and 3 ch)**, 3 tr into next dc, rep from * to end, ending last rep at **, 2 tr into last dc, turn.
Row 29: 5 ch (counts as 1 dtr and 1 ch), tr2tog into tr at base of 5 ch, *3 ch, miss (1 tr and 2 ch), 1 dc into next dc, 3 ch, miss (3 ch and 1 tr)**, (tr2tog, 3 ch and tr2tog) into next tr, rep from * to end, ending last rep at **, (tr2tog, 1 ch and 1 dtr) into top of 3 ch at beg of previous row, turn.
Rows 30 to 33: As rows 26 to 29.
Row 34: As row 26.
Row 35: 3 ch (counts as 1 tr), 1 tr into dc at base of 3 ch, *2 tr into next ch sp, 1 tr into each of next 3 tr, 2 tr into next ch sp, 1 tr into next dc, rep from * to end, turn. 98 [106: 122: 130: 146] sts.
Row 36: 4 ch (counts as 1 tr and 1 ch), miss first 2 tr, *tr4tog into next tr**, 2 ch, miss 2 tr, rep from * to end, ending last rep at **, 1 ch, miss 1 tr, 1 tr into top of 3 ch at beg of previous row, turn.
Row 37: 3 ch (counts as 1 tr), miss tr at base of 3 ch, 1 tr into next ch sp, *1 tr into next tr4tog**, 2 tr into next ch sp, rep from * to end, ending last rep at **, 1 tr into next ch sp, 1 tr into 3rd of 4 ch at beg of previous row, turn.
Row 38: 3 ch (counts as 1 tr), miss tr at base of 3 ch, 1 tr into each tr to end, working last tr into top of 3 ch at beg of previous row, turn.
Rows 39 and 40: As row 38.
Row 41: 1 ch (does NOT count as st), 1 dc into each tr to end, working last dc into top of 3 ch at beg of previous row, turn.
Row 42: 6 ch (counts as 1 ttr and 1 ch), miss first 2 dc, *ttr4tog into next dc**, 2 ch, miss 2 dc, rep from * to end, ending last rep at **, 1 ch, miss 1 dc, 1 ttr into last dc, turn.
Row 43: 1 ch (does NOT count as st), 1 dc into first ttr, 1 dc into next ch sp, *1 dc into next ttr4tog**, 2 dc into next ch sp, rep from * to end, ending last rep at **, 1 dc into next ch sp, 1 dc into 5th of 6 ch at beg of previous row, turn.
Row 44: As row 8.
Rows 45 and 46: As row 38.

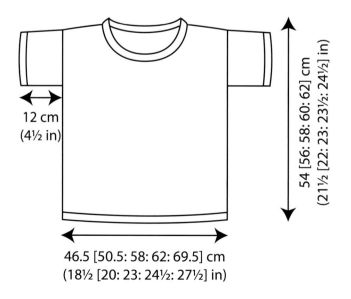

12 cm
(4½ in)

54 [56: 58: 60: 62] cm
(21½ [22: 23: 23½: 24½] in)

46.5 [50.5: 58: 62: 69.5] cm
(18½ [20: 23: 24½: 27½] in)

Rows 47 and 48: As rows 36 and 37.
Sizes S, L and XXL only
Row 49: 3 ch (counts as 1 tr), miss tr at base of 3 ch, ★1 tr into next tr, 1 ch, miss 2 tr, 4 tr into next tr, 1 ch, miss 2 tr, rep from ★ to last st, 2 tr into top of 3 ch at beg of previous row, turn. 16 [-: 20: –: 24] patt reps.
Sizes M and XL only
Row 49: 3 ch (counts as 1 tr), miss (tr at base of 3 ch and next tr), ★1 tr into next tr★★, 1 ch, miss 2 tr, 4 tr into next tr, 1 ch, miss 2 tr, rep from ★ to end, ending last rep at ★★, miss 1 tr, 1 tr into top of 3 ch at beg of previous row, turn. – [17: –: 21: –] patt reps.
All sizes
Row 50: 3 ch (counts as 1 tr), miss tr at base of 3 ch, ★1 tr into next tr★★, 2 ch, miss 1 ch, tr4tog over next 4 tr, 2 ch, miss 1 ch, rep from ★ to end, ending last rep at ★★, 1 tr into top of 3 ch at beg of previous row, turn.
Row 51: 3 ch (counts as 1 tr), miss tr at base of 3 ch, 2 tr into next tr, ★1 ch, miss 2 tr, 1 tr into next tr4tog, 1 ch, miss 2 ch★★, 4 tr into next tr, rep from ★ to end, ending last rep at ★★, 2 tr into next tr, 1 tr into top of 3 ch at beg of previous row, turn.
Row 52: 3 ch (counts as 1 tr), miss tr at base of 3 ch, tr2tog over next 2 tr, ★2 ch, miss 1 ch, 1 tr into next tr, 2 ch, miss 1 ch★★, tr4tog over next 4 tr, rep from ★ to end, ending last rep at ★★, tr2tog over next 2 tr, 1 tr into top of 3 ch at beg of previous row, turn.
Row 53: 3 ch (counts as 1 tr), miss tr at base of 3 ch, 1 tr into next tr2tog, ★1 ch, miss 2 tr, 4 tr into next tr, 1 ch, miss 2 ch★★, 1 tr into next tr4tog, rep from ★ to end, ending last rep at ★★, 1 tr into next tr2tog, 1 tr into top of 3 ch at beg of previous row, turn.
Rows 50 to 53 form patt for rest of back.
Cont in patt as now set until back meas approx 51 [53: 55: 57: 59] cm, ending after a rep of patt row 51 [53: 53: 51: 51].
Shape back neck
Next row: Work 4½ [5: 6: 6½: 7½] patt reps ending last rep after "tr4tog over next 4 tr, 2 ch, miss 1 ch, 1 tr into next tr", now work 2 ch, miss 1 ch, tr4tog over next 4 tr and turn, leaving rem sts unworked.
Next row: 3 ch (counts as first tr), miss (tr4tog at base of 3 ch and next 2 ch), 2 tr into next tr, 1 ch, miss 2 tr, 1 tr into next tr4tog, patt to end. 4½ [5: 6: 6½: 7½] patt reps.
Fasten off.
Return to last complete row worked, miss next 5 [5: 6: 6: 7] groups of 4 tr after last one worked into for first side of neck, miss next

(1 ch, 1 tr and 1 ch), attach yarn to first tr of next 4 tr group and cont as folls: 3 ch (does NOT count as st), miss tr at base of 3 ch, tr3tog over next 3 tr, 2 ch, miss 1 ch, 1 tr into next tr, patt to end, turn.
Next row: Patt until tr has been worked into first tr4tog of previous row, 1 ch, miss 2 ch, 2 tr into next tr, 1 tr into top of tr3tog at beg of previous row. 4½ [5: 6: 6½: 7½] patt reps.
Fasten off.

FRONT
Work as given for back until 10 rows less have been worked than on back to shoulder fasten-off point, ending after a rep of patt row 51 [53: 53: 51: 51].
Shape front neck
Row 1: Work 5½ [6: 7: 7½: 8½] patt reps ending last rep after "tr4tog over next 4 tr, 2 ch, miss 1 ch, 1 tr into next tr", now work 2 ch, miss 1 ch, tr4tog over next 4 tr and turn, leaving rem sts unworked.
Row 2: 3 ch (does NOT count as st), miss (tr4tog and 2 ch), 4 tr into next tr, patt to end, turn.
Row 3: Patt until tr4tog has been worked over first group of 4 tr at beg of previous row, turn.
Rows 4 and 5: As rows 2 and 3.
Row 6: 3 ch (counts as 1 tr), miss (tr4tog and 2 ch), 4 tr into next tr, patt to end, turn.
Row 7: Patt until tr4tog has been worked over first group of 4 tr at beg of previous row, 1 tr into top of 3 ch at beg of previous row, turn.
Row 8: 3 ch (counts as 1 tr), 1 tr into next tr4tog, patt to end, turn.
4½ [5: 6: 6½: 7½] patt reps.
Keeping patt correct as now set, work a further 2 rows.
Fasten off.
Return to last complete row worked, miss next 3 [3: 4: 4: 5] groups of 4 tr after last one worked into for first side of neck, miss next (1 ch, 1 tr and 1 ch), attach yarn to first tr of next 4 tr group and cont as folls:
Row 1: 3 ch (does NOT count as st), miss tr at base of 3 ch, tr3tog over next 3 tr, 2 ch, miss 1 ch, 1 tr into next tr, patt to end, turn.
Row 2: Patt until 1 tr has been worked into first tr4tog of previous row, 1 ch, miss 2 ch, 3 tr into next tr, tr2tog working first "leg" into same tr as previous 3 tr, missing 2 ch, and working 2nd "leg" into top of tr3tog at beg of previous row, turn.
Row 3: 3 ch (does NOT count as st), miss tr2tog at base of 3 ch, tr3tog over next 3 tr, 2 ch, miss 1 ch, 1 tr into next tr, patt to end, turn.

Rows 4 and 5: As rows 2 and 3.
Row 6: Patt until 1 tr has been worked into first tr4tog of previous row, 1 ch, miss 2 ch, 4 tr into next tr, miss 2 ch, 1 tr into top of tr3tog at beg of previous row, turn.
Row 7: 3 ch (counts as 1 tr), miss tr at base of 3 ch, tr4tog over next 4 tr, patt to end, turn.
Row 8: Patt until 1 tr has been worked into first tr3tog at beg of previous row, 1 tr into top of 3 ch at beg of previous row, turn.
4½ [5: 6: 6½: 7½] patt reps.
Keeping patt correct as now set, work a further 2 rows.
Fasten off.

SLEEVES
Using 3.00mm (US C2) crochet hook make 67 [75: 75: 83: 83] ch.
Row 1 (WS): 1 dc into 2nd ch from hook, 1 dc into each ch to end, turn.
66 [74: 74: 82: 82] sts.
Beg with row 2, now work in patt as given for back until patt row 15 has been completed. (Sleeve should meas approx 11 cm.)
Fasten off.

MAKING UP
Press as described on the information page. Join both shoulder seams using back stitch, or mattress stitch if preferred.
Neck edging
With RS facing and using 3.00mm (US C2) crochet hook, attach yarn at neck edge of left shoulder seam, 1 ch (does NOT count as st), work 1 round of dc evenly around entire neck edge, ensuring number of dc worked is divisible by 6 and ending with ss to first dc, do NOT turn.
Next round (RS): Miss dc where ss was worked and next 2 dc, ★6 tr into next dc, miss 2 dc★★, 1 ss into next dc, miss 2 dc, rep from ★ to end, ending last rep at ★★, 1 ss into same place as ss at end of previous round.
Fasten off.
Mark points along side seam edges 17 [19: 19: 21: 21] cm either side of shoulder seams to denote base of armhole openings. See information page for finishing instructions, setting in sleeves using the straight cast-off method.
Cuff edgings (both alike)
Work as given for neck edging, attaching yarn at base of sleeve seam.
Hem edging
Work as given for neck edging, attaching yarn at base of left side seam.

RHODES
LISA RICHARDSON
Main image page 22 & 23

●●●

YARN

	S	M	L	XL	XXL	
To fit bust						
81-86	91-97	102-107	112-117	122-127 cm		
32-34	36-38	40-42	44-46	48-50 in		

Kidsilk Haze and Fine Lace

A KSH Cream 634						
6	7	7	8	8	x 25gm
B FL P'laine 928						
3	4	4	4	5	x 50gm
C FL Cameo 920						
1	1	1	1	1	x 50gm
D FL Antique 921						
1	1	1	1	1	x 50gm
E FL Quaint 925						
1	1	1	1	1	x 50gm
F FL Vamp 935						
1	1	1	1	1	x 50gm
G KSH Shadow 653						
1	1	1	1	1	x 25gm
H KSH Grace 580						
1	1	1	1	1	x 25gm
I KSH Blushes 583						
1	1	1	1	1	x 25gm
J KSH Brick 649						
1	1	1	1	1	x 25gm
K KSH Candy Girl 606						
1	1	1	1	1	x 25gm

NEEDLES
1 pair 2¼mm (no 13) (US 1) needles
1 pair 2¾mm (no 12) (US 2) needles

TENSION
29 sts and 38 rows to 10 cm measured over st st using 2¾mm (US 2) needles and one strand each of Kidsilk Haze and Fine Lace held together.

BACK
Using 2¼mm (US 1) needles and one strand each of yarns A and B held together cast on 130 [146: 162: 178: 202] sts.
Row 1 (RS): K2, *P2, K2, rep from * to end.
Row 2: P2, *K2, P2, rep from * to end.
These 2 rows form rib.
Cont in rib for a further 14 rows, inc [dec: inc: inc: dec] 1 st at end of last row and ending with RS facing for next row.
131 [145: 163: 179: 201] sts.
Change to 2¾mm (US 2) needles.**
Beg with a K row, work in st st until back meas 29 [30: 31: 32: 33] cm, ending with RS facing

for next row.
Shape armholes
Cast off 5 [6: 7: 8: 9] sts at beg of next 2 rows.
121 [133: 149: 163: 183] sts.
Dec 1 st at each end of next 5 [7: 9: 11: 13] rows, then on foll 3 [4: 6: 7: 10] alt rows.
105 [111: 119: 127: 137] sts.
Cont straight until armhole meas 20 [21: 22: 23: 24] cm, ending with RS facing for next row.
Shape back neck and shoulders
Next row (RS): Cast off 6 [7: 8: 9: 10] sts, K until there are 25 [27: 29: 32: 35] sts on right needle and turn, leaving rem sts on a holder.
Work each side of neck separately.
Dec 1 st at neck edge of next 5 rows, ending with RS facing for next row, **and at same time** cast off 6 [7: 8: 9: 10] sts at beg of 2nd row, then 7 [7: 8: 9: 10] sts at beg of foll alt row.
Cast off rem 7 [8: 8: 9: 10] sts.
With RS facing, rejoin yarns to rem sts, cast off centre 43 [43: 45: 45: 47] sts, K to end.
Complete to match first side, reversing shapings.

FRONT
Work as given for back to **.
Beg with a K row, work in st st until front meas 9 [10: 11: 12: 12] cm, ending with RS facing for next row.
Place chart
Next row (RS): K23 [30: 39: 47: 58], work next 85 sts as row 1 of chart, K23 [30: 39: 47: 58].
Next row: P23 [30: 39: 47: 58], work next 85 sts as row 2 of chart, P23 [30: 39: 47: 58].
These 2 rows set the sts - centre 85 sts in patt from chart with edge sts still in st st using one strand each of yarns A and B held together.
(**Note**: All contrast colours on chart are 2 strands of yarn held together – one strand each of Kidsilk Haze and Fine Lace.)
Working rem 98 rows of chart and then completing front in st st using one strand each of yarns A and B held together, cont as folls:
Work as given for back from ** until 20 [20: 24: 24: 28] rows less have been worked than on back to beg of shoulder shaping, ending with RS facing for next row.

Shape front neck
Next row (RS): K37 [40: 44: 48: 53] and turn, leaving rem sts on a holder.
Work each side of neck separately.
Dec 1 st at neck edge of next 6 rows, then on foll 4 alt rows, then on 1 [1: 2: 2: 3] foll 4th rows. 26 [29: 32: 36: 40] sts.
Work 1 row, ending with RS facing for next row.
Shape shoulder
Cast off 6 [7: 8: 9: 10] sts at beg of next and foll alt row, then 7 [7: 8: 9: 10] sts at beg of foll alt row.
Work 1 row.
Cast off rem 7 [8: 8: 9: 10] sts.
With RS facing, rejoin yarns to rem sts, cast off centre 31 sts, K to end.
Complete to match first side, reversing shapings.

SLEEVES
Using 2¼mm (US 1) needles and one strand each of yarns A and B held together cast on 70 [70: 74: 74: 74] sts.
Work in rib as given for back for 16 rows, dec [inc: dec: dec: inc] 1 st at end of last row and ending with RS facing for next row.
69 [71: 73: 73: 75] sts.
Change to 2¾mm (US 2) needles.
Beg with a K row, work in st st, shaping sides by inc 1 st at each end of 5th and every foll 6th row to 77 [83: 89: 105: 115] sts, then on every foll 8th row until there are 105 [109: 113: 117: 121] sts.
Cont straight until sleeve meas 45 [46: 47: 47: 47] cm, ending with RS facing for next row.
Shape top
Cast off 5 [6: 7: 8: 9] sts at beg of next 2 rows.
95 [97: 99: 101: 103] sts.
Dec 1 st at each end of next 5 rows, then on every foll alt row until 55 sts rem, then on foll 9 rows, ending with RS facing for next row.
37 sts.
Cast off 4 sts at beg of next 4 rows.
Cast off rem 21 sts.

MAKING UP
Press as described on the information page.
Join right shoulder seam using back stitch, or

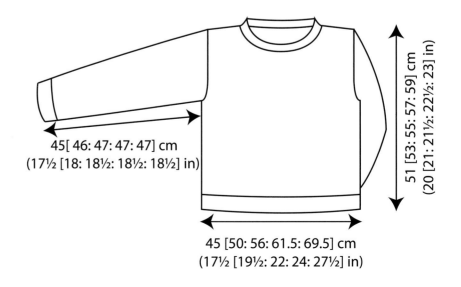

45[46: 47: 47: 47] cm
(17½ [18: 18½: 18½: 18½] in)

45 [50: 56: 61.5: 69.5] cm
(17½ [19½: 22: 24: 27½] in)

51 [53: 55: 57: 59] cm
(20 [21: 21½: 22½: 23] in)

mattress stitch if preferred.

Neckband

With RS facing, using 2¼mm (US 1) needles and one strand each of yarns A and B held together, pick up and knit 21 [21: 24: 24: 29] sts down left side of neck, 31 sts from front, 21 [21: 24: 24: 29] sts up right side of neck, then 53 [53: 55: 55: 57] sts from back. 126 [126: 134: 134: 146] sts.

Beg with row 2, work in rib as given for back for 9 rows, ending with RS facing for next row.

Cast off in rib.

See information page for finishing instructions, setting in sleeves using the set-in method.

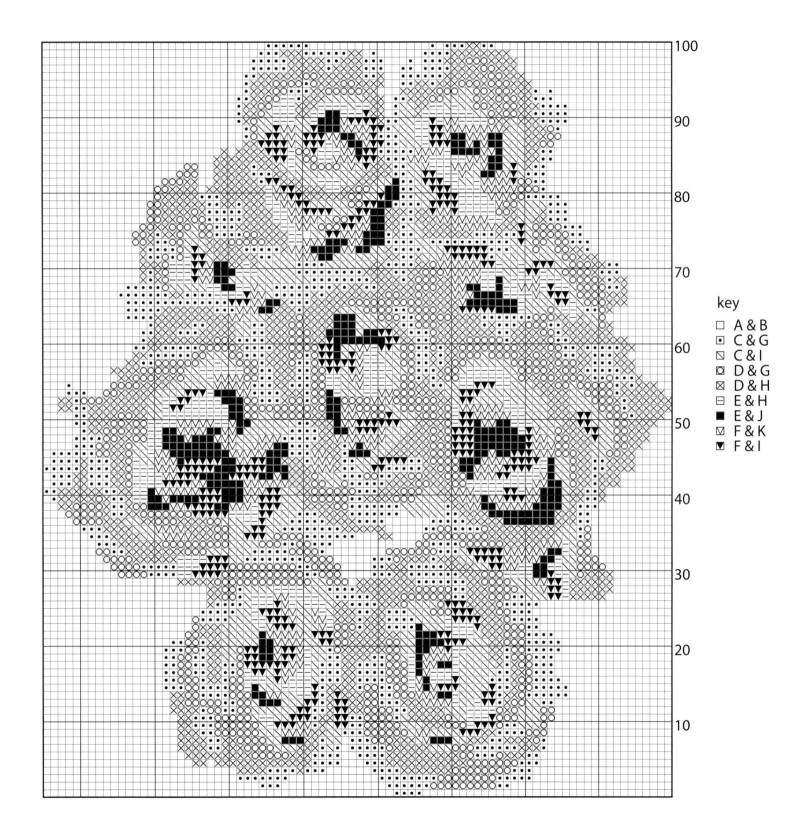

key
☐ A & B
⊡ C & G
⊠ C & I
◩ D & G
⊠ D & H
⊟ E & H
■ E & J
☒ F & K
▼ F & I

SAMOS
VIBE ULRIK
Main image page 24 & 25

● ● ●

YARN

S	M	L	XL	XXL

To fit bust
81–86 91–97 102–107 112–117 122–127 cm
32–34 36–38 40–42 44–46 48–50 in

Fine Lace

4	4	5	5	6	x 50gm

(photographed in Leaf 931)

NEEDLES

1 pair 4mm (no 8) (US 6) needles

TENSION

21 sts and 29 rows to 10 cm measured over st
st, 19½ sts and 27 rows to 10 cm measured
over lace patt, both using 4mm (US 6) needles
and yarn DOUBLE.

Pattern note: Take care to ensure each dec of
patt is matched by an inc. If there are
insufficient sts to work both, work end sts of
rows in st st.

BACK

Using 4mm (US 6) needles and yarn
DOUBLE cast on 29 [39: 53: 69: 85] sts.
Row 1 (RS): K2, *P1, K1, rep from * to last
st, K1.
Row 2: K1, *P1, K1, rep from * to end.
These 2 rows form rib.
Work in rib for a further 3 rows, ending with
WS facing for next row.
Row 6 (WS): Rib 3 [3: 3: 2: 1], work 2 tog,
(rib 5 [8: 7: 7: 7], work 2 tog) 3 [3: 5: 7: 9]
times, rib 3 [4: 3: 2: 1]. 25 [35: 47: 61: 75] sts.
Now shape side edges as folls:
Row 1 (RS): K2, M1, K to last 2 sts, M1, K2.
Row 2: K1, P to last st, K1.
Rows 3 and 4: As rows 1 and 2.
Row 5: As row 1.
Row 6: K1, P1, M1P, P to last 2 sts, M1P, P1, K1.
Row 7: Knit.
Rows 8 and 9: As rows 6 and 7.
Row 10: As row 6. 37 [47: 59: 73: 87] sts.
Rep last 10 rows 5 times more, then first 4 of
these rows again, ending with RS facing for
next row. 101 [111: 123: 137: 151] sts.
Place markers at both ends of last row. (Back
should meas 24 cm.)
Beg with a K row, cont straight in st st until
back meas 28 [29: 30: 31: 32] cm **measuring
at centre of work**, ending with RS facing for
next row.

Shape armholes

Cast off 3 [4: 5: 6: 7] sts at beg of next 2 rows.
95 [103: 113: 125: 137] sts.
Dec 1 st at each end of next 3 [3: 5: 5: 7] rows,
then on foll 2 [4: 4: 7: 7] alt rows.
85 [89: 95: 101: 109] sts.
Cont straight until armhole meas 17 [18: 19:
20: 21] cm, ending with RS facing for next row.

Shape shoulders and back neck

Cast off 4 [4: 5: 5: 6] sts at beg of next 2 rows.
77 [81: 85: 91: 97] sts.
Next row (RS): Cast off 4 [4: 5: 5: 6] sts, K
until there are 17 [19: 19: 22: 23] sts on right
needle and turn, leaving rem sts on a holder.
Work each side of neck separately.
Dec 1 st at neck edge of next 4 rows **and at
same time** cast off 4 [5: 5: 6: 6] sts at beg of
2nd and foll alt row.
Work 1 row, ending with RS facing for next row.
Cast off rem 5 [5: 5: 6: 7] sts.
With RS facing, rejoin yarn to rem sts, cast off
centre 35 [35: 37: 37: 39] sts, K to end.
Complete to match first side, reversing shapings.

FRONT

Using 4mm (US 6) needles and yarn
DOUBLE cast on 115 [127: 139: 157: 171] sts.
Work in rib as given for back for 5 rows,
ending with **WS** facing for next row.
Row 6 (WS): Rib 6 [7: 8: 7: 9], work 2 tog,
(rib 3, work 2 tog) 20 [22: 24: 28: 30] times, rib
7 [8: 9: 8: 10]. 94 [104: 114: 128: 140] sts.
Beg and ending rows as indicated, repeating the
34 st patt rep 2 [3: 3: 3: 4] times across each
row and repeating the 24 row patt rep
throughout, cont in patt from appropriate chart
for size being knitted as folls:
Cont straight until back meas 28 [29: 30: 31:
32] cm, ending with RS facing for next row.

Shape armholes

Keeping patt correct, cast off 3 [4: 5: 6: 7] sts at
beg of next 2 rows. 88 [96: 104: 116: 126] sts.
Dec 1 st at each end of next 3 [3: 5: 5: 7] rows,
then on foll 2 [4: 3: 6: 5] alt rows.
78 [82: 88: 94: 102] sts.
Cont straight until armhole meas 15 [16: 16:
17: 17] cm, ending with RS facing for next row.

Shape front neck

Next row (RS): Patt 28 [30: 33: 36: 40] sts
and turn, leaving rem sts on a holder.

Work each side of neck separately.
Keeping patt correct, dec 1 st at neck edge of
next 4 [4: 6: 6: 6] rows, then on foll 0 [0: 0: 0:
1] alt row. 24 [26: 27: 30: 33] sts.
Work 1 row, ending with RS facing for next row.

Shape shoulder

Cast off 4 [4: 4: 5: 5] sts at beg of next and foll
3 [2: 1: 3: 0] alt rows, then – [5: 5: –: 6] sts at beg
of foll – [1: 2: –: 3] alt rows **and at same time**
dec 1 st at neck edge of next and 3 foll alt rows.
Work 1 row.
Cast off rem 4 [5: 5: 6: 6] sts.
With RS facing, rejoin yarn to rem sts, cast off
centre 22 sts, patt to end.
Complete to match first side, reversing shapings.

SLEEVES

Using 4mm (US 6) needles and yarn
DOUBLE cast on 77 [81: 85: 89: 93] sts.
Row 1 (RS): K1, *P1, K1, rep from * to end.
Row 2: P1, *K1, P1, rep from * to end.
These 2 rows form rib.
Cont in rib until sleeve meas 2 cm, ending
with RS facing for next row.

Shape top

Cast off 3 [4: 5: 6: 7] sts at beg of next 2 rows.
71 [73: 75: 77: 79] sts.
Dec 1 st at each end of next 5 rows, then on
every foll alt row until 49 sts rem, then on foll
9 rows, ending with RS facing for next row.
31 sts.
Cast off 4 sts at beg of next 4 rows.
Cast off rem 15 sts.

MAKING UP

Press as described on the information page.
Join right shoulder seam using back stitch, or
mattress stitch if preferred.
Side panels (both alike)
With RS facing, using 4mm (US 6) needles
and yarn DOUBLE, pick up and knit 73 sts
evenly along shaped side edge of back, between
cast-on edge and marker.
Beg with row 2, work in rib as given for back
for 24 cm, ending with RS facing for next row.
Cast off in rib.
Neckband
With RS facing, using 4mm (US 6) needles
and yarn DOUBLE, pick up and knit 16 [16:
18: 18: 20] sts down left side of neck, 29 sts

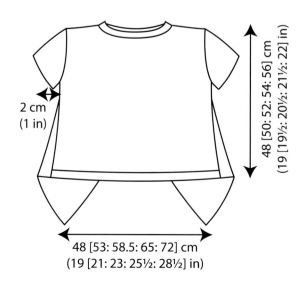

2 cm
(1 in)

48 [50: 52: 54: 56] cm
(19 [19½: 20½: 21½: 22] in)

48 [53: 58.5: 65: 72] cm
(19 [21: 23: 25½: 28½] in)

from front, 16 [16: 18: 18: 20] sts up right side of neck, then 48 [48: 50: 50: 52] sts from back. 109 [109: 115: 115: 121] sts.
Beg with row 2, work in rib as given for sleeves for 5 rows, ending with RS facing for next row.
Cast off in rib.
See information page for finishing instructions, setting in sleeves using the set-in method. (**Note**: When joining side seams, front side seam edge is attached to back side seam edge above marker **and** to row-end edge of side panel. Cast-off edge of side panel matches cast-on edge of front, and rem row-end edge and cast-off edge of side panel are left unattached.)

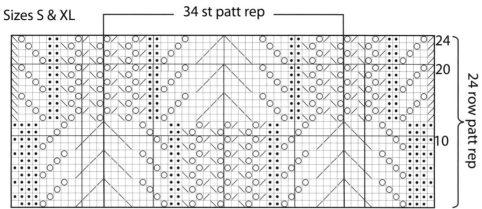

Sizes S & XL

34 st patt rep

24 row patt rep

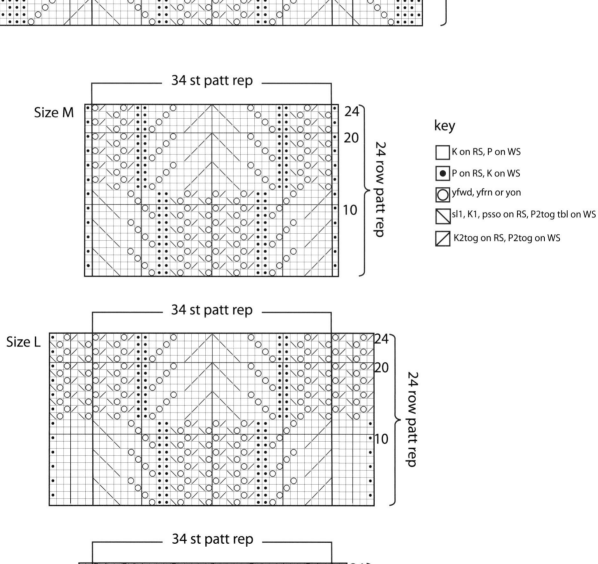

Size M

34 st patt rep

24 row patt rep

key

- ☐ K on RS, P on WS
- ▣ P on RS, K on WS
- Ⓞ yfwd, yfrn or yon
- ◹ sl1, K1, psso on RS, P2tog tbl on WS
- ◿ K2tog on RS, P2tog on WS

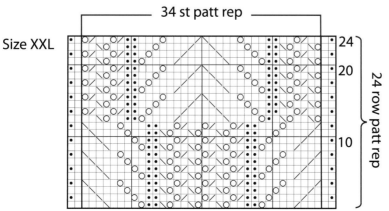

Size L

34 st patt rep

24 row patt rep

Size XXL

34 st patt rep

24 row patt rep

SANTORINI

MARIE WALLIN

Main image page 4, 6 & 7

YARN

	S-M	L-XL	XXL	
To fit bust				
	81-97	102-117	122-127	cm
	32-38	40-46	48-50	in

Purelife Revive and Wool Cotton

A Rev Pumice 461				
	9	12	13	x 50gm
B WCo Pier 983				
	1	1	1	x 50gm
C WCo Wind Break 984				
	1	1	1	x 50gm
D WCo French Navy 909				
	1	1	1	x 50gm
E WCo Brolly 980				
	1	1	1	x 50gm
F WCo Cafe 985				
	1	1	1	x 50gm
G WCo Antique 900				
	1	1	1	x 50gm
H WCo Bilberry 969				
	1	1	1	x 50gm
I WCo Rich 911				
	1	1	1	x 50gm
J WCo Ship Shape 955				
	1	1	1	x 50gm
K WCo Elf 946				
	1	1	1	x 50gm
L WCo Deepest Olive 907				
	1	1	1	x 50gm
M WCo Flower 943				
	1	1	1	x 50gm

NEEDLES

1 pair 3¼mm (no 10) (US 3) needles
1 pair 4mm (no 8) (US 6) needles

TENSION

22 sts and 30 rows to 10 cm measured over st st using 4mm (US 6) needles.

BACK

Using 3¼mm (US 3) needles and yarn A cast on 108 [136: 152] sts.
Row 1 (RS): K3, *P2, K2, rep from * to last st, K1.
Row 2: K1, P2, *K2, P2, rep from * to last st, K1.
These 2 rows form rib.
Cont in rib for a further 6 rows, dec 0 [1: 1] st at each end of last row and ending with RS facing for next row. 108 [134: 150] sts.
Change to 4mm (US 6) needles.

Beg with a K row, work in st st throughout as folls:
Work 22 rows, inc 1 st at each end of 13th of these rows and ending with RS facing for next row. 110 [136: 152] sts.

Shape side vents
Cast on 5 sts at beg of next 2 rows.
120 [146: 162] sts.
Inc 1 st at each end of 5th and 5 foll 16th rows. 132 [158: 174] sts.
Cont straight until back meas 44 [46: 47] cm, ending with RS facing for next row.
★★Place markers at both ends of last row to denote base of armhole openings.
Cont straight until work meas 22 [24: 25] cm from markers, ending with RS facing for next row.

Shape shoulders
Cast off 2 [2: 3] sts at beg of next 24 [6: 24] rows, then - [3: -] sts at beg of foll - [18: -] rows. 84 [92: 102] sts.

Shape back neck
Next row (RS): Cast off 2 [3: 4] sts, K until there are 12 [14: 17] sts on right needle and turn, leaving rem sts on a holder.
Work each side of neck separately.
Dec 1 st at neck edge of next 5 rows, ending with RS facing for next row, **and at same time** cast off 2 [3: 4] sts at beg of 2nd and foll alt row.
Cast off rem 3 [3: 4] sts.
With RS facing, rejoin yarn to rem sts, cast off centre 56 [58: 60] sts, K to end.
Complete to match first side, reversing shapings.

FRONT

Using 3¼mm (US 3) needles and yarn A cast on 108 [136: 152] sts.
Work in rib as given for back for 8 rows, inc 1 [0: 0] st at each end of last row and ending with RS facing for next row. 110 [136: 152] sts.
Change to 4mm (US 6) needles.
Beg with a K row, work in st st throughout as folls:

Work 10 rows, ending with RS facing for next row.

Shape side vents
Cast on 5 sts at beg of next 2 rows.
120 [146: 162] sts.
Inc 1 st at each end of 5th and 3 foll 16th rows. 128 [154: 170] sts.
Work 11 rows, ending with RS facing for next row.

Place motif
Next row (RS): K19 [32: 40], work next 90 sts as row 1 of chart, K19 [32: 40].
Next row: P19 [32: 40], work next 90 sts as row 2 of chart, P19 [32: 40].
These 2 rows set the sts - central 90 sts in patt from chart with edge sts in st st using yarn A.
Working rem 85 rows of chart and then completing front in st st using yarn A **only**, cont as folls:
Inc 1 st at each end of 3rd and foll 16th row. 132 [158: 174] sts.
Cont straight until front meas 40 [42: 43] cm, ending with RS facing for next row. (**Note**: Back is 4 cm longer than front.)
Complete as given for back from ★★.

SLEEVES

Using 3¼mm (US 3) needles and yarn A cast on 92 [100: 104] sts.
Work in rib as given for back for 4 rows, inc 0 [1: 1] st at each end of last row and ending with RS facing for next row. 92 [102: 106] sts.
Change to 4mm (US 6) needles.
Beg with a K row, work in st st until sleeve meas 12 cm, ending with RS facing for next row.
Cast off.

MAKING UP

Press as described on the information page.
Join right shoulder seam using back stitch, or mattress stitch if preferred.
Neckband
With RS facing, using 3¼mm (US 3) needles

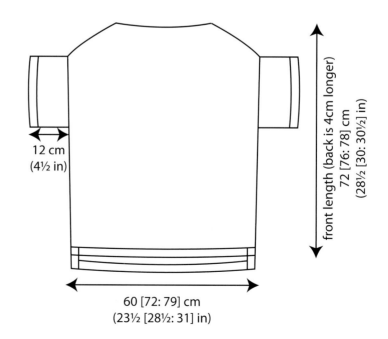

12 cm
(4½ in)

front length (back is 4cm longer)
72 [76: 78] cm
(28½ [30: 30½] in)

60 [72: 79] cm
(23½ [28½: 31] in)

and yarn A, pick up and knit 5 sts down left side of front neck, 56 [58: 60] sts from front, 5 sts up right side of front neck, 5 sts down right side of back neck, 56 [58: 60] sts from back, then 5 sts up left side of back neck.
132 [136: 140] sts.
Cast off knitwise (on **WS**).
Join left shoulder and neckband seam.
Front side vent borders (both alike)
With RS facing, using 3¼mm (US 3) needles and yarn A, pick up and knit 16 sts evenly

along row-end edge of front side vent, between original cast-on edge and cast-on sts at top of vent.
Beg with row 2, work in rib as given for back for 6 rows, ending with **WS** facing for next row.
Cast off in rib (on **WS**).
Back side vent borders (both alike)
With RS facing, using 3¼mm (US 3) needles and yarn A, pick up and knit 24 sts evenly along row-end edge of back side vent, between

original cast-on edge and cast-on sts at top of vent.
Beg with row 2, work in rib as given for back for 6 rows, ending with **WS** facing for next row.
Cast off in rib (on **WS**).
Sew row-end edges of vent borders to cast-on sts at top of vent.
See information page for finishing instructions, setting in sleeves using the straight cast-off method.

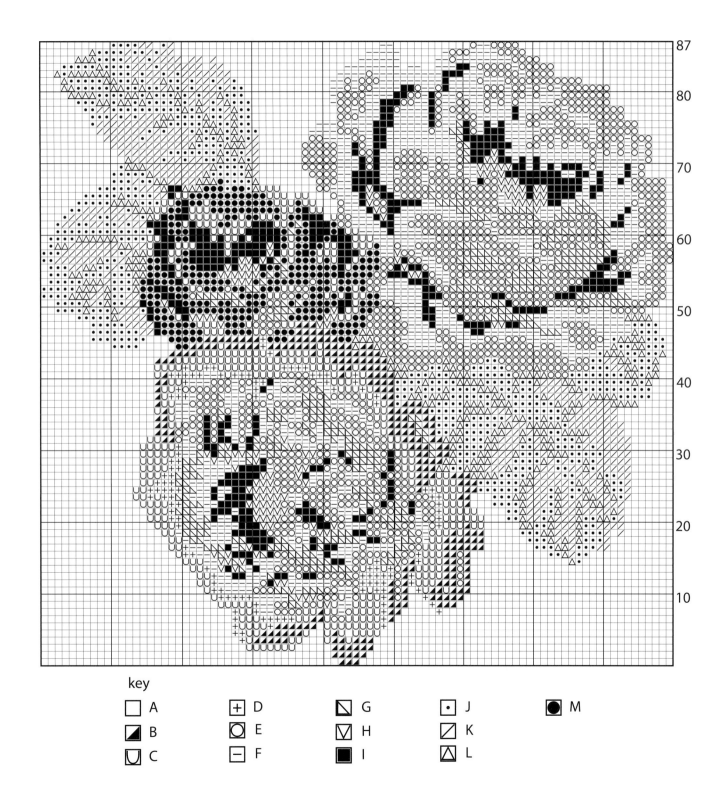

key

☐	A	⊞	D	◹	G	·	J	◉	M
◿	B	⊕	E	▽	H	╱	K		
⊔	C	⊟	F	■	I	◺	L		

CRETE
MARTIN STOREY
Main image page 16 & 17

YARN

	S	M	L	XL	XXL
To fit bust					
81-86	91-97	102-107	112-117	122-127	cm
32-34	36-38	40-42	44-46	48-50	in

Wool Cotton 4ply

7	8	9	10	11	x 50gm

(photographed in Antique 480)

NEEDLES

1 pair 3¼mm (no 10) (US 3) needles

BEADS - approx 112 [112: 128: 128: 156]
small glass beads size 8, col 34, silver lined from Debbie Abrahams. Please see information page for contact details.

TENSION

28 sts and 36 rows to 10 cm measured over st st using 3¼mm (US 3) needles.

SPECIAL ABBREVIATION

bead 1 = place a bead by taking yarn to RS of work and slipping bead up next to st just worked, slip next st purlwise from left needle to right needle and take yarn back to WS of work, leaving bead sitting in front of slipped st on RS.

Beading note: Before starting to knit, thread beads onto yarn. To do this, thread a fine sewing needle (one that will easily pass through the beads) with sewing thread. Knot ends of thread and then pass end of yarn through this loop. Thread a bead onto sewing thread and then gently slide it along and onto knitting yarn. Continue in this way until required number of beads are on yarn. Do not place beads on edge sts of rows as this will interfere with seaming.

Pattern note: When working border patt from chart, take care to ensure each dec of patt is matched by an inc. If there are insufficient sts to work both, work end sts of rows in st st.

BACK

Using 3¼mm (US 3) needles cast on 133 [147: 163: 181: 199] sts.
Beg and ending rows as indicated and repeating the 15 st patt rep 7 [9: 9: 11: 11] times across each row, cont in patt from chart as folls:
Work 24 [24: 26: 26: 28] rows, ending with RS facing for next row.
Keeping patt correct, dec 1 st at each end of

next and 3 foll 6th rows.
125 [139: 155: 173: 191] sts.
Work 5 [5: 3: 3: 1] rows, ending with RS facing for next row - all 48 rows of chart are now completed.
Beg with a K row, cont in st st as folls:
Dec 1 st at each end of next [next: 3rd: 3rd: 5th] and 3 foll 6th rows, then on 3 foll 4th rows. 111 [125: 141: 159: 177] sts.
Work 19 [21: 21: 23: 23] rows, ending with RS facing for next row.
Inc 1 st at each end of next and 4 foll 10th rows. 121 [135: 151: 169: 187] sts.
Cont straight until back meas 62 [64: 66: 68: 70] cm, ending with RS facing for next row.
Shape back neck
Next row (RS): K36 [43: 50: 59: 67] and turn, leaving rem sts on a holder.
Work each side of neck separately.
Dec 1 st at neck edge of next 3 rows, ending with RS facing for next row.
33 [40: 47: 56: 64] sts.
Shape shoulder
Cast off 10 [12: 15: 18: 20] sts at beg of next and foll alt row **and at same time** dec 1 st at neck edge of next 3 rows.
Work 1 row.
Cast off rem 10 [13: 14: 17: 21] sts.
With RS facing, rejoin yarn to rem sts, cast off centre 49 [49: 51: 51: 53] sts, K to end.
Complete to match first side, reversing shapings.

FRONT

Work as given for back until front meas 44 [46: 47: 49: 50] cm, ending with RS facing for next row.
Divide for front opening
Next row (RS): K60 [67: 75: 84: 93] and turn, leaving rem sts on a holder.
Work each side of opening separately.
Dec 1 st at front opening edge of next row.
59 [66: 74: 83: 92] sts.
Cont straight until 39 [39: 43: 43: 47] rows less have been worked than on back to beg of shoulder shaping, ending with **WS** facing for next row.
Shape front neck
Cast off 13 sts at beg of next row.

46 [53: 61: 70: 79] sts.
Dec 1 st at neck edge of next 11 rows, then on foll 3 alt rows, then on 2 [2: 3: 3: 4] foll 4th rows. 30 [37: 44: 53: 61] sts.
Work 13 rows, ending with RS facing for next row.
Shape shoulder
Cast off 10 [12: 15: 18: 20] sts at beg of next and foll alt row.
Work 1 row.
Cast off rem 10 [13: 14: 17: 21] sts.
With RS facing, rejoin yarn to rem sts, K2tog, K to end. 60 [67: 75: 84: 93] sts.
Complete to match first side, reversing shapings.

SLEEVES

Using 3¼mm (US 3) needles cast on 73 [75: 79: 79: 81] sts.
Beg and ending rows as indicated and repeating the 15 st patt rep 3 [5: 5: 5: 5] times across each row, cont in patt from chart as folls:
Inc 1 st at each end of 11th [9th: 7th: 5th: 5th] and 3 [3: 2: 3: 7] foll 12th [10th: 8th: 6th: 6th] rows, then on - [-: 2: 3: -] foll - [-: 10th: 8th: -] rows, taking inc sts into patt.
81 [83: 89: 93: 97] sts.
Work 1 [9: 5: 1: 1] rows, ending with RS facing for next row - all 48 rows of chart are now completed.
Beg with a K row, cont in st st as folls:
Inc 1 st at each end of 11th [next: 5th: 7th: 5th] and every foll 12th [10th: 10th: 8th: 6th] row to 87 [95: 101: 107: 105] sts, then on every foll 14th [-: -: -: 8th] row until there are 89 [-: -: -: 113] sts.
Cont straight until sleeve meas 32 [33: 34: 34: 34] cm, ending with RS facing for next row.
Cast off.

MAKING UP

Press as described on the information page.
Join both shoulder seams using back stitch, or mattress stitch if preferred.
Front opening edging
With RS facing and using 3¼mm (US 3) needles, beg and ending at top of front opening, pick up and knit 22 sts down left side of opening, 1 st from base of opening, then

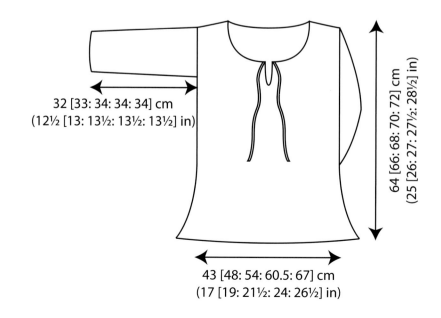

32 [33: 34: 34: 34] cm
(12½ [13: 13½: 13½: 13½] in)

64 [66: 68: 70: 72] cm
(25 [26: 27: 27½: 28½] in)

43 [48: 54: 60.5: 67] cm
(17 [19: 21½: 24: 26½] in)

22 sts up other side of opening. 45 sts.
Cast off knitwise (on **WS**).

Neckband

With RS facing and using 3¼mm (US 3)
needles, beg and ending at front opening edges,
pick up and knit 53 [53: 57: 57: 61] sts up right
side of neck, 61 [61: 63: 63: 65] sts from back,
then 53 [53: 57: 57: 61] sts down left side of
neck. 167 [167: 177: 177: 187] sts.
Cast off knitwise (on **WS**).
Mark points along side seam edges 17 [18: 19:
20: 21] cm either side of shoulder seams to
denote base of armhole openings. See
information page for finishing instructions,
setting in sleeves using the straight cast-off
method.

Ties

Make 2 twisted cords or crochet chains, each
30 cm long, and attach to ends of neckband to
form neck ties.

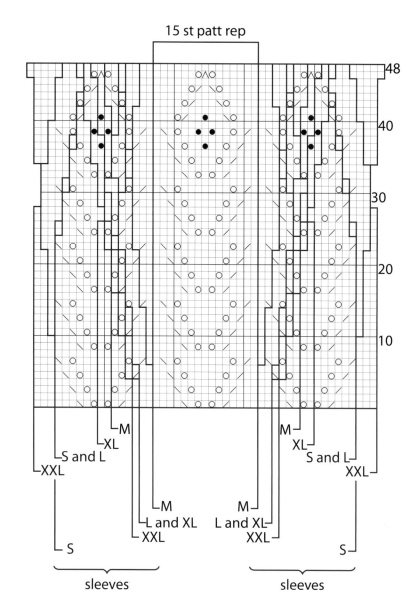

15 st patt rep

sleeves   sleeves

key

- ☐ K on RS, P on WS
- ⟲ yfwd
- ⧄ K2tog
- ⧅ sl1, K1, psso
- ⟋⟍ sl1, K2tog, psso
- ⬤ bead 1

CORFU

KAFFE FASSETT

Main image page 18 & 19

● ● ●

YARN

	S	M	L	XL	XXL	
To fit bust						
	81-86	91-97	102-107	112-117	122-127	cm
	32-34	36-38	40-42	44-46	48-50	in

**Purelife Revive, Wool Cotton and Wool
Cotton 4ply**

	S	M	L	XL	XXL	
A Purelife Revive Grit 473						
	4	4	5	5	6	x 50gm
B Wool Cotton Clear 941						
	3	4	4	5	6	x 50gm
C Wool Cotton Flower 943						
	1	1	1	1	1	x 50gm
D Wool Cotton Brolly 980						
	1	1	1	1	1	x 50gm
E ★Wool Cotton 4ply Old Rose 498						
	1	1	1	1	1	x 50gm
F Purelife Revive Firestone 470						
	1	1	1	1	1	x 50gm
G Wool Cotton Cafe 985						
	1	1	1	1	1	x 50gm
H ★Wool Cotton 4ply Leaf 491						
	1	1	1	1	1	x 50gm

★Use Wool Cotton 4ply DOUBLE throughout

NEEDLES

1 pair 3¼mm (no 10) (US 3) needles
1 pair 3¾mm (no 9) (US 5) needles

TENSION

22 sts and 25 rows to 10 cm measured over
patterned st st using 3¾mm (US 5) needles.

BACK

Using 3¼mm (US 3) needles and yarn A cast
on 101 [113: 125: 139: 155] sts.

Work in g st for 6 rows, ending with RS facing
for next row.
Change to 3¾mm (US 5) needles.
Beg and ending rows as indicated, using the
intarsia technique as described on the
information page and repeating the 110 row
patt rep throughout, cont in patt from chart,
which is worked entirely in st st beg with a K
row, as folls:
Cont straight until back meas 46.5 [48.5:
50.5: 52.5: 54.5] cm, ending with RS facing for
next row.

Shape back neck and shoulders

Next row (RS): Cast off 9 [11: 13: 15: 18] sts,
patt until there are 22 [26: 29: 34: 38] sts on
right needle and turn, leaving rem sts on a
holder.
Work each side of neck separately.
Dec 1 st at neck edge of next 3 rows, ending
with RS facing for next row, **and at same
time** cast off 9 [11: 13: 15: 18] sts at beg of
2nd row.
Cast off rem 10 [12: 13: 16: 17] sts.
With RS facing, slip centre 39 [39: 41:
41: 43] sts onto a holder, rejoin yarns to rem
sts, patt to end.
Complete to match first side, reversing shapings.

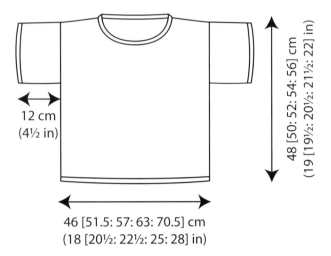

12 cm
(4½ in)

48 [50: 52: 54: 56] cm
(19 [19½: 20½: 21½: 22] in)

46 [51.5: 57: 63: 70.5] cm
(18 [20½: 22½: 25: 28] in)

FRONT

Work as given for back until 16 [16: 18: 18: 20] rows less have been
worked than on back to beg of shoulder shaping, ending with RS
facing for next row.

Shape front neck

Next row (RS): Patt 39 [45: 51: 58: 66] sts and turn, leaving rem
sts on a holder.

Work each side of neck separately.

Keeping patt correct, dec 1 st at neck edge of next 8 rows, then on
foll 3 [3: 4: 4: 5] alt rows. 28 [34: 39: 46: 53] sts.

Work 1 row, ending with RS facing for
next row.

Shape shoulder

Cast off 9 [11: 13: 15: 18] sts at beg of next and foll alt row.

Work 1 row.

Cast off rem 10 [12: 13: 16: 17] sts.

With RS facing, slip centre 23 sts onto a holder, rejoin yarns to
rem sts, patt to end.

Complete to match first side, reversing shapings.

SLEEVES

Using 3¼mm (US 3) needles and yarn A cast on 75 [79: 83: 89:
93] sts.

Work in g st for 6 rows, ending with RS facing for next row.

Change to 3¾mm (US 5) needles.

Beg and ending rows as indicated, cont in patt from chart until
sleeve meas 12 cm, ending with RS facing for next row.

Cast off.

MAKING UP

Press as described on the information page.

Join right shoulder seam using back stitch, or mattress stitch if
preferred.

Neckband

With RS facing, using 3¼mm (US 3) needles and yarn A, pick up
and knit 16 [16: 18: 18: 20] sts down left side of front neck, K
across 23 sts on front holder, pick up and knit 16 [16: 18: 18: 20] sts
up right side of front neck, and 3 sts down right side of back neck,
K across 39 [39: 41: 41: 43] sts on back holder, then pick up and
knit 3 sts up left side of back neck.

100 [100: 106: 106: 112] sts.

Work in g st for 4 rows, ending with **WS** facing for next row.

Cast off knitwise (on **WS**).

Join left shoulder and neckband seam. Mark points along side seam
edges 18 [19: 20: 21: 22] cm either side of shoulder seams to
denote base of armholes. See information page for finishing
instructions, setting in sleeves using the straight cast-off method.

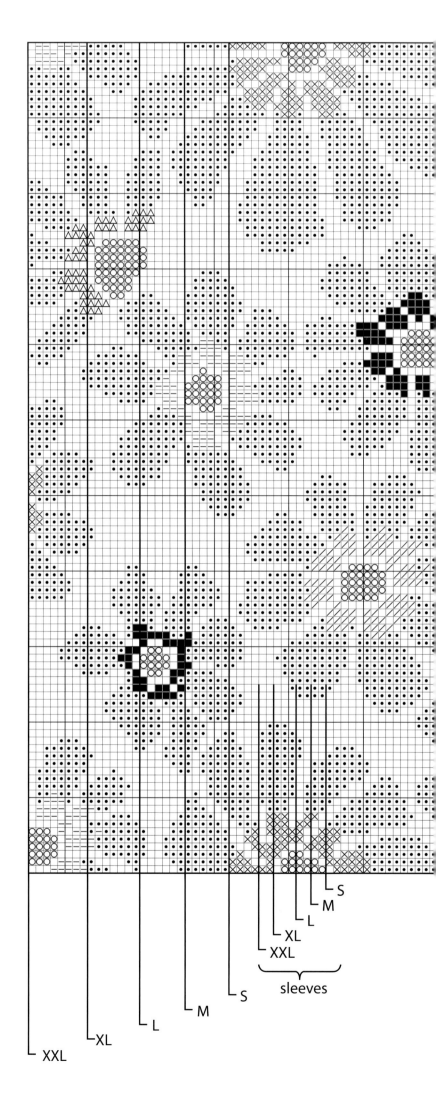

S
M
L
XL
XXL
sleeves

S
M
L
XL
XXL

110 row patt rep

key

	A		E
•	B	■	F
⊠	C	◩	G
◉	D	⊟	H

sleeves

S
M
L
XL
XXL

S
M
L
XL
XXL

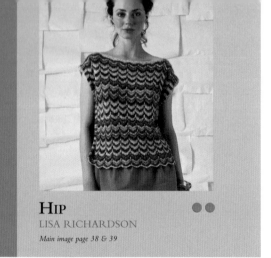

HIP
LISA RICHARDSON
Main image page 38 & 39

YARN

	S	M	L	XL	XXL	
To fit bust						
	81-86	91-97	102-107	112-117	122-127	cm
	32-34	36-38	40-42	44-46	48-50	in

Panama, Kidsilk Haze and Siena 4ply

	S	M	L	XL	XXL	
A Pan Orchid 304						
	2	2	2	2	2	x 50gm
B KSH Splendour 579						
	1	1	1	1	1	x 25gm
C Sie Sloe 670						
	1	1	1	2	2	x 50gm
D KSH Meadow 581						
	1	1	1	1	1	x 25gm
E Pan Aster 310						
	1	1	2	2	2	x 50gm
F Sie Madras 675						
	1	1	2	2	2	x 50gm
G Pan Nightshade 312						
	1	1	1	2	2	x 50gm
H KSH Ultra 659						
	1	1	1	1	1	x 25gm

NEEDLES
1 pair 2¼mm (no 13) (US 1) needles
1 pair 3mm (no 11) (US 2/3) needles

TENSION
34 sts and 35 rows to 10 cm measured over patt using 3mm (US 2/3) needles.

STRIPE SEQUENCE
Row 1 (WS): Using yarn A.
Rows 2 and 3: Using yarn B.
Rows 4 and 5: Using yarn C.
Rows 6 and 7: Using yarn D.
Rows 8 and 9: Using yarn E.
Rows 10 and 11: Using yarn F.
Rows 12 and 13: Using yarn G.
Rows 14 and 15: Using yarn H.
Rows 16 and 17: Using yarn E.
Rows 18 and 19: Using yarn B.
Rows 20 and 21: Using yarn F.
Rows 22 and 23: Using yarn A.
Rows 24 and 25: Using yarn C.
Rows 26 and 27: Using yarn G.
Rows 28 and 29: Using yarn D.
Rows 30 and 31: Using yarn A.
Rows 32 and 33: Using yarn H.
Rows 34 and 35: Using yarn C.
Rows 36 and 37: Using yarn F.
Rows 38 and 39: Using yarn D.
Rows 40 and 41: Using yarn B.
Rows 42 and 43: Using yarn G.
Rows 44 and 45: Using yarn E.
Rows 46 and 47: Using yarn H.
Row 48: Using yarn A.
These 48 rows form stripe sequence and are repeated.

BACK
Using 3mm (US 2/3) needles and yarn A cast on 153 [171: 191: 211: 235] sts.
Beg with stripe row 1, now work in stripe sequence throughout (see above) in patt as folls:
Row 1 (WS): Purl.
Row 2: K11 [8: 6: 10: 10], ★yfwd, K4, sl 1, K2tog, psso, K4, yfwd, K1, rep from ★ to last 10 [7: 5: 9: 9] sts, K10 [7: 5: 9: 9].
These 2 rows form patt.
Cont in patt for a further 7 rows, ending with RS facing for next row.
Keeping stripes and patt correct, dec 1 st at each end of next and 4 foll 6th rows.
143 [161: 181: 201: 225] sts.
Work 13 [13: 15: 15: 17] rows, ending with RS facing for next row.
Inc 1 st at each end of next and 4 foll 10th rows, taking inc sts into patt.
153 [171: 191: 211: 235] sts.
Cont straight until back meas 29 [30: 31: 32: 33] cm, ending with RS facing for next row.
Shape armholes
Keeping stripes and patt correct, cast off 3 sts at beg of next 2 rows. 147 [165: 185: 205: 229] sts.
Cont straight until armhole meas 21 [22: 23: 24: 25] cm, ending with RS facing for next row.
Shape shoulders
Cast off 9 [12: 15: 18: 22] sts at beg of next 4 rows, then 10 [13: 15: 19: 21] sts at beg of foll 2 rows.
Cast off rem 91 [91: 95: 95: 99] sts.

FRONT
Work as given for back until 10 [10: 12: 12: 14] rows less have been worked than on back to beg of shoulder shaping, ending with RS facing for next row.
Shape front neck
Next row (RS): Patt 37 [46: 55: 65: 76] sts and turn, leaving rem sts on a holder.
Work each side of neck separately.
Keeping stripes and patt correct, dec 1 st at neck edge of next 8 rows, then on foll 0 [0: 1: 1: 2] alt rows. 29 [38: 46: 56: 66] sts.
Work 1 row, ending with RS facing for next row.

Shape shoulder
Cast off 9 [12: 15: 18: 22] sts at beg of next and foll alt row **and at same time** dec 1 st at neck edge of next row.
Work 1 row.
Cast off rem 10 [13: 15: 19: 21] sts.
With RS facing, rejoin appropriate yarn to rem sts, cast off centre 73 [73: 75: 75: 77] sts, patt to end.
Complete to match first side, reversing shapings.

MAKING UP
Press as described on the information page.
Join right shoulder seam using back stitch, or mattress stitch if preferred.
Neckband
With RS facing, using 2¼mm (US 1) needles and yarn A, pick up and knit 10 [10: 12: 12: 14] sts down left side of neck, 60 [60: 62: 62: 64] sts from front, 10 [10: 12: 12: 14] sts up right side of neck, then 75 [75: 77: 77: 79] sts from back. 155 [155: 163: 163: 171] sts.
Work in g st for 4 rows, ending with **WS** facing for next row.
Cast off knitwise (on **WS**).
Join left shoulder and neckband seam.
Armhole borders (both alike)
With RS facing, using 2¼mm (US 1) needles and yarn A, pick up and knit 118 [124: 128: 134: 140] sts evenly along row-end edge of armhole openings, beg and ending at inner edge of cast-off sts at base of armhole.
Work in g st for 4 rows, ending with **WS** facing for next row.
Cast off knitwise (on **WS**).
Sew row-end edges of armhole borders to cast-off sts at base of armhole openings.
See information page for finishing instructions.

51 [53: 55: 57: 59] cm
(20 [21: 21½: 22½: 23] in)

45 [50.5: 56: 62: 69] cm
(17½ [20: 22: 24½: 27] in)

HALKIDIKI
MARIE WALLIN
Main image page 28, 29 & 30

● ● ●

YARN

	S	M	L	XL	XXL	
To fit bust						
	81-86	91-97	102-107	112-117	122-127	cm
	32-34	36-38	40-42	44-46	48-50	in

Kidsilk Haze and Fine Lace

	S	M	L	XL	XXL	
A KSH Cream 634						
	3	3	3	4	4	x 25gm
B FL Porcelaine 928						
	2	2	2	2	3	x 50gm
C KSH Ghost 642						
	2	2	2	3	3	x 25gm
D FL Cobweb 922						
	1	1	1	2	2	x 50gm
E KSH Blushes 583						
	1	1	1	1	1	x 25gm
F FL Quaint 925						
	1	1	1	1	1	x 50gm
G KSH Ultra 659						
	1	1	1	1	1	x 25gm
H FL Jewel 936						
	1	1	1	1	1	x 50gm
I KSH Forest Green 651						
	1	1	1	1	1	x 25gm
J FL Patina 924						
	1	1	1	1	1	x 50gm
K KSH Ember 644						
	1	1	1	1	1	x 25gm
L FL Ochre 930						
	1	1	1	1	1	x 50gm
M ★KSH Trance 582						
	1	1	1	1	1	x 25gm

★Use yarn M DOUBLE throughout.

NEEDLES
1 pair 2¾mm (no 12) (US 2) needles
1 pair 3¼mm (no 10) (US 3) needles

BUTTONS – 1 x BN1121 from Bedecked.
Please see information page for contact details.

TENSION
29 sts and 38 rows to 10 cm measured over patterned st st using 2¾mm (US 2) needles and one strand of Fine Lace and one strand of Kidsilk Haze held together. 25 sts and 34 rows to 10 cm measured over st st using 3¼mm (US 3) needles and one strand of Kidsilk Haze.

BACK
Using 2¾mm (US 2) needles and one strand each of yarns C and D held together, work picot cast-on as folls: ★cast on 5 sts, cast off

2 sts, slip st on right needle back onto left needle, rep from ★ until there are 123 [135: 153: 171: 192] sts on left needle, cast on 2 sts. 125 [137: 155: 173: 194] sts.
Next row (WS): (Inc in first st) 0 [1: 1: 1: 1] times, K to last 0 [1: 1: 1: 0] st, (inc in last st) 0 [1: 1: 1: 0] times.
125 [139: 157: 175: 195] sts.★★
Beg with a K row, now work in striped st st as folls:
Rows 1 to 4: Using one strand each of yarns A and B held together.
Rows 5 to 8: Using one strand each of yarns C and D held together.
These 8 rows form striped st st.
★★★Cont in striped st st, dec 1 st at each end of foll 15th [17th: 17th: 19th: 19th] row, then on 5 foll 8th rows. 113 [127: 145: 163: 183] sts.
Work 17 [19: 21: 21: 23] rows, ending with RS facing for next row.
Inc 1 st at each end of next and 5 foll 10th rows. 125 [139: 157: 175: 195] sts.
Work 15 [15: 17: 19: 19] rows, ending with RS facing for next row. (Back should meas approx 39 [40: 41: 42: 43] cm.)
Shape armholes
Keeping stripes correct, cast off 6 [7: 8: 9: 10] sts at beg of next 2 rows.
113 [125: 141: 157: 175] sts.
Dec 1 st at each end of next 7 [9: 11: 13: 15] rows, then on foll 3 [4: 6: 7: 9] alt rows.
93 [99: 107: 117: 127] sts.★★★
Work 21 [21: 19: 19: 17] rows, ending with RS facing for next row.
Divide for back opening
Keeping stripes correct, cont as folls:
Next row (RS): K46 [49: 53: 58: 63] and turn, leaving rem sts on a holder.
Work each side of back separately.
Next row (WS): K1, P to end.
Next row: Knit.
These 2 rows set the sts – back opening edge st worked as a K st on every row with all other sts still in st st.
Cont as set for a further 27 rows, ending with RS facing for next row. (Armhole meas approx 17.5 [18.5: 19.5: 20.5: 21.5] cm.)
Shape back neck and shoulder
Keeping stripes correct, cont as folls:

Next row (RS): K26 [29: 32: 37: 41] and turn, leaving rem 20 [20: 21: 21: 22] sts on a holder (for neckband).
Dec 1 st at neck edge of next 6 rows, ending with **WS** facing for next row, **and at same time** cast off 5 [6: 6: 8: 9] sts at beg of 2nd and foll alt row, then 5 [6: 7: 8: 9] sts at beg of foll alt row.
Work 1 row.
Cast off rem 5 [5: 7: 7: 8] sts.
With RS facing, rejoin appropriate yarns to rem sts, K2tog, K to end. 46 [49: 53: 58: 63] sts.
Keeping stripes correct, cont as folls:
Next row (WS): P to last st, K1.
Next row: Knit.
These 2 rows set the sts – back opening edge st worked as a K st on every row with all other sts still in st st.
Complete to match first side, reversing shapings and working first row of back neck shaping as folls:
Next row (RS): Break yarn. Slip first 20 [20: 21: 21: 22] sts onto a holder (for neckband), rejoin yarns and K to end.
26 [29: 32: 37: 41] sts.

FRONT
Work as given for back to ★★.
Beg and ending rows as indicated and using the **intarsia** technique as described on the information page, cont in patt from chart, which is worked entirely in st st beg with a K row, as folls:
Work 8 rows, ending with RS facing for next row.
Keeping chart correct, now work as given for back from ★★★ to ★★★.
Work 29 [29: 23: 23: 17] rows, ending with RS facing for next row.
Shape front neck
Next row (RS): Patt 33 [36: 40: 45: 50] sts and turn, leaving rem sts on a holder.
Work each side of neck separately.
Keeping patt correct, dec 1 st at neck edge of next 8 rows, then on foll 4 alt rows, then on 1 [1: 2: 2: 3] foll 4th rows.
20 [23: 26: 31: 35] sts.
Work 3 rows, ending with RS facing for next row.
Shape shoulder
Keeping patt correct, cast off 5 [6: 6: 8: 9] sts at beg of next and foll alt row, then 5 [6: 7: 8: 9] sts

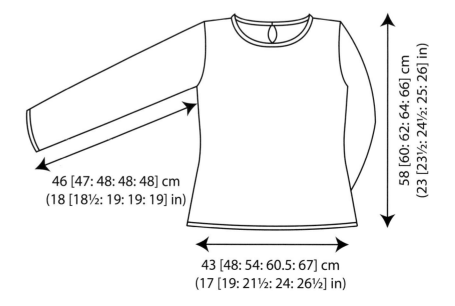

46 [47: 48: 48: 48] cm
(18 [18½: 19: 19: 19] in)

58 [60: 62: 64: 66] cm
(23 [23½: 24½: 25: 26] in)

43 [48: 54: 60.5: 67] cm
(17 [19: 21½: 24: 26½] in)

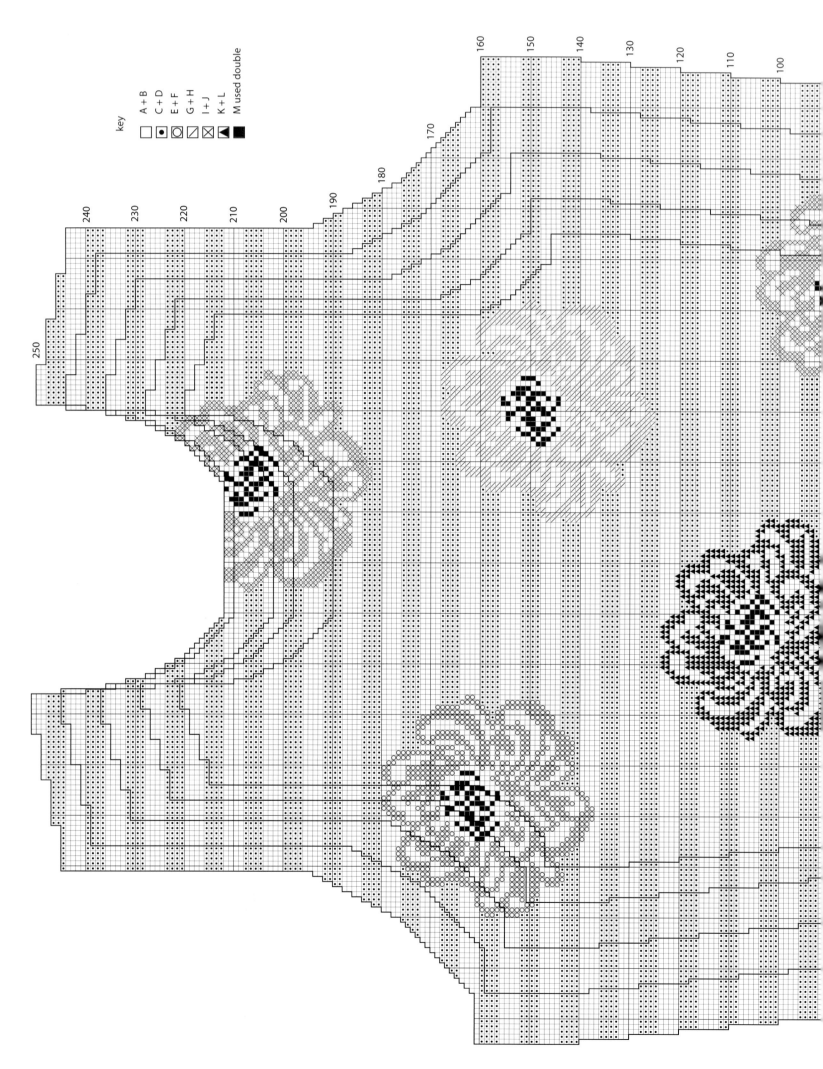

at beg of foll alt row.
Work 1 row.
Cast off rem 5 [5: 7: 7: 8] sts.
With RS facing, slip centre 27 sts onto a holder (for neckband), rejoin appropriate yarns to rem sts, patt to end. 33 [36: 40: 45: 50] sts.
Complete to match first side, reversing shapings.

SLEEVES
Using 2³⁄4mm (US 2) needles and one strand each of yarns C and D held together, work picot cast-on as folls: ★cast on 5 sts, cast off 2 sts, slip st on right needle back onto left needle, rep from ★ until there are 48 [51: 51: 51: 54] sts on left needle, cast on 2 sts.
50 [53: 53: 53: 56] sts.
Next row (WS): (Inc in first st) 1 [0: 1: 1: 1] times, K to last 0 [0: 1: 1: 0] st, (inc in last st) 0 [0: 1: 1: 0] times. 51 [53: 55: 55: 57] sts.
Break off yarns C and D and join in **ONE** strand of yarn A.
Change to 3¹⁄4mm (US 3) needles.
Beg with a K row and using a **SINGLE** strand of yarn A **only**, work in st st, shaping sides by inc 1 st at each end of 7th [5th: 5th: 5th: 5th] and every foll 8th [8th: 6th: 6th: 6th] row to 83 [89: 63: 79: 89] sts, then on every foll 10th [-: 8th: 8th: 8th] row until there are 85 [-: 93: 97: 101] sts.
Cont straight until sleeve meas 46 [47: 48: 48: 48] cm, ending with RS facing for next row.
Shape top
Cast off 5 [6: 7: 8: 9] sts at beg of next 2 rows.
75 [77: 79: 81: 83] sts.
Dec 1 st at each end of next 5 rows, then on every foll alt row until 43 sts rem, then on foll 9 rows, ending with RS facing for next row.
25 sts.
Cast off 5 sts at beg of next 2 rows.
Cast off rem 15 sts.

MAKING UP
Press as described on the information page.
Join both shoulder seams using back stitch, or mattress stitch if preferred.
Neckband
With RS facing, using 2³⁄4mm (US 2) needles and one strand each of yarns C and D held together, K across 20 [20: 21: 21: 22] sts on left back neck holder, pick up and knit 6 sts up left side of back neck, and 24 [24: 27: 27: 33] sts down left side of front neck, K across 27 sts on front holder, pick up and knit 24 [24: 28: 28: 32] sts up right side of front neck, and 6 sts down right side of back neck, then K across 20 [20: 21: 21: 22] sts on right back neck holder. 127 [127: 136: 136: 148] sts.
Now work picot cast-off as folls: cast off 2 sts, ★slip st on right needle back onto left needle, cast on 2 sts, cast off 5 sts, rep from ★ to end, casting off rem 4 sts at end of last rep.
See information page for finishing instructions, setting in sleeves using the set-in method. Make button loop at one end of neckband and attach button to other end to fasten back opening.

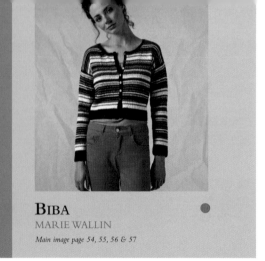

BIBA
MARIE WALLIN
Main image page 54, 55, 56 & 57

YARN

	S	M	L	XL	XXL	
To fit bust						
	81–86	91–97	102–107	112–117	122–127	cm
	32–34	36–38	40–42	44–46	48–50	in

Siena 4ply

	S	M	L	XL	XXL	
A Black 674						
	4	5	6	6	7	x 50gm
B Cream 652						
	2	3	3	3	4	x 50gm
C Alpine 671						
	1	1	1	1	1	x 50gm
D Tandoori 676						
	1	1	1	1	1	x 50gm
E Beacon 668						
	1	1	1	1	2	x 50gm
F Mariner 672						
	1	1	1	1	1	x 50gm
G Madras 675						
	1	1	1	2	2	x 50gm

NEEDLES
1 pair 2¼mm (no 13) (US 1) needles
1 pair 3mm (no 11) (US 2/3) needles

BUTTONS – 7 x 1018 from Coats Crafts.
Please see information page for contact details.

TENSION
28 sts and 38 rows to 10 cm measured over st st using 3mm (US 2/3) needles.

STRIPE SEQUENCE
Rows 1 and 2: Using yarn A.
Rows 3 to 8: Using yarn B.
Rows 9 and 10: Using yarn C.
Rows 11 to 13: Using yarn B.
Row 14: Using yarn D.
Rows 15 to 17: Using yarn E.
Rows 18 and 19: Using yarn A.
Row 20: Using yarn F.
Rows 21 to 24: Using yarn A.
Rows 25 and 26: Using yarn G.
Rows 27 and 28: Using yarn A.
Rows 29 and 30: Using yarn B.
Rows 31 and 32: Using yarn A.
Rows 33 and 34: Using yarn C.
Rows 35 and 36: Using yarn A.
Rows 37 and 38: Using yarn F.
Rows 39 and 40: Using yarn A.
Rows 41 and 42: Using yarn D.
Rows 43 and 44: Using yarn A.
Rows 45 to 47: Using yarn G.
Row 48: Using yarn E.
Rows 49 and 50: Using yarn B.
Row 51: Using yarn F.
Rows 52 to 54: Using yarn A.
Row 55: Using yarn C.
Rows 56 to 59: Using yarn B.
Row 60: Using yarn G.
Rows 61 and 62: Using yarn B.
Row 63: Using yarn A.
Rows 64 and 65: Using yarn E.
Row 66: Using yarn A.
Rows 67 to 69: Using yarn F.
Rows 70 and 71: Using yarn B.
Rows 72 and 73: Using yarn D.
Rows 74 and 75: Using yarn A.
Row 76: Using yarn G.
Rows 77 to 79: Using yarn E.
Rows 80 to 83: Using yarn A.
Rows 84 to 86: Using yarn C.
Rows 87 and 88: Using yarn G.
These 88 rows form stripe sequence and are repeated throughout.

BACK
Using 2¼mm (US 1) needles and yarn A cast on 111 [125: 143: 159: 179] sts.
Row 1 (RS): K1, *P1, K1, rep from * to end.
Row 2: As row 1.
These 2 rows form moss st.
Cont in moss st until back meas 5 cm, ending with RS facing for next row.
Change to 3mm (US 2/3) needles.
Beg with stripe row 1 and a K row, cont in st st in stripe sequence (see above) as folls:
Inc 1 st at each end of 3rd and 5 foll 14th rows. 123 [137: 155: 171: 191] sts.
Cont straight until back meas 42 [44: 46: 48: 50] cm, ending with RS facing for next row.
Shape shoulders and back neck
Next row (RS): Cast off 7 [8: 10: 11: 13] sts, K until there are 35 [41: 47: 54: 61] sts on right needle and turn, leaving rem sts on a holder.
Work each side of neck separately.
Keeping stripes correct, dec 1 st at neck edge of next 6 rows **and at same time** cast off 7 [8: 10: 12: 13] sts at beg of 2nd and foll 2 [0: 2: 2: 0] alt rows, then - [9: -: -: 14] sts at beg of foll - [2: -: -: 2] alt rows.
Work 1 row.
Cast off rem 8 [9: 11: 12: 14] sts.

With RS facing, slip centre 39 [39: 41: 41: 43] sts onto a holder, rejoin appropriate yarn to rem sts, K to end.
Complete to match first side, reversing shapings.

LEFT FRONT
Using 2¼mm (US 1) needles and yarn A cast on 55 [61: 71: 79: 89] sts.
Work in moss st as given for back for 5 cm, inc 0 [1: 0: 0: 0] st at end of last row and ending with RS facing for next row.
55 [62: 71: 79: 89] sts.
Change to 3mm (US 2/3) needles.
Beg with stripe row 1 and a K row, cont in st st in stripe sequence (see above) as folls:
Inc 1 st at beg of 3rd and 5 foll 14th rows.
61 [68: 77: 85: 95] sts.
Cont straight until 30 [30: 32: 32: 34] rows less have been worked than on back to beg of shoulder shaping, ending with RS facing for next row.
Shape front neck
Next row (RS): K52 [59: 68: 76: 86] and turn, leaving rem 9 sts on a holder (for neckband).
Keeping stripes correct, dec 1 st at neck edge of next 8 rows, then on foll 6 [6: 7: 7: 8] alt rows, then on 2 foll 4th rows.
36 [43: 51: 59: 68] sts.
Work 1 row, ending with RS facing for next row.
Shape shoulder
Cast off 7 [8: 10: 11: 13] sts at beg of next and foll 3 [1: 3: 0: 1] alt rows, then - [9: -: 12: 14] sts at beg of foll - [2: -: 3: 2] alt rows.
Work 1 row.
Cast off rem 8 [9: 11: 12: 14] sts.

RIGHT FRONT
Using 2¼mm (US 1) needles and yarn A cast on 55 [61: 71: 79: 89] sts.
Work in moss st as given for back for 5 cm, inc 0 [1: 0: 0: 0] st at beg of last row and ending with RS facing for next row.
55 [62: 71: 79: 89] sts.
Change to 3mm (US 2/3) needles.
Beg with stripe row 1 and a K row, cont in st st in stripe sequence (see above) as folls:
Inc 1 st at end of 3rd and 5 foll 14th rows.

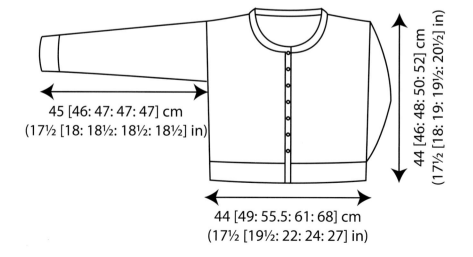

45 [46: 47: 47: 47] cm
(17½ [18: 18½: 18½: 18½] in)

44 [49: 55.5: 61: 68] cm
(17½ [19½: 22: 24: 27] in)

44 [46: 48: 50: 52] cm
(17½ [18: 19: 19½: 20½] in)

61 [68: 77: 85: 95] sts.
Complete to match left front, reversing shapings and working first row of neck shaping as folls:

Shape front neck

Next row (RS): Break yarn. Slip first 9 sts onto a holder (for neckband), rejoin yarn and K to end. 52 [59: 68: 76: 86] sts.

SLEEVES
Using 2¼mm (US 1) needles and yarn A cast on 57 [59: 61: 61: 63] sts.
Work in moss st as given for back for 5 cm, ending with RS facing for next row.
Change to 3mm (US 2/3) needles.
Beg with stripe row 1 and a K row, cont in st st in stripe sequence (see above) as folls:
Inc 1 st at each end of 7th [5th: 5th: 5th: 3rd] and every foll 8th [6th: 6th: 6th: 4th] row to 83 [67: 81: 105: 73] sts, then on every foll 10th [8th: 8th: 8th: 6th] row until there are 89 [95: 101: 107: 113] sts.
Cont straight until sleeve meas 45 [46: 47: 47: 47] cm, ending with RS facing for next row.
Cast off.

MAKING UP
Press as described on the information page. Join both shoulder seams using back stitch, or mattress stitch if preferred.

Neckband
With RS facing, using 2¼mm (US 1) needles and yarn A, K across 9 sts on right front holder, pick up and knit 30 [30: 32: 32: 34] sts up right side of front neck, and 6 sts down right side of back neck, K across 39 [39: 41: 41: 43] sts on back holder, pick up and knit 6 sts up left side of back neck, and 30 [30: 32: 32: 34] sts down left side of front neck, then K across 9 sts on left front holder. 129 [129: 135: 135: 141] sts.
Work in moss st as given for back for 5 rows, ending with RS facing for next row.
Cast off in moss st.

Button band
With RS facing, using 2¼mm (US 1) needles and yarn A, pick up and knit 99 [105: 111: 115: 119] sts evenly down entire left front opening edge, from top of neckband to cast-on edge.

Work in moss st as given for back for 5 rows, ending with RS facing for next row.
Cast off in moss st.

Buttonhole band
With RS facing, using 2¼mm (US 1) needles and yarn A, pick up and knit 99 [105: 111: 115: 119] sts evenly up entire right front opening edge, from cast-on edge to top of neckband.
Work in moss st as given for back for one row, ending with RS facing for next row.
Row 2 (RS): Moss st 28 [28: 28: 32: 30] sts, *yrn (to make a buttonhole), work 2 tog, moss st 9 [10: 11: 11: 12], rep from * 5 times more, yrn (to make 7th buttonhole) work 2 tog, moss st 3 sts.
Work in moss st for a further 3 rows, ending with RS facing for next row.
Cast off in moss st.
Mark points along side seam edges 17 [18: 19: 20: 21] cm either side of shoulder seams to denote base of armhole openings. See information page for finishing instructions, setting in sleeves using the straight cast-off method.

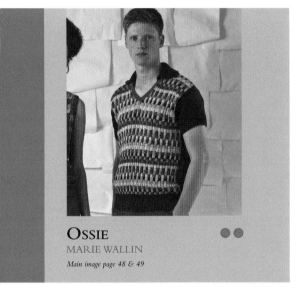

OSSIE
MARIE WALLIN
Main image page 48 & 49

YARN

	XS	S	M	L	XL	XXL	2XL	
To fit chest								
	97	102	107	112	117	122	127	cm
	38	40	42	44	46	48	50	in
Cotton Glacé								
A Nightshade 746								
	6	7	7	8	8	9	9	x 50gm
B Twilight 829								
	1	1	1	1	1	1	2	x 50gm
C Sky 749								
	1	1	2	2	2	2	2	x 50gm
D Dawn Grey 831								
	2	2	2	2	2	2	3	x 50gm
E Toffee 843								
	1	1	1	1	1	1	1	x 50gm
F Oyster 730								
	1	1	1	1	1	1	2	x 50gm
G Dijon 739								
	1	1	1	1	1	1	1	x 50gm
H Baked Red 837								
	1	1	1	1	1	1	1	x 50gm

NEEDLES
1 pair 2¼mm (no 13) (US 1) needles
1 pair 3mm (no 11) (US 2/3) needles
2¼mm (no 13) (US 1) circular needle, 60 cm long

TENSION
25 sts and 33 rows to 10 cm measured over st st, 30 sts and 30 rows to 10 cm measured over patterned st st, both using 3mm (US 2/3) needles.

BACK
Using 2¼mm (US 1) needles and yarn A cast on 122 [130: 138: 146: 150: 158: 166] sts.
Row 1 (RS): K2, *P2, K2, rep from * to end.
Row 2: P2, *K2, P2, rep from * to end.
These 2 rows form rib.
Cont in rib for a further 28 rows, inc [inc: dec: dec: inc: dec: dec] 1 st at end of last row and

ending with RS facing for next row.
123 [131: 137: 145: 151: 157: 165] sts.
Change to 3mm (US 2/3) needles.
Beg with a K row, now work in st st throughout as folls:
Cont straight until back meas 39 [40: 41: 39: 39: 39: 41] cm, ending with RS facing for next row.

Shape armholes
Cast off 5 sts at beg of next 2 rows.
113 [121: 127: 135: 141: 147: 155] sts.
Dec 1 st at each end of next and foll 6 alt rows.
99 [107: 113: 121: 127: 133: 141] sts.
Cont straight until armhole meas 19 [21: 23: 25: 27: 27: 28] cm, ending with RS facing for next row.

Shape shoulders and back neck
Next row (RS): Cast off 7 [7: 8: 9: 10: 10: 11] sts, K until there are 25 [28: 30: 32: 34: 36: 39] sts

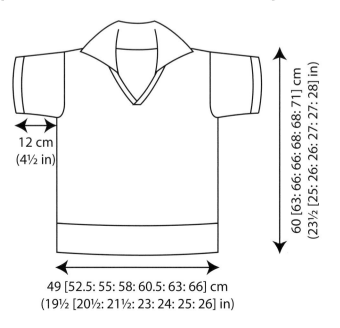

60 [63: 66: 66: 68: 68: 71] cm
(23½ [25: 26: 26: 27: 27: 28] in)

12 cm
(4½ in)

49 [52.5: 55: 58: 60.5: 63: 66] cm
(19½ [20½: 21½: 23: 24: 25: 26] in)

on right needle and turn, leaving rem sts on a holder.

Work each side of neck separately.

Dec 1 st at neck edge of next 4 rows, ending with **WS** facing for next row, **and at same time** cast off 7 [8: 8: 9: 10: 10: 11] sts at beg of 2nd row, then 7 [8: 9: 9: 10: 11: 12] sts at beg of foll alt row.

Work 1 row.

Cast off rem 7 [8: 9: 10: 10: 11: 12] sts.

With RS facing, slip centre 35 [37: 37: 39: 39: 41: 41] sts onto a holder, rejoin yarn to rem sts, K to end.

Complete to match first side, reversing shapings.

FRONT

Using 2¼mm (US 1) needles and yarn A cast on 122 [130: 138: 146: 150: 158: 166] sts.

Work in rib as given for back for 29 rows, ending with **WS** facing for next row.

Row 30 (WS): Rib 2 [2: 4: 3: 3: 4: 3], (rib 2 [2: 3: 3: 2: 3: 3], M1, rib 5, M1, rib 2) 13 [14: 13: 14: 16: 15: 16] times, rib 3 [2: 4: 3: 3: 4: 3]. 148 [158: 164: 174: 182: 188: 198] sts.

Change to 3mm (US 2/3) needles.

Beg and ending rows as indicated and using the **fairisle** technique as described on the information page, repeating the 8 st patt rep 18 [19: 20: 21: 22: 23: 24] times across each row and repeating the 44 row patt repeat throughout, cont in patt from chart, which is worked entirely in st st beg with a K row, as folls:

Cont straight until front matches back to beg of armhole shaping, ending with RS facing for next row.

Shape armholes

Keeping patt correct, cast off 6 sts at beg of next 2 rows.

136 [146: 152: 162: 170: 176: 186] sts.

Dec 1 st at each end of next 5 rows, then on foll 3 alt rows.

120 [130: 136: 146: 154: 160: 170] sts.

Work 1 [5: 9: 15: 17: 17: 17] rows, ending with RS facing for next row.

Divide for neck

Next row (RS): Patt 58 [63: 66: 71: 75: 78: 83] sts and turn, leaving rem sts on a holder.

Work each side of neck separately.

Keeping patt correct, dec 1 st at neck edge of next 10 [10: 8: 10: 6: 8: 6] rows, then on foll 14 [15: 17: 16: 20: 19: 21] alt rows.

34 [38: 41: 45: 49: 51: 56] sts.

Cont straight until front matches back to beg of shoulder shaping, ending with RS facing for next row.

Shape shoulder

Cast off 8 [9: 10: 11: 12: 12: 14] sts at beg of next and foll 1 [1: 2: 2: 2: 0: 2] alt rows, then 9 [10: -: -: -: 13: -] sts at beg of foll 1 [1: -: -: -: 2: -] alt rows.

Work 1 row.

Cast off rem 9 [10: 11: 12: 13: 13: 14] sts.

With RS facing, rejoin appropriate yarns to rem sts, cast off centre 4 sts, patt to end.

Complete to match first side, reversing shapings.

SLEEVES

Using 2¼mm (US 1) needles and yarn A cast on 70 [78: 90: 98: 110: 110: 114] sts.

Work in rib as given for back for 10 rows, dec [inc: dec: inc: dec: dec: inc] 1 st at end of last row and ending with RS facing for next row. 69 [79: 89: 99: 109: 109: 115] sts.

Change to 3mm (US 2/3) needles.

Beg with a K row, now work in st st throughout as folls:

Inc 1 st at each end of 3rd and 4 foll 4th rows, then on foll 6 alt rows.

91 [101: 111: 121: 131: 131: 137] sts.

Work 1 row, ending with RS facing for next row. (Sleeve should meas 12 cm.)

Shape top

Cast off 5 sts at beg of next 2 rows.

81 [91: 101: 111: 121: 121: 127] sts.

Dec 1 st at each end of next and foll 5 alt rows, then on foll row, ending with RS facing for next row.

Cast off rem 67 [77: 87: 97: 107: 107: 113] sts.

MAKING UP

Press as described on the information page.

Join both shoulder seams using back stitch, or mattress stitch if preferred.

Neckband

With RS facing, using 2¼mm (US 1) circular needle and yarn H, beg and ending either side of cast-off sts at base of front neck, pick up and knit 49 [52: 54: 55: 57: 58: 60] sts up right side of front neck and 5 sts down right side of back neck, K across 35 [37: 37: 39: 39: 41: 41] sts on back holder inc 1 st at centre, pick up and knit 5 sts up left side of back neck and 49 [52: 54: 55: 57: 58: 60] sts down left side of front neck. 144 [152: 156: 160: 164: 168: 172] sts.

Row 1 (WS): K1, P2, *K2, P2, rep from * to last st, K1.

Row 2: K3, *P2, K2, rep from * to last st, K1. These 2 rows form rib.

Cont in rib until neckband meas 2 cm from pick-up row, ending with RS facing for next row.

Cast off in rib.

Lay one end of neckband over other end as in photograph and neatly sew row-end edges in place to cast-off sts at base of front neck.

Collar

Using 2¼mm (US 1) needles and yarn A cast on 116 [120: 120: 124: 124: 128: 128] sts.

Beg with row 2, work in rib as given for neckband for 14 cm, ending with RS facing for next row.

Cast off in rib.

Mark points along inside of neckband pick-up row 10 cm down from shoulder seams. Easing in slight fullness, sew collar to pick-up row between these points.

See information page for finishing instructions, setting in sleeves using the shallow set-in method.

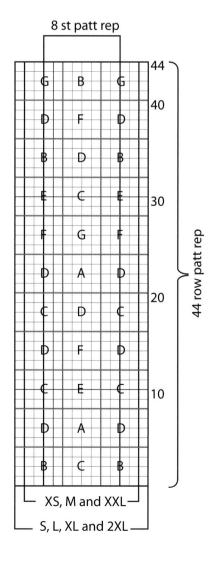

MARILYN

GALINA CARROLL

Main image page 50 & 51

YARN

	S	M	L	XL	XXL	
To fit bust						
	81-86	91-97	102-107	112-117	122-127	cm
	32-34	36-38	40-42	44-46	48-50	in

Purelife Revive and Summerspun

A Rev Pumice 461					
	5	6	6	7	8	x 50gm

B Sum Piccadilly 111					
	1	1	1	1	1	x 50gm

C Sum Greenwich 122					
	1	1	1	1	2	x 50gm

NEEDLES

1 pair 3¼mm (no 10) (US 3) needles
1 pair 4mm (no 8) (US 6) needles
3¼mm (no 10) (US 3) circular needle, 60 cm long

TENSION

22 sts and 30 rows to 10 cm measured over st st using 4mm (US 6) needles.

Pattern note: When working rows 7 and 19 of front patt from chart, take care to ensure each dec of patt is matched by an inc. If there are insufficient sts to work both, work end sts of rows in st st.

BACK

Using 3¼mm (US 3) needles and yarn A cast on 93 [103: 117: 129: 145] sts.
Row 1 (RS): K1 [0: 1: 1: 0], *P1, K2, rep from * to last 2 [1: 2: 2: 1] sts, P1, K1 [0: 1: 1: 0].
Row 2: P1 [0: 1: 1: 0], *K1, P2, rep from * to last 2 [1: 2: 2: 1] sts, K1, P1 [0: 1: 1: 0].
These 2 rows form rib.
Cont in rib until back meas 9 cm, ending with RS facing for next row.
Change to 4mm (US 6) needles.
Beg with a K row, work in st st for 10 [12: 12: 14: 14] rows, ending with RS facing for next row.
Dec 1 st at each end of next and 3 foll 4th rows. 85 [95: 109: 121: 137] sts.
Work 9 [9: 11: 11: 11] rows, ending with RS facing for next row.
Inc 1 st at each end of next and 3 foll 12th rows. 93 [103: 117: 129: 145] sts.
Cont straight until back meas 38 [39: 40: 41: 42] cm, ending with RS facing for next row.
Shape armholes
Cast off 3 [4: 5: 6: 7] sts at beg of next 2 rows. 87 [95: 107: 117: 131] sts.

Dec 1 st at each end of next 3 [5: 5: 7: 7] rows, then on foll 3 [3: 6: 5: 8] alt rows. 75 [79: 85: 93: 101] sts.
Cont straight until armhole meas 16 [17: 18: 19: 20] cm, ending with RS facing for next row.
Break yarn and leave sts on a holder.

FRONT

Using 3¼mm (US 3) needles and yarn A cast on 93 [103: 117: 129: 145] sts.
Work in rib as given for back for 9 cm, inc [dec: inc: inc: inc] 1 st at centre of last row and ending with RS facing for next row. 94 [102: 118: 130: 146] sts.
Change to 4mm (US 6) needles.
Beg and ending rows as indicated, using the **fairisle** technique as described on the information page, repeating the 4 st patt rep 20 [22: 26: 28: 32] times across each row and repeating the 24 row patt repeat throughout, cont in patt from chart, which is worked mainly in st st beg with a K row, as folls:
Work 10 [12: 12: 14: 14] rows, ending with RS facing for next row.
Keeping patt correct, dec 1 st at each end of next and 3 foll 4th rows.
86 [94: 110: 122: 138] sts.
Work 9 [9: 11: 11: 11] rows, ending with RS facing for next row.
Inc 1 st at each end of next and 3 foll 12th rows, taking inc sts into patt.
94 [102: 118: 130: 146] sts.
Cont straight until front matches back to beg of armhole shaping, ending with RS facing for next row.
Shape armholes
Keeping patt correct, cast off 3 [4: 5: 6: 7] sts at beg of next 2 rows. 88 [94: 108: 118: 132] sts.
Dec 1 st at each end of next 3 [5: 5: 7: 7] rows, then on foll 3 [3: 6: 5: 8] alt rows.
76 [78: 86: 94: 102] sts.
Cont straight until armhole meas 16 [17: 18: 19: 20] cm, dec [inc: dec: dec: dec] 1 st at centre of last row and ending with RS facing for next row. 75 [79: 85: 93: 101] sts.
Break yarn and leave sts on a holder.

MAKING UP

Press as described on the information page.
Join side seams using back stitch, or mattress stitch if preferred.
Armhole borders (both alike)
With RS facing, using 3¼mm (US 3) needles and yarn A, beg and ending at sts left on holders, pick up and knit 76 [82: 90: 96: 102] sts evenly around armhole opening edge.
Cast off knitwise (on **WS**).
Neatly sew row-end edges of armhole borders together at upper edge.
Neckband
With RS facing, using 3¼mm (US 3) circular needle and yarn A, pick up and knit 1 st from row-end edge of left armhole border (mark this st with a coloured thread), K across 75 [79: 85: 93: 101] sts on front holder, pick up and knit 1 st from row-end edge of right armhole border (mark this st with a coloured thread), then K across 75 [79: 85: 93: 101] sts on back holder. 152 [160: 172: 188: 204] sts.

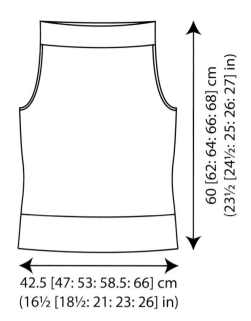

60 [62: 64: 66: 68] cm
(23½ [24½: 25: 26: 27] in)

42.5 [47: 53: 58.5: 66] cm
(16½ [18½: 21: 23: 26] in)

key

- ☐ A
- ▨ B
- ▨ C
- ⊠ K2tog
- ⊠ sl1, K1, psso
- ⊡ yfwd

4 st patt rep

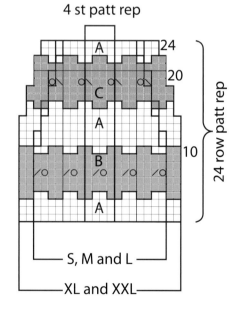

S, M and L
XL and XXL

Round 1 (RS): *K marked st, K1 [0: 0: 1: 2], (P1, K2) 24 [26: 28: 30: 32] times, P1, K1 [0: 0: 1: 2], rep from * once more.
Rep last round until neckband meas 6 cm from pick-up round.
Cast off in patt.
See information page for finishing instructions.

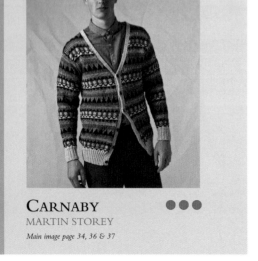

CARNABY

MARTIN STOREY

Main image page 34, 36 & 37

●●●

YARN

	XS	S	M	L	XL	XXL	2XL	
To fit chest								
	97	102	107	112	117	122	127	cm
	38	40	42	44	46	48	50	in

Siena 4ply

A Frost 653								
	4	5	5	5	6	6	6	x 50gm
B Black 674								
	4	5	5	6	6	6	7	x 50gm
C Sloe 670								
	2	2	3	3	3	3	3	x 50gm
D Madras 675								
	1	1	1	1	1	1	1	x 50gm
E Tandoori 676								
	1	1	1	1	1	1	2	x 50gm
F Mariner 672								
	1	2	2	2	2	2	2	x 50gm
G Alpine 671								
	2	2	2	2	2	2	2	x 50gm

NEEDLES

1 pair 2¼mm (no 13) (US 1) needles
1 pair 3mm (no 11) (US 2/3) needles

BUTTONS – 6 x RW5022 (18mm) reverse side used from Bedecked. Please see information page for contact details.

TENSION

28 sts and 32 rows to 10 cm measured over patterned st st using 3mm (US 2/3) needles.

BACK

Using 2¼mm (US 1) needles and yarn A cast on 142 [150: 158: 170: 174: 182: 190] sts.
Row 1 (RS): K2, *P2, K2, rep from * to end.
Row 2: P2, *K2, P2, rep from * to end.
These 2 rows form rib.
Cont in rib until back meas 7 cm, inc [inc: inc: dec: dec: inc: inc] 1 st at end of last row and ending with RS facing for next row.
143 [151: 159: 169: 173: 183: 191] sts.
Change to 3mm (US 2/3) needles.
Beg and ending rows as indicated, using the **fairisle** technique as described on the information page, repeating the 24 st patt rep 5 [5: 5: 7: 7: 7: 7] times across each row and the 54 row patt repeat throughout, cont in patt from chart, which is worked entirely in st st beg with a K row, as folls:
Cont straight until back meas 45 [46: 47: 45: 45: 45: 47] cm, ending with RS facing for next row.

Shape armholes

Keeping patt correct, cast off 5 sts at beg of next 2 rows.
133 [141: 149: 159: 163: 173: 181] sts.
Dec 1 st at each end of next and foll 8 alt rows.
115 [123: 131: 141: 145: 155: 163] sts.
Cont straight until armhole meas 19 [21: 23: 25: 27: 27: 28] cm, ending with RS facing for next row.

Shape shoulders and back neck

Next row (RS): Cast off 8 [9: 10: 11: 11: 12: 13] sts, patt until there are 29 [31: 34: 37: 39: 42: 45] sts on right needle and turn, leaving rem sts on a holder.
Work each side of neck separately.
Keeping patt correct, dec 1 st at neck edge of next 4 rows, ending with **WS** facing for next row, **and at same time** cast off 8 [9: 10: 11: 11: 12: 13] sts at beg of 2nd row, then 8 [9: 10: 11: 12: 13: 14] sts at beg of foll alt row.
Work 1 row.
Cast off rem 9 [9: 10: 11: 12: 13: 14] sts.
With RS facing, rejoin appropriate yarns to rem sts, cast off centre 41 [43: 43: 45: 45: 47: 47] sts, patt to end.
Complete to match first side, reversing shapings.

LEFT FRONT

Using 2¼mm (US 1) needles and yarn A cast on 67 [71: 75: 83: 83: 87: 91] sts.
Row 1 (RS): K2, *P2, K2, rep from * to last st, K1.
Row 2: K1, P2, *K2, P2, rep from * to end.
These 2 rows form rib.
Cont in rib until left front meas 7 cm, inc [inc: inc: dec: –: inc: inc] 1 [1: 1: 2: –: 1: 1] sts evenly across last row and ending with RS facing for next row. 68 [72: 76: 81: 83: 88: 92] sts.
Change to 3mm (US 2/3) needles.
Beg and ending rows as indicated and repeating the 24 st patt rep 2 [2: 2: 3: 3: 3: 3] times across each row, cont in patt from chart as folls:
Cont straight until 4 rows less have been worked than on back to beg of armhole shaping, ending with RS facing for next row.

Shape armholes

Keeping patt correct, cast off 5 sts at beg of next 2 rows.

Shape front slope

Keeping patt correct, dec 1 st at end of next and foll alt row. 66 [70: 74: 79: 81: 86: 90] sts.
Work 1 row.

Shape armhole

Keeping patt correct, cast off 5 sts at beg and dec 1 st at end of next row.
60 [64: 68: 73: 75: 80: 84] sts.
Work 1 row.
Dec 1 st at armhole edge of next and foll 8 alt rows **and at same time** dec 1 st at front slope edge of next and foll 8 [8: 5: 4: 1: 3: 1] alt rows, then on 0 [0: 1: 2: 3: 2: 3] foll 4th rows.
42 [46: 52: 57: 61: 65: 70] sts.
Dec 1 st at front slope edge **only** on 2nd [4th: 2nd: 4th: 2nd: 2nd: 2nd] and foll 1 [0: 0: 0: 0: 0: 0] alt row, then on 7 [9: 11: 12: 14: 14: 15] foll 4th rows. 33 [36: 40: 44: 46: 50: 54] sts.
Cont straight until left front matches back to beg of shoulder shaping, ending with RS facing for next row.

Shape shoulder

Cast off 8 [9: 10: 11: 11: 12: 13] sts at beg of next and foll alt row, then 8 [9: 10: 11: 12: 13: 14] sts at beg of foll alt row.
Work 1 row.
Cast off rem 9 [9: 10: 11: 12: 13: 14] sts.

RIGHT FRONT

Using 2¼mm (US 1) needles and yarn A cast on 67 [71: 75: 83: 83: 87: 91] sts.
Row 1 (RS): K3, *P2, K2, rep from * to end.
Row 2: P2, *K2, P2, rep from * to last st, K1.
These 2 rows form rib.
Complete to match left front, reversing shapings.

SLEEVES

Using 2¼mm (US 1) needles and yarn A cast on 62 [66: 66: 70: 70: 74: 74] sts.
Work in rib as given for back for 7 cm, inc [dec: inc: dec: inc: dec: inc] 1 st at end of last row and ending with RS facing for next row.
63 [65: 67: 69: 71: 73: 75] sts.
Change to 3mm (US 2/3) needles.
Beg and ending rows as indicated and repeating

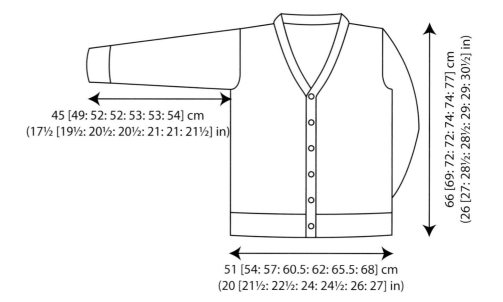

45 [49: 52: 52: 53: 53: 54] cm
(17½ [19½: 20½: 20½: 21: 21: 21½] in)

51 [54: 57: 60.5: 62: 65.5: 68] cm
(20 [21½: 22½: 24: 24½: 26: 27] in)

66 [69: 72: 72: 74: 74: 77] cm
(26 [27: 28½: 28½: 29: 29: 30½] in)

the 24 st patt rep 2 [2: 2: 2: 2: 3: 3] times across each row, cont in patt from chart as folls:
Inc 1 st at each end of 5th [5th: 5th: 3rd: 3rd: 3rd: 3rd] and every foll 4th [4th: 4th: alt: alt: alt: alt] row to 71 [85: 107: 73: 87: 85: 93] sts, then on every foll 6th [6th: 6th: 4th: 4th: 4th: 4th] row until there are 101 [111: 123: 135: 145: 145: 151] sts, taking inc sts into patt.
Cont straight until sleeve meas 45 [49: 52: 52: 53: 53: 54] cm, ending with RS facing for next row.

Shape top
Keeping patt correct, cast off 5 sts at beg of next 2 rows.
91 [101: 113: 125: 135: 135: 141] sts.
Dec 1 st at each end of next and foll 7 alt rows, then on foll row, ending with RS facing for next row.

Cast off rem 73 [83: 95: 107: 117: 117: 123] sts.

MAKING UP
Press as described on the information page. Join both shoulder seams using back stitch, or mattress stitch if preferred.

Button band
Using 2¼mm (US 1) needles and yarn A cast on 12 sts.
Row 1 (RS): K3, (P2, K2) twice, K1.
Row 2: K1, (P2, K2) twice, P2, K1.
These 2 rows form rib.
Cont in rib until band, when slightly stretched, fits up right front opening edge, up right front slope and across to centre back neck, ending with RS facing for next row.
Cast off in rib.

Slip stitch band in place. Mark positions for 6 buttons on this band - first to come 2 cm up from cast-on edge, last to come just below beg of front slope shaping, and rem 4 buttons evenly spaced between.

Buttonhole band
Work to match button band, making buttonholes to correspond with positions marked for buttons as folls:
Buttonhole row (RS): K3, P2, yon, K2tog (to make a buttonhole), P2, K3.
When this band is complete, slip stitch this band in place up left front opening edge, joining cast-off ends of bands at centre back neck.
See information page for finishing instructions, setting in sleeves using the shallow set-in method.

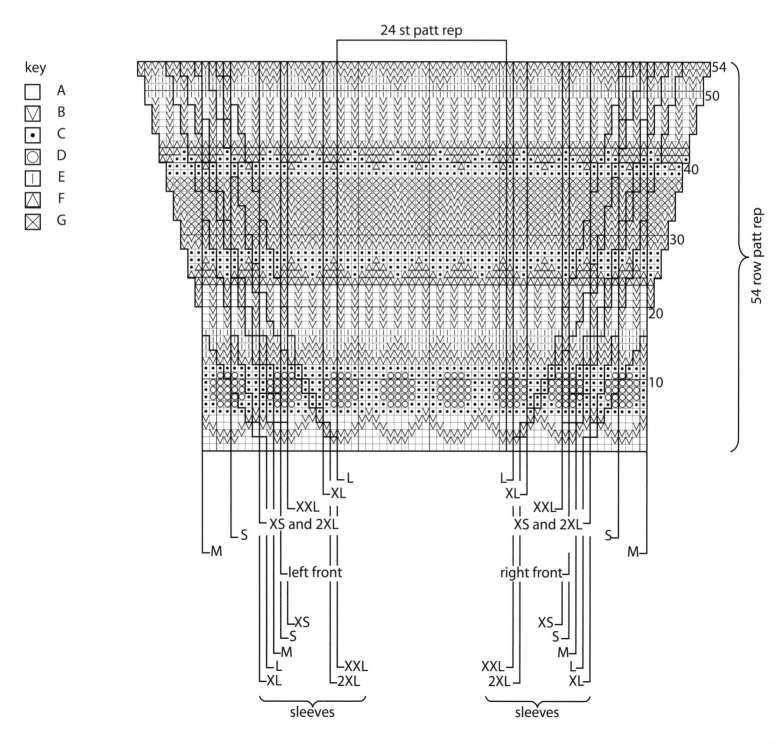

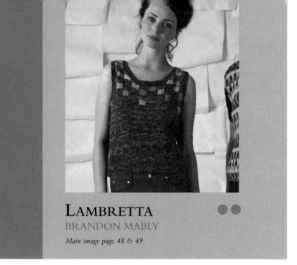

LAMBRETTA
BRANDON MABLY
Main image page 48 & 49

YARN

	S	M	L	XL	XXL	
To fit bust						
	81-86	91-97	102-107	112-117	122-127	cm
	32-34	36-38	40-42	44-46	48-50	in

Summerspun and Wool Cotton

A SS Bayswater 120
| 5 | 5 | 6 | 7 | 8 | x 50gm |

B WCo Flower 943
| 1 | 1 | 1 | 1 | 1 | x 50gm |

C WCo Elf 946
| 1 | 1 | 1 | 1 | 1 | x 50gm |

D WCo Mocha 965
| 1 | 1 | 1 | 1 | 1 | x 50gm |

E WCo Cafe 985
| 1 | 1 | 1 | 1 | 1 | x 50gm |

F WCo Brolly 980
| 1 | 1 | 1 | 1 | 1 | x 50gm |

G WCo Cypress 968
| 1 | 1 | 1 | 1 | 1 | x 50gm |

H WCo Pier 983
| 1 | 1 | 1 | 1 | 1 | x 50gm |

I WCo Rich 911
| 1 | 1 | 1 | 1 | 1 | x 50gm |

J WCo Clear 941
| 1 | 1 | 1 | 1 | 1 | x 50gm |

NEEDLES
1 pair 3¼mm (no 10) (US 3) needles
1 pair 4mm (no 8) (US 6) needles

TENSION
22 sts and 30 rows to 10 cm measured over st st, 22 sts and 28 rows to 10 cm measured over patterned st st, both using 4mm (US 6) needles.

BACK
Using 3¼mm (US 3) needles and yarn A cast on 95 [105: 119: 133: 147] sts.
Row 1 (RS): K1, *P1, K1, rep from * to end.
Row 2: P1, *K1, P1, rep from * to end.
These 2 rows form rib.
Cont in rib, dec 1 st at each end of 7th and 3 foll 6th rows. 87 [97: 111: 125: 139] sts.
Work in rib for a further 3 rows, ending with RS facing for next row.
Change to 4mm (US 6) needles.
Beg with a K row, work in st st until back meas 13 [14: 15: 16: 17] cm, ending with RS facing for next row.
Inc 1 st at each end of next and 3 foll 12th rows. 95 [105: 119: 133: 147] sts.
Work 7 rows, ending with RS facing for next row.

Beg and ending rows as indicated and using the **intarsia** technique as described on the information page, cont in patt from chart, which is worked entirely in st st beg with a K row, as folls:
Work 10 rows, ending with RS facing for next row. (Back should meas approx 31 [32: 33: 34: 35] cm.)
Shape armholes
Keeping patt correct, cast off 6 [6: 8: 9: 10] sts at beg of next 2 rows.
83 [93: 103: 115: 127] sts.**
Dec 1 st at each end of next 5 [7: 7: 9: 11] rows, then on foll 6 [6: 8: 9: 9] alt rows.
61 [67: 73: 79: 87] sts.
Work 27 [29: 27: 25: 27] rows, ending after chart row 56 [60: 62: 64: 68] and with RS facing for next row. (Armhole should meas approx 16.5 [17.5: 18.5: 19.5: 20.5] cm.)
Shape back neck and shoulders
Next row (RS): Patt 12 [15: 17: 20: 23] sts and turn, leaving rem sts on a holder.
Work each side of neck separately.
Dec 1 st at neck edge of next 4 rows, ending with **WS** facing for next row, **and at same time** cast off 4 [5: 6: 8: 9] sts at beg of 4th row.
Work 1 row.
Cast off rem 4 [6: 7: 8: 10] sts.
With RS facing, slip centre 37 [37: 39: 39: 41] sts onto a holder, rejoin yarns to rem sts, patt to end.
Complete to match first side, reversing shapings.

FRONT
Work as given for back to **.
Dec 1 st at each end of next 5 [7: 7: 9: 11] rows, then on foll 5 [6: 6: 6: 6] alt rows.
63 [67: 77: 85: 93] sts.
Work 1 row, ending with RS facing for next row.
Shape front neck
Next row (RS): (Work 2 tog) 1 [0: 1: 1: 1] times, patt 18 [22: 25: 29: 33] sts and turn, leaving rem sts on a holder.
19 [22: 26: 30: 34] sts.
Work each side of neck separately. (**Note:** Front neck shaping is **NOT** shown on chart.)
Keeping patt correct, dec 1 st at neck edge of next 6 rows, then on foll 4 [4: 5: 5: 6] alt rows, then on foll 4th row **and at same time** dec 0 [0: 1: 1: 1] st at armhole edge of 0 [0: 2nd: 2nd: 2nd] and foll 0 [0: 0: 1: 1] alt row.
8 [11: 13: 16: 19] sts.
Work 13 rows, ending after chart row 60 [64: 66: 68: 72] and with RS facing for next row.
Shape shoulder
Cast off 4 [5: 6: 8: 9] sts at beg of next row.
Work 1 row.
Cast off rem 4 [6: 7: 8: 10] sts.
With RS facing, slip centre 23 sts onto a holder, rejoin yarns to rem sts, patt to last 2 [0: 2: 2: 2] sts, (work 2 tog) 1 [0: 1: 1: 1] times. 19 [22: 26: 30: 34] sts.
Complete to match first side, reversing shapings.

MAKING UP
Press as described on the information page.
Join right shoulder seam using back stitch, or mattress stitch if preferred.
Neckband
With RS facing, using 3¼mm (US 3) needles and yarn A, pick up and knit 32 [32: 34: 34: 36] sts down left side of front neck, K across 23 sts on front holder, pick up and knit 32 [32: 34: 34: 36] sts up right side of front neck and 5 sts down right side of back neck, K across 37 [37: 39: 39: 41] sts on back holder, then pick up and knit 6 sts up left side of back neck.
135 [135: 141: 141: 147] sts.
Beg with row 2, work in rib as given for back for 5 rows, ending with RS facing for next row.
Cast off in rib.
Join left shoulder and neckband seam.
Armhole borders (both alike)
With RS facing, using 3¼mm (US 3) needles and yarn A, pick up and knit 91 [97: 105: 111: 117] sts evenly all round armhole edge.
Beg with row 2, work in rib as given for back for 5 rows, ending with RS facing for next row.
Cast off in rib.
See information page for finishing instructions.

50 [52: 54: 56: 58] cm
(19½ [20½: 21½: 22: 23] in)

43 [47.5: 54: 60.5: 67] cm
(17 [18½: 21½: 24: 26½] in)

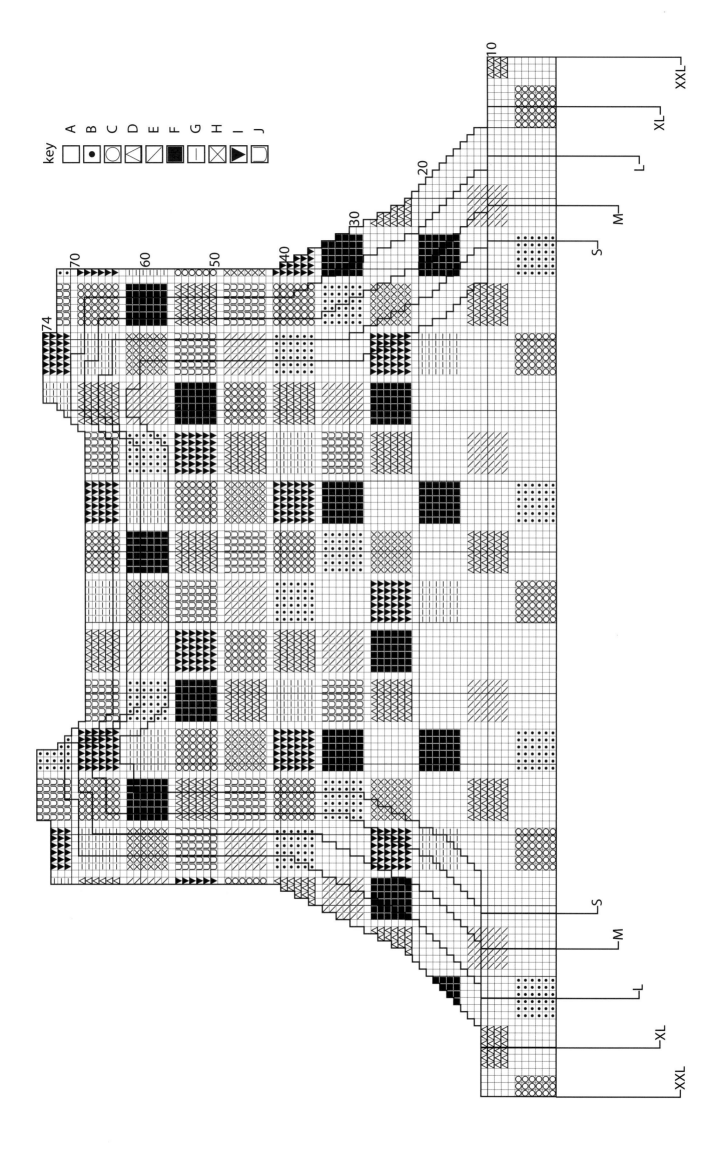

key
A □
B •
C ○
D ◁
E ◨
F ■
G |
H ⊠
I ▶
J ◻

PIXIE
KAFFE FASSETT

Main image page 46 & 47

● ● ●

YARN

	S	M	L	XL	XXL	
To fit bust						
	81-86	91-97	102-107	112-117	122-127	cm
	32-34	36-38	40-42	44-46	48-50	in

Kidsilk Haze and Siena 4ply

	S	M	L	XL	XXL	
A KSH Meadow 581						
	4	5	5	6	7	x 25gm
B Sie Cream 652						
	1	1	1	1	1	x 50gm
C Sie Korma 677						
	1	1	1	1	1	x 50gm
D Sie Beacon 668						
	1	1	1	1	1	x 50gm
E Sie Chilli 666						
	1	1	1	1	1	x 50gm
F Sie Lipstick 680						
	1	1	1	1	1	x 50gm
G Sie Sorbet 683						
	1	1	1	1	1	x 50gm
H Sie Alpine 671						
	1	1	1	1	1	x 50gm
I Sie Greengage 661						
	1	1	1	1	1	x 50gm
K Sie Madras 675						
	1	1	1	1	1	x 50gm

NEEDLES

1 pair 2¾mm (no 12) (US 2) needles
1 pair 3¼mm (no 10) (US 3) needles
2.00mm (no 14) (US B1) crochet hook

TENSION

25 sts and 34 rows to 10 cm measured over patterned st st using 3¼mm (US 3) needles.

CROCHET ABBREVIATIONS

ch = chain; **dc** = double crochet; **ss** = slip stitch; **tr** = treble.

BACK

Using 2¾mm (US 2) needles and yarn A cast on 113 [125: 141: 155: 173] sts.
Row 1 (RS): K1, *P1, K1, rep from * to end.
Row 2: P1, *K1, P1, rep from * to end.
These 2 rows form rib.
Cont in rib for a further 4 rows, ending with RS facing for next row.
Change to 3¼mm (US 3) needles.

Beg and ending rows as indicated, using the **intarsia** technique as described on the information page and repeating the 56 row patt rep throughout, cont in patt from chart, which is worked entirely in st st beg with a K row, as folls:
Cont straight until back meas 52 [54: 56: 58: 60] cm, ending with RS facing for next row.

Shape back neck and shoulders

Next row (RS): Cast off 7 [9: 10: 12: 14] sts, patt until there are 26 [30: 36: 41: 47] sts on right needle and turn, leaving rem sts on a holder.
Work each side of neck separately.
Dec 1 st at neck edge of next 4 rows, ending with **WS** facing for next row, **and at same time** cast off 7 [9: 10: 12: 14] sts at beg of 2nd row, then 7 [9: 11: 12: 14] sts at beg of foll alt row.
Work 1 row.
Cast off rem 8 [8: 11: 13: 15] sts.
With RS facing, rejoin yarns to rem sts, cast off centre 47 [47: 49: 49: 51] sts, patt to end.
Complete to match first side, reversing shapings.

FRONT

Work as given for back until 14 [14: 16: 16: 18] rows less have been worked than on back to beg of shoulder shaping, ending with RS facing for next row.

Shape front neck

Next row (RS): Patt 39 [45: 53: 60: 69] sts and turn, leaving rem sts on a holder.
Work each side of neck separately.
Keeping patt correct, dec 1 st at neck edge of next 8 rows, then on foll 2 [2: 3: 3: 4] alt rows. 29 [35: 42: 49: 57] sts.
Work 1 row, ending with RS facing for next row.

Shape shoulder

Cast off 7 [9: 10: 12: 14] sts at beg of next and foll alt row, then 7 [9: 11: 12: 14] sts at beg of foll alt row.

Work 1 row.
Cast off rem 8 [8: 11: 13: 15] sts.
With RS facing, rejoin yarns to rem sts, cast off centre 35 sts, patt to end.
Complete to match first side, reversing shapings.

SLEEVES

Using 3¼mm (US 3) needles and yarn A cast on 85 [91: 95: 101: 105] sts.
Beg and ending rows as indicated, cont in patt from chart as folls:
Cont straight until sleeve meas 12 cm, ending with RS facing for next row.
Cast off.

MAKING UP

Press as described on the information page.
Join both shoulder seams using back stitch, or mattress stitch if preferred.
Mark points along side seam edges 18 [19: 20: 21: 22] cm either side of shoulder seams to denote base of armhole openings. See information page for finishing instructions, setting in sleeves using the straight cast-off method.

Neck edging

With RS facing, using 2.00mm (US B1) crochet hook and yarn A, attach yarn at neck edge of left shoulder seam, 1 ch (does NOT count as st), work 1 round of dc evenly around entire neck edge, ensuring number of dc worked is divisible by 4 and ending with ss to first dc.
Next round (RS): 1 ch (does NOT count as st), 1 dc into first dc, *miss 1 dc, 5 tr into next dc, miss 1 dc, 1 dc into next dc, rep from * to end, replacing dc at end of last rep with ss to first dc.
Fasten off.

Cuff edgings (both alike)

Beg and ending at sleeve seam, work edging around cast-on edge of sleeve in same way as neck edging.

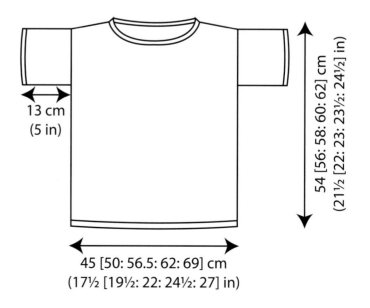

13 cm
(5 in)

54 [56: 58: 60: 62] cm
(21½ [22: 23: 23½: 24½] in)

45 [50: 56.5: 62: 69] cm
(17½ [19½: 22: 24½: 27] in)

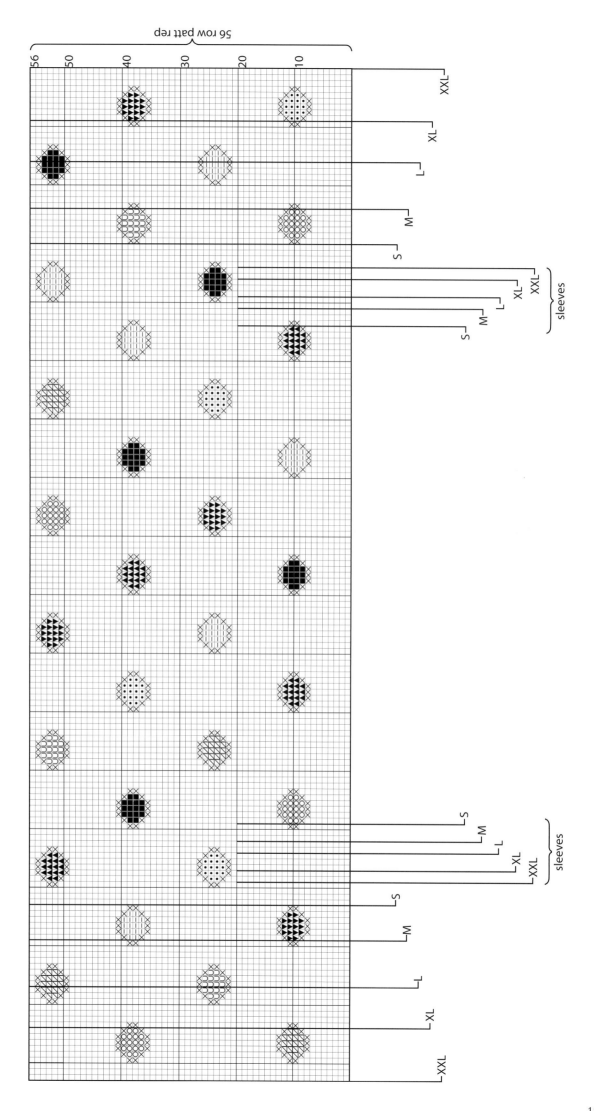

56 row patt rep

key

A □
B ⊠
C •
D ○
E ◀

F □
G ■
H ▶
I □
K ◩

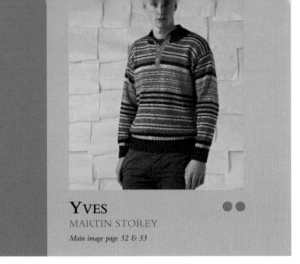

YVES
MARTIN STOREY
Main image page 52 & 53

YARN

	XS	S	M	L	XL	XXL	2XL	
To fit chest								
	97	102	107	112	117	122	127	cm
	38	40	42	44	46	48	50	in

Cotton Glacé

A Dawn Grey 831								
	5	5	6	6	6	6	7	x 50gm
B Nightshade 746								
	5	5	6	6	6	6	7	x 50gm
C Ivy 812								
	1	1	2	2	2	2	2	x 50gm
D Heather 828								
	2	2	2	2	3	3	3	x 50gm
E Green Slate 844								
	2	2	2	2	2	2	2	x 50gm
F Cobalt 850								
	2	2	2	2	2	2	2	x 50gm

NEEDLES
1 pair 2¼mm (no 13) (US 1) needles
1 pair 3mm (no 11) (US 2/3) needles

BUTTONS – 4 x RW5022 from Bedecked.
Please see information page for contact details.

TENSION
25 sts and 33 rows to 10 cm measured over st st using 3mm (US 2/3) needles.

STRIPE SEQUENCE
Rows 1 to 6: Using yarn A.
Rows 7 to 12: Using yarn B.
Rows 13 to 20: Using yarn C.
Rows 21 to 23: Using yarn A.
Rows 24 and 25: Using yarn B.
Rows 26 to 28: Using yarn A.
Rows 29 to 36: Using yarn D.
Rows 37 to 52: As rows 21 to 36.
Rows 53 to 60: As rows 21 to 28.
Rows 61 to 64: Using yarn B.
Rows 65 to 68: Using yarn E.
Rows 69 to 84: As rows 61 to 68, twice.
Rows 85 and 86: Using yarn A.
Row 87: Using yarn B.
Rows 88 and 89: Using yarn A.
Rows 90 to 95: Using yarn F.
Rows 96 to 106: As rows 85 to 95.
Rows 107 to 111: As rows 85 to 89.
Rows 112 to 116: Using yarn F.
These 116 rows form stripe sequence and are repeated throughout.

BACK
Using 2¼mm (US 1) needles and yarn B cast on 126 [134: 142: 146: 154: 162: 166] sts.
Row 1 (RS): K2, *P2, K2, rep from * to end.
Row 2: P2, *K2, P2, rep from * to end.
These 2 rows form rib.
Cont in rib until back meas 7 cm, dec [dec: dec: inc: dec: dec: inc] 1 st at end of last row and ending with RS facing for next row.
125 [133: 141: 147: 153: 161: 167] sts.
Change to 3mm (US 2/3) needles.
Beg with stripe row 1 and a K row, now work in st st in stripe sequence (see above) throughout as folls:
Cont straight until back meas 41 [42: 43: 41: 41: 41: 43] cm, ending with RS facing for next row.
Shape armholes
Keeping stripes correct, cast off 5 sts at beg of next 2 rows.
115 [123: 131: 137: 143: 151: 157] sts.**
Dec 1 st at each end of next and foll 6 alt rows.
101 [109: 117: 123: 129: 137: 143] sts.
Work 47 [55: 61: 67: 75: 75: 77] rows, ending with RS facing for next row. (Armhole should meas approx 19 [21: 23: 25: 27: 27: 28] cm.)
Shape shoulders and back neck
Next row (RS): Cast off 7 [8: 9: 9: 10: 11: 11] sts, K until there are 26 [28: 31: 33: 35: 37: 40] sts on right needle and turn, leaving rem sts on a holder.
Work each side of neck separately.
Keeping stripes correct, dec 1 st at neck edge of next 4 rows, ending with **WS** facing for next row, **and at same time** cast off 7 [8: 9: 9: 10: 11: 12] sts at beg of 2nd row, then 7 [8: 9: 10: 10: 11: 12] sts at beg of foll alt row.
Work 1 row.
Cast off rem 8 [8: 9: 10: 11: 11: 12] sts.
With RS facing, slip centre 35 [37: 37: 39: 39: 41: 41] sts onto a holder, rejoin appropriate yarn to rem sts, K to end.
Complete to match first side, reversing shapings.

FRONT
Sizes XS
Work as given for back until 8 rows less have been worked than on back to beg of armhole shaping, ending with RS facing for next row.
Divide for front opening
Next row (RS): K59 and turn, leaving rem sts on a holder.

Work each side of front opening separately.
Work 7 rows, ending with RS facing for next row.
Shape armhole
Keeping stripes correct, cast off 5 sts at beg of next row. 54 sts.
Sizes S
Work as given for back to beg of armhole shaping.
Shape armhole and divide for front opening
Next row (RS): Cast off 5 sts, K until there are 58 sts on right needle and turn, leaving rem sts on a holder.
Work each side of front opening separately.
Sizes M, L, XL, XXL and 2XL only
Work as given for back to **.
Dec 1 st at each end of next and foll – [-: 1: 3: 6: 6: 6] alt rows.
– [-: 127: 129: 129: 137: 143] sts.
Work 1 row, ending with RS facing for next row.
Divide for front opening
Next row (RS): (K2tog) – [-: 1: 1: 0: 0: 0] times, K– [-: 58: 59: 61: 65: 68] and turn, leaving rem sts on a holder.
– [-: 59: 60: 61: 65: 68] sts.
Work each side of front opening separately.
Sizes XS, S, M and L only
Work 1 row, ending with RS facing for next row.
Dec 1 st at armhole edge of next and foll 6 [6: 3: 1: -: -: -] alt rows. 47 [51: 55: 58: -: -: -] sts.
All sizes
Work 19 [27: 33: 37: 41: 41: 41] rows, ending with RS facing for next row.
Shape front neck
Next row (RS): K42 [45: 49: 52: 55: 59: 62] and turn, leaving rem 5 [6: 6: 6: 6: 6: 6] sts on a holder.
Keeping stripes correct, dec 1 st at neck edge of next 6 rows, then on foll 5 [5: 5: 6: 6: 7: 7] alt rows, then on 2 foll 4th rows.
29 [32: 36: 38: 41: 44: 47] sts.
Work 3 [3: 3: 3: 5: 3: 5] rows, ending with RS facing for next row.
Shape shoulder
Cast off 7 [8: 9: 9: 10: 11: 11] sts at beg of next and foll 2 [2: 2: 1: 2: 2: 0] alt rows, then – [-: -: -: 10: -: -: 12] sts at beg of foll – [-: -: 1: -: -: 2] alt rows.
Work 1 row.
Cast off rem 8 [8: 9: 10: 11: 11: 12] sts.
With RS facing, rejoin appropriate yarn to rem sts, cast off centre 7 sts, K to last 0 [0: 2: 2: 0: 0: 0] sts, (K2tog) 0 [0: 1: 1: 0: 0: 0] times.

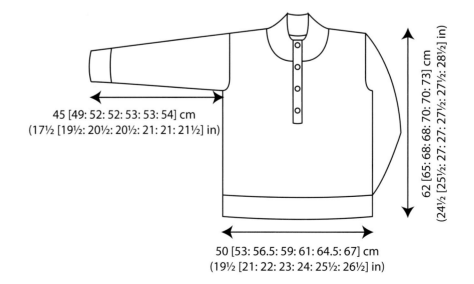

45 [49: 52: 52: 53: 53: 54] cm
(17½ [19½: 20½: 20½: 21: 21: 21½] in)

62 [65: 68: 68: 70: 70: 73] cm
(24½ [25½: 27: 27: 27½: 27½: 28½] in)

50 [53: 56.5: 59: 61: 64.5: 67] cm
(19½ [21: 22: 23: 24: 25½: 26½] in)

Complete to match first side, reversing shapings and working first row of neck shaping as folls:

Shape front neck

Next row (RS): Break yarn. Slip first 5 [6: 6: 6: 6: 6: 6] sts on a holder, rejoin appropriate yarn and K to end.
42 [45: 49: 52: 55: 59: 62] sts.

SLEEVES

Using 2¼mm (US 1) needles and yarn B cast on 58 [58: 62: 62: 66: 66: 70] sts.
Work in rib as given for back for 7 cm, dec [inc: dec: inc: dec: inc: dec] 1 st at end of last row and ending with RS facing for next row.
57 [59: 61: 63: 65: 67: 69] sts.
Change to 3mm (US 2/3) needles.
Beg with stripe row 1 and a K row, now work in st st in stripe sequence (see above) throughout as folls:
Inc 1 st at each end of 3rd and every foll 4th row to 81 [75: 79: 87: 97: 105: 117] sts, then on every foll 6th row until there are 101 [105: 111: 115: 121: 125: 131] sts.
Cont straight until sleeve meas 45 [49: 52: 52: 53: 53: 54] cm, ending with RS facing for next row.

Shape top

Keeping stripes correct, cast off 5 sts at beg of next 2 rows.
91 [95: 101: 105: 111: 115: 121] sts.

Dec 1 st at each end of next and foll 5 alt rows, then on foll row, ending with RS facing for next row.
Cast off rem 77 [81: 87: 91: 97: 101: 107] sts.

MAKING UP

Press as described on the information page. Join both shoulder seams using back stitch, or mattress stitch if preferred.

Neckband

With RS facing, using 2¼mm (US 1) needles and yarn B, K across 5 [6: 6: 6: 6: 6: 6] sts on right front holder, pick up and knit 28 [28: 28: 31: 31: 32: 32] sts up right side of front neck and 5 sts down right side of back neck, K across 35 [37: 37: 39: 39: 41: 41] sts on back holder inc 1 st at centre, pick up and knit 5 sts up left side of back neck and 28 [28: 28: 31: 31: 32: 32] sts down left side of front neck, then K across 5 [6: 6: 6: 6: 6: 6] sts on left front holder.
112 [116: 116: 124: 124: 128: 128] sts.
Row 1 (WS): K1, P2, *K2, P2, rep from * to last st, K1.
Row 2: K3, *P2, K2, rep from * to last st, K1.
These 2 rows form rib.
Cont in rib until neckband meas 7 cm from pick-up row, ending with RS facing for next row.
Cast off in rib.

Button band

With RS facing, using 2¼mm (US 1) needles and yarn E, beg at base of front opening, pick up and knit 60 sts evenly up right side of front opening to top of neckband.
Beg with row 1, work in rib as given for neckband for 9 rows, ending with RS facing for next row.
Cast off in rib.

Buttonhole band

With RS facing, using 2¼mm (US 1) needles and yarn E, beg at top of neckband, pick up and knit 60 sts evenly down left side of front opening to base of front opening.
Beg with row 1, work in rib as given for neckband for 4 rows, ending with **WS** facing for next row.
Row 5 (WS): Rib 10, *work 2 tog, yrn (to make a buttonhole), rib 13, rep from * twice more, work 2 tog, yrn (to make 4th buttonhole), rib 3.
Cont in rib for 4 rows more, ending with RS facing for next row.
Cast off in rib.
Lay buttonhole band over button band and neatly sew in place to cast-off sts at base of opening.
See information page for finishing instructions, setting in sleeves using the shallow set-in method.

PIERRE

MARIE WALLIN

Main image page 42 & 43

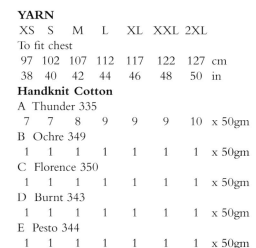

YARN

	XS	S	M	L	XL	XXL	2XL	
To fit chest								
	97	102	107	112	117	122	127	cm
	38	40	42	44	46	48	50	in

Handknit Cotton

	XS	S	M	L	XL	XXL	2XL	
A Thunder 335								
	7	7	8	9	9	9	10	x 50gm
B Ochre 349								
	1	1	1	1	1	1	1	x 50gm
C Florence 350								
	1	1	1	1	1	1	1	x 50gm
D Burnt 343								
	1	1	1	1	1	1	1	x 50gm
E Pesto 344								
	1	1	1	1	1	1	1	x 50gm
F Atlantic 346								
	1	1	1	1	1	1	1	x 50gm
G Turkish Plum 277								
	7	8	8	9	10	10	11	x 50gm

NEEDLES

1 pair 3¾mm (no 9) (US 5) needles
1 pair 4mm (no 8) (US 6) needles

TENSION

22 sts and 26 rows to 10 cm measured over rib when slightly stretched using 4mm (US 6) needles.

BACK and FRONT (both alike)

Using 3¾mm (US 5) needles and yarn A cast on 110 [114: 122: 130: 134: 138: 146] sts.
Row 1 (RS): P2, *K2, P2, rep from * to end.
Row 2: K2, *P2, K2, rep from * to end.
These 2 rows form rib.
Work in rib for a further 22 rows, ending with RS facing for next row.
Change to 4mm (US 6) needles.
Cont in rib until work meas 39 [40: 41: 39: 39: 39: 41] cm, ending with RS facing for next row.

Shape armholes

Keeping rib correct, cast off 5 sts at beg of next 2 rows. 100 [104: 112: 120: 124: 128: 136] sts.

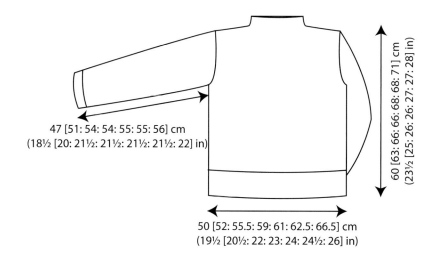

47 [51: 54: 54: 55: 55: 56] cm
(18½ [20: 21½: 21½: 21½: 21½: 22] in)

50 [52: 55.5: 59: 61: 62.5: 66.5] cm
(19½ [20½: 22: 23: 24: 24½: 26] in)

60 [63: 66: 66: 68: 68: 71] cm
(23½ [25: 26: 26: 27: 27: 28] in)

Dec 1 st at each end of next and foll 6 alt rows.
86 [90: 98: 106: 110: 114: 122] sts.
Work 1 row, ending with RS facing for next row.
Break off yarn A and join in yarn B.
Work 4 rows.
Break off yarn B and join in yarn C.
Work 4 rows.
Break off yarn C and join in yarn D.
Work 4 rows.
Break off yarn D and join in yarn E.
Work 4 rows.
Break off yarn E and join in yarn F.
Work 4 rows.
Break off yarn F and join in yarn G.
Complete work using yarn G **only**.
Cont straight until armhole meas 19 [21: 23: 25: 27: 27: 28] cm, ending with RS facing for next row.
Shape shoulders and funnel neck
Cast off 7 [8: 9: 10: 11: 11: 12] sts at beg of next 4 rows, then 8 [7: 9: 10: 10: 11: 13] sts at beg of foll 2 rows. 42 [44: 44: 46: 46: 48: 48] sts.

Dec 1 st at each end of next and foll 4th row.
38 [40: 40: 42: 42: 44: 44] sts.
Work a further 3 rows, ending with RS facing for next row.
Cast off **loosely** in rib.

SLEEVES
Using 3¾mm (US 5) needles and yarn G cast on 48 [50: 52: 54: 56: 58: 60] sts.
Row 1 (RS): P1 [0: 1: 0: 1: 0: 1], K2, *P2, K2, rep from * to last 1 [0: 1: 0: 1: 0: 1] st, P1 [0: 1: 0: 1: 0: 1].
Row 2: K1 [0: 1: 0: 1: 0: 1], P2, *K2, P2, rep from * to last 1 [0: 1: 0: 1: 0: 1] st, K1 [0: 1: 0: 1: 0: 1].
These 2 rows form rib.
Work in rib for a further 6 rows, ending with RS facing for next row.
Change to 4mm (US 6) needles.
Cont in rib, shaping sides by inc 1 st at each end of 5th [3rd: 3rd: 3rd: 3rd: 3rd: 3rd] and every foll 6th [6th: 4th: 4th: 4th: 4th: 4th] row

to 74 [88: 64: 90: 108: 104: 110] sts, then on every foll 8th [-: 6th: 6th: 6th: 6th: 6th] row until there are 80 [-: 96: 106: 114: 114: 118] sts, taking inc sts into rib.
Cont straight until sleeve meas 47 [51: 54: 54: 55: 55: 56] cm, ending with RS facing for next row.
Shape top
Keeping rib correct, cast off 5 sts at beg of next 2 rows. 70 [78: 86: 96: 104: 104: 108] sts.
Dec 1 st at each end of next and foll 5 alt rows, then on foll row, ending with RS facing for next row.
Cast off rem 56 [64: 72: 82: 90: 90: 94] sts.

MAKING UP
Press as described on the information page.
Join both shoulder and funnel neck seams using back stitch, or mattress stitch if preferred.
See information page for finishing instructions, setting in sleeves using the shallow set-in method.

MOD
RUTH GREEN
Main image page 42 & 43

YARN

	S	M	L	XL	XXL	
To fit bust						
	81-86	91-97	102-107	112-117	122-127	cm
	32-34	36-38	40-42	44-46	48-50	in

Handknit Cotton

	S	M	L	XL	XXL	
A Linen 205						
	5	5	6	6	7	x 50gm
B Cloud 345						
	2	2	3	3	3	x 50gm
C Bleached 263						
	3	3	4	4	4	x 50gm
D Raspberry 356						
	2	2	3	3	3	x 50gm
E Gooseberry 219						
	2	2	3	3	3	x 50gm
F Black 252						
	2	2	2	2	3	x 50gm
G Violet 353						
	1	1	1	1	1	x 50gm

NEEDLES
1 pair 3¾mm (no 9) (US 5) needles
1 pair 4mm (no 8) (US 6) needles

TENSION
20 sts and 28 rows to 10 cm measured over patterned st st using 4mm (US 6) needles.

BACK & FRONT ALIKE
Using 3¾mm (US 5) needles and yarn A cast on 122 [130: 142: 154: 170] sts.
Row 1 (RS): K2, *P2, K2, rep from * to end.
Row 2: P2, *K2, P2, rep from * to end.
These 2 rows form rib.
Cont in rib for a further 20 rows, dec 1 [0: 0: 0: 1] st at each end of last row and ending with RS facing for next row.
120 [130: 142: 154: 168] sts.

Change to 4mm (US 6) needles.
Beg and ending rows as indicated and using the **intarsia** technique as described on the information page, cont in patt from chart for back, which is worked entirely in st st beg with a K row, as folls:
Cont straight until chart row 102 [106: 112: 118: 124] has been completed, ending with RS facing for next row. (Back should meas approx 44 [46: 48: 50: 52] cm.)
Shape back neck and shoulders
Next row (RS): Patt 44 [49: 54: 60: 66] sts and turn, leaving rem sts on a holder.
Work each side of neck separately.
Dec 1 st at neck edge of next 6 rows, ending with **WS** facing for next row, **and at same time** cast off 13 [14: 16: 18: 20] sts at beg of 4th and foll alt row.

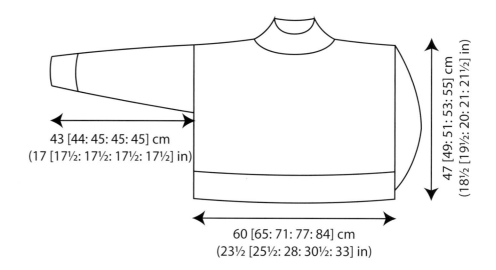

43 [44: 45: 45: 45] cm
(17 [17½: 17½: 17½: 17½] in)

47 [49: 51: 53: 55] cm
(18½ [19½: 20: 21: 21½] in)

60 [65: 71: 77: 84] cm
(23½ [25½: 28: 30½: 33] in)

Work 1 row.
Cast off rem 12 [15: 16: 18: 20] sts.
With RS facing, slip centre 32 [32: 34: 34: 36] sts onto a holder, rejoin appropriate yarns to rem sts, patt to end.
Complete to match first side, reversing shapings.

SLEEVES
Using 3¾mm (US 5) needles and yarn A cast on 40 [42: 44: 44: 46] sts.

Row 1 (RS): P1 [0: 1: 1: 0], K2, *P2, K2, rep from * to last 1 [0: 1: 1: 0] st, P1 [0: 1: 1: 0].
Row 2: K1 [0: 1: 1: 0], P2, *K2, P2, rep from * to last 1 [0: 1: 1: 0] st, K1 [0: 1: 1: 0].
These 2 rows form rib.
Work in rib for a further 4 [4: 4: 4: 2] rows, ending with RS facing for next row.
Cont in rib, inc 1 st at each end of next and 2 [2: 2: 3: 4] foll 6th [6th: 6th: 4th: 4th] rows,

taking inc sts into rib. 46 [48: 50: 52: 56] sts.
Work 3 [3: 3: 3: 1] rows, ending with RS facing for next row.
Change to 4mm (US 6) needles.
Beg and ending rows as indicated and using the **intarsia** technique as described on the information page, cont in patt from chart for sleeve, which is worked entirely in st st beg with a K row, as folls:
Inc 1 st at each end of 3rd [3rd: 3rd: next: 3rd]

Sleeve Chart

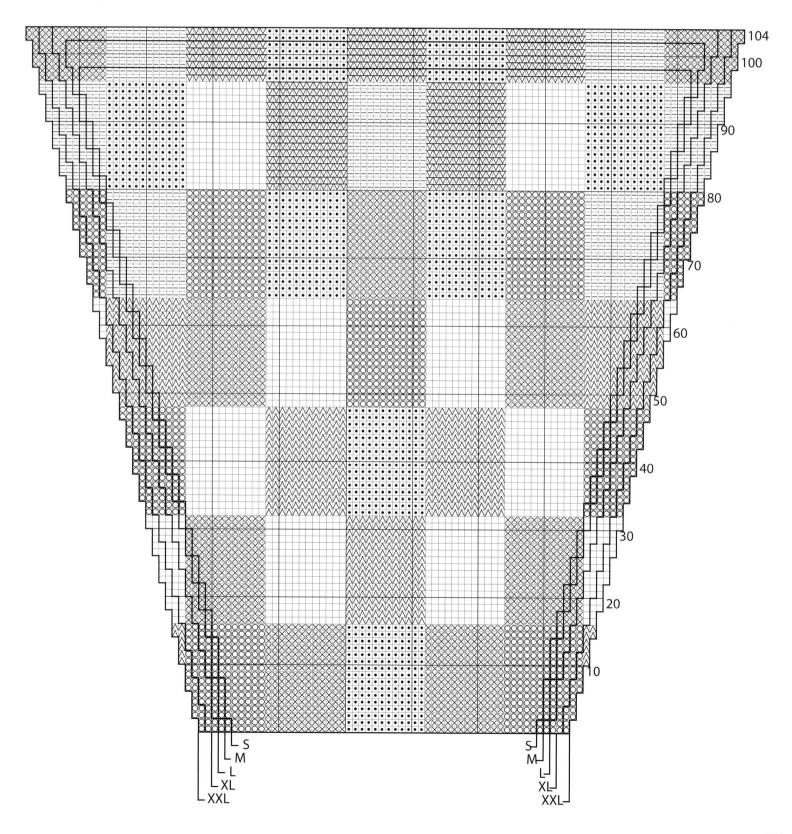

127

and 2 [2: 1: 0: 0] foll 6th rows, then on every foll 4th row until there are 92 [96: 100: 104: 108] sts, taking inc sts into patt.

Work 3 [3: 3: 3: 1] rows, ending after chart row 98 [102: 104: 104: 104] and with RS facing for next row. (Sleeve should meas approx 43 [44: 45: 45: 45] cm.)

Cast off.

MAKING UP

Press as described on the information page. Join right shoulder seam using back stitch, or mattress stitch if preferred.

Neckband

With RS facing, using 3¾mm (US 5) needles and yarn F, pick up and knit 8 [8: 11: 11: 12] sts down left side of front neck, K across 30 sts on front holder, pick up and knit 8 [8: 11: 11: 12] sts up right side of front neck and 6 sts down right side of back neck, K across 32 [32: 34: 34: 36] sts on back holder, then pick up and knit 6 sts up left side of back neck.

90 [90: 98: 98: 102] sts.

Beg with row 2, work in rib as given for back for 17 rows, ending with RS facing for next row.

Cast off in rib.

Join left shoulder and neckband seam. Mark points along side seam edges of back and front 24 [25: 26: 27: 28] cm either side of shoulder seams to denote base of armhole openings. See information page for finishing instructions, setting in sleeves using the straight cast-off method.

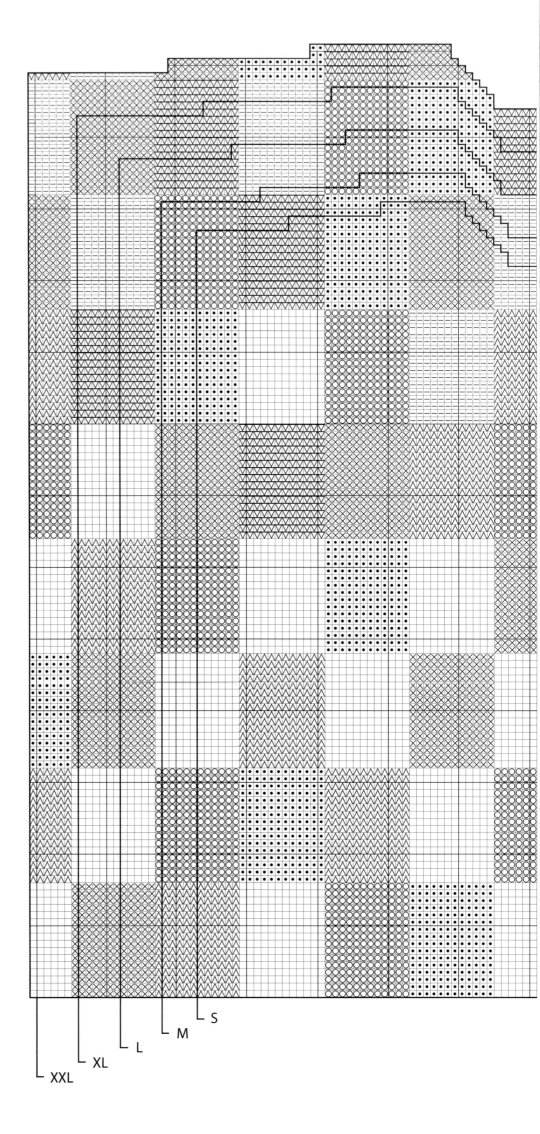

Back / Front Chart

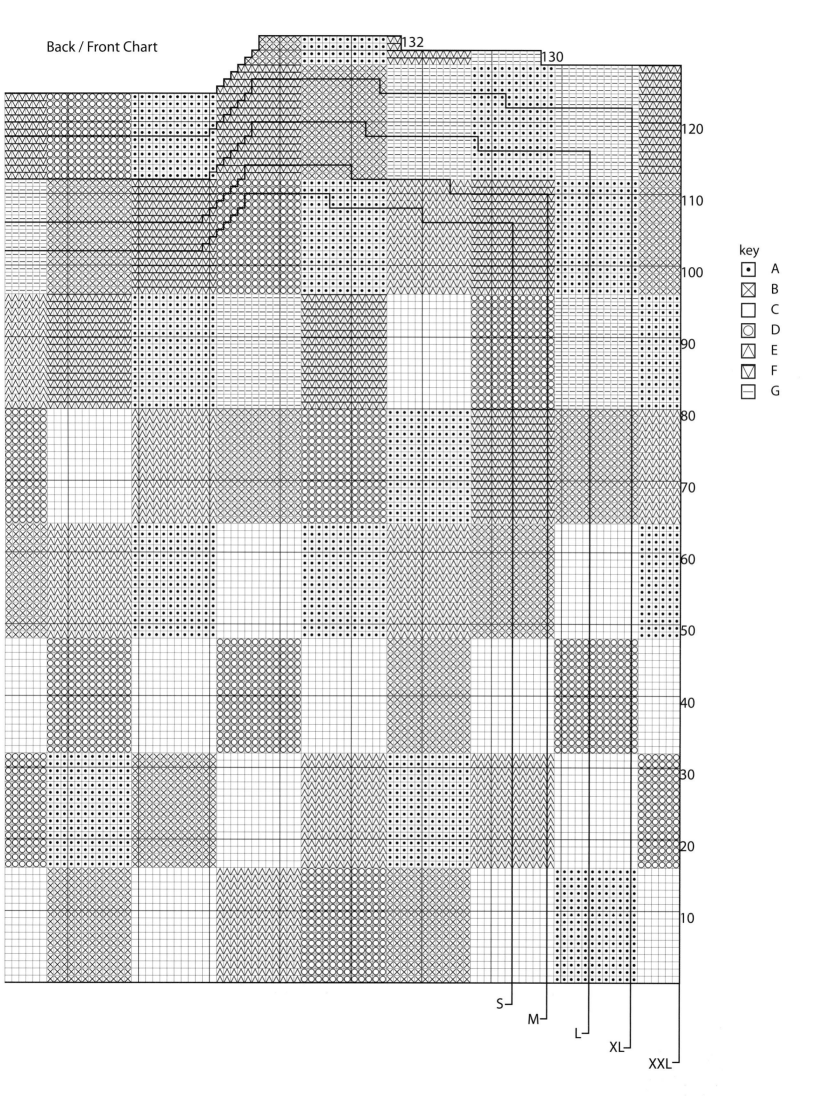

132

130

120

110

100

90

80

70

60

50

40

30

20

10

key
A
B
C
D
E
F
G

S
M
L
XL
XXL

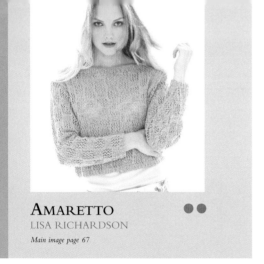

AMARETTO
LISA RICHARDSON

Main image page 67

YARN

	S	M	L	XL	XXL
To fit bust					
81-86	91-97	102-107	112-117	122-127	cm
32-34	36-38	40-42	44-46	48-50	in

Panama

| 8 | 9 | 10 | 11 | 12 | x 50gm |

(photographed in Blush 318)

NEEDLES

1 pair 2¾mm (no 12) (US 2) needles
1 pair 3¼mm (no 10) (US 3) needles

BEADS - approx 2,600 [3,000: 3,300: 3,700: 4,200] size 6, col 216 beads from Debbie Abrahams. Please see information page for contact details.

TENSION

25 sts and 34 rows to 10 cm measured over patt using 3¼mm (US 3) needles.

SPECIAL ABBREVIATIONS

bead 1 = place a bead by taking yarn to RS of work (this is front of work on RS rows, or back of work on WS rows), slip bead up next to st just worked and slip next st purlwise from left needle to right needle, leaving bead sitting in front of slipped st on RS of work (this is front of work on RS rows, or back of work on WS rows), and then take yarn back to WS of work (this is back of work on RS rows, or front of work on WS rows). (**Note**: Beads are placed on RS **and** WS rows, but beads should always "sit" on RS of work.)

Beading note: Before starting to knit, thread beads onto yarn. To do this, thread a fine sewing needle (one that will easily pass through the beads) with sewing thread. Knot ends of thread and then pass end of yarn through this loop. Thread a bead onto sewing thread and then gently slide it along and onto knitting yarn. Continue in this way until required number of beads are on yarn. Do not place beads on edge sts of rows as this will interfere with seaming.

Pattern note: When working lacy squares of patt from chart, take care to ensure each dec of patt is matched by an inc. If there are insufficient sts to work both, work end sts of rows in st st.

BACK

Using 2¾mm (US 2) needles cast on 115 [127:

141: 157: 175] sts.
Row 1 (RS): P0 [0: 1: 0: 0], K1, *P2, K1, rep from * to last 0 [0: 1: 0: 0] sts, P0 [0: 1: 0: 0].
Row 2: K0 [0: 1: 0: 0], P1, *K2, P1, rep from * to last 0 [0: 1: 0: 0] sts, K0 [0: 1: 0: 0].
These 2 rows form rib.
Work in rib for a further 5 rows, ending with **WS** facing for next row.
Change to 3¼mm (US 3) needles.
Row 8 (WS): Purl.
Beg and ending rows as indicated, repeating the 18 st patt rep 5 [7: 7: 7: 9] times across each row and the 24 row patt repeat throughout, cont in patt from chart as folls:
Inc 1 st at each end of 15th and 2 foll 16th rows, taking inc sts into patt.
121 [133: 147: 163: 181] sts.
Cont straight until back meas 21 [22: 23: 24: 25] cm, ending with RS facing for next row.
Shape armholes
Keeping patt correct, cast off 5 sts at beg of next 2 rows. 111 [123: 137: 153: 171] sts.
Dec 1 st at each end of next and foll 6 alt rows. 97 [109: 123: 139: 157] sts.
Cont straight until armhole meas 22 [23: 24: 25: 26] cm, ending with RS facing for next row.
Shape back neck and shoulders
Next row (RS): Cast off 4 [5: 7: 9: 11] sts, patt until there are 17 [22: 26: 32: 38] sts on right needle and turn, leaving rem sts on a holder.
Work each side of neck separately.
Keeping patt correct, dec 1 st at neck edge of next 5 rows, ending with RS facing for next row, **and at same time** cast off 4 [5: 7: 9: 11] sts at beg of 2nd row, then 4 [6: 7: 9: 11] sts at beg of foll alt row.
Cast off rem 4 [6: 7: 9: 11] sts.
With RS facing, slip centre 55 [55: 57: 57: 59] sts onto a holder, rejoin yarn to rem sts, patt to end.
Complete to match first side, reversing shapings.

FRONT

Work as given for back until 14 [14: 16: 16: 18] rows less have been worked than on back to beg of shoulder shaping, ending with RS facing for next row.
Shape front neck
Next row (RS): Patt 26 [32: 39: 47: 56] sts and turn, leaving rem sts on a holder.
Work each side of neck separately.

Keeping patt correct, dec 1 st at neck edge of next 8 rows, then on foll 2 [2: 3: 3: 4] alt rows. 16 [22: 28: 36: 44] sts.
Work 1 row, ending with RS facing for next row.
Shape shoulder
Cast off 4 [5: 7: 9: 11] sts at beg of next and foll alt row, then 4 [6: 7: 9: 11] sts at beg of foll alt row.
Work 1 row.
Cast off rem 4 [6: 7: 9: 11] sts.
With RS facing, slip centre 45 sts onto a holder, rejoin yarn to rem sts, patt to end.
Complete to match first side, reversing shapings.

SLEEVES

Using 2¾mm (US 2) needles cast on 51 [53: 55: 55: 57] sts.
Row 1 (RS): P1 [2: 0: 0: 1], K1, *P2, K1, rep from * to last 1 [2: 0: 0: 1] sts, P1 [2: 0: 0: 1].
Row 2: K1 [2: 0: 0: 1], P1, *K2, P1, rep from * to last 1 [2: 0: 0: 1] sts, K1 [2: 0: 0: 1].
These 2 rows form rib.
Work in rib for a further 5 rows, ending with **WS** facing for next row.
Change to 3¼mm (US 3) needles.
Row 8 (WS): Purl.
Beg and ending rows as indicated, repeating the 18 st patt rep 2 [2: 3: 3: 3] times across each row and the 24 row patt repeat throughout, cont in patt from chart as folls:
Inc 1 st at each end of 3rd and every foll 4th row until there are 83 [95: 99: 117: 125] sts, then on 11 [8: 8: 2: 0] foll 6th rows, taking inc sts into patt. 105 [111: 115: 121: 125] sts.
Cont straight until sleeve meas 45 [46: 47: 47: 47] cm, ending with RS facing for next row.
Shape top
Keeping patt correct, cast off 5 sts at beg of next 2 rows. 95 [101: 105: 111: 115] sts.
Dec 1 st at each end of next and foll 5 alt rows, then on foll row, ending with RS facing for next row.
Cast off rem 81 [87: 91: 97: 101] sts.

MAKING UP

Press as described on the information page.
Join right shoulder seam using back stitch, or mattress stitch if preferred.
Neckband
With RS facing and 2¾mm (US 2) needles, pick up and knit 14 [14: 16: 16: 18] sts down left side of front neck, K across 45 sts on front

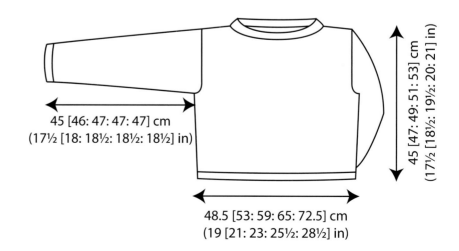

45 [46: 47: 47: 47] cm
(17½ [18: 18½: 18½: 18½] in)

48.5 [53: 59: 65: 72.5] cm
(19 [21: 23: 25½: 28½] in)

45 [47: 49: 51: 53] cm
(17½ [18½: 19½: 20: 21] in)

holder, pick up and knit 14 [14: 16: 16: 18] sts up right side of front neck, and 7 sts down right side of back neck, K across 55 [55: 57: 57: 59] sts on back holder, then pick up and knit 8 sts up left side of back neck.

143 [143: 149: 149: 155] sts.
Row 1 (WS): K2, ★P1, K2, rep from ★ to end.
Row 2: P2, ★K1, P2, rep from ★ to end.
These 2 rows form rib.
Cont in rib for a further 5 rows, ending with

RS facing for next row.
Cast off in rib.
See information page for finishing instructions, setting in sleeves using the shallow set-in method.

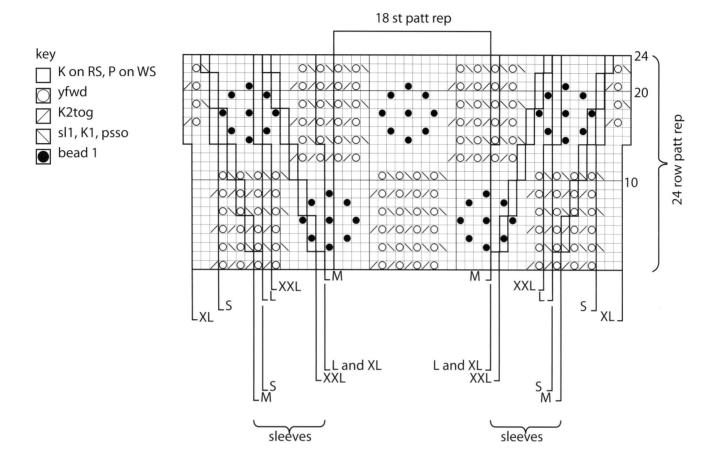

18 st patt rep

key
☐ K on RS, P on WS
◯ yfwd
◩ K2tog
◪ sl1, K1, psso
● bead 1

24 row patt rep

sleeves

sleeves

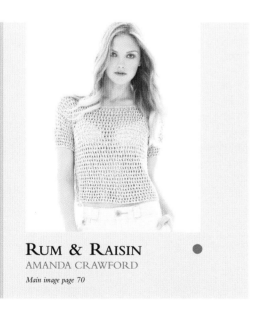

RUM & RAISIN
AMANDA CRAWFORD
Main image page 70

YARN
	S	M	L	XL	XXL

To fit bust
81–86 91–97 102–107 112–117 122–127 cm
32–34 36–38 40–42 44–46 48–50 in
Panama
 4 5 6 6 7 x 50gm
(photographed in Blue Fog 317)

NEEDLES
1 pair 3¾mm (no 9) (US 5) needles

TENSION
19 sts and 40 rows to 10 cm measured over patt using 3¾mm (US 5) needles.

BACK
Using 3¾mm (US 5) needles cast on 91 [101: 113: 123: 137] sts.
Now work in patt as folls:
Rows 1 to 3: Purl.

Row 4 (RS): K1, ★yfwd, sl 1, K1, psso, rep from ★ to end.
Rows 5 to 7: Purl.
Row 8: K1, ★K2tog, yfwd, rep from ★ to last 2 sts, K2.
These 8 rows form patt.
Cont in patt until back meas 42 [44: 46: 48: 50] cm, ending with RS facing for next row.
Shape back neck
Next row (RS): Patt 25 [30: 35: 40: 46] sts and turn, leaving rem sts on a holder.

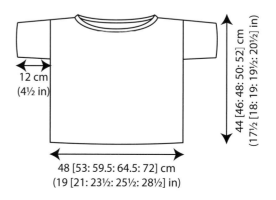

12 cm
(4½ in)

44 [46: 48: 50: 52] cm
(17½ [18: 19: 19½: 20½] in)

48 [53: 59.5: 64.5: 72] cm
(19 [21: 23½: 25½: 28½] in)

Work each side of neck separately.
Keeping patt correct, dec 1 st at neck edge of next 3 rows, ending with RS facing for next row. 22 [27: 32: 37: 43] sts.
Shape shoulder
Cast off 6 [8: 10: 11: 13] sts at beg of next and foll alt row **and at same time** dec 1 st at neck edge of next 3 rows.
Work 1 row.
Cast off rem 7 [8: 9: 12: 14] sts.
With RS facing, slip centre 41 [41: 43: 43: 45] sts onto a holder, rejoin yarn to rem sts, patt to end.
Complete to match first side, reversing shapings.

FRONT
Work as given for back until 20 [20: 24: 24: 28] rows less have been worked than on back to beg of shoulder shaping, ending with RS facing for next row.
Shape front neck
Next row (RS): Patt 31 [36: 42: 47: 54] sts and turn, leaving rem sts on a holder.
Work each side of neck separately.

Keeping patt correct, dec 1 st at neck edge of next 8 rows, then on foll 3 alt rows, then on 1 [1: 2: 2: 3] foll 4th rows. 19 [24: 29: 34: 40] sts.
Work 1 row, ending with RS facing for next row.
Shape shoulder
Cast off 6 [8: 10: 11: 13] sts at beg of next and foll alt row.
Work 1 row.
Cast off rem 7 [8: 9: 12: 14] sts.
With RS facing, slip centre 29 sts onto a holder, rejoin yarn to rem sts, patt to end.
Complete to match first side, reversing shapings.

SLEEVES
Using 3¾mm (US 5) needles cast on 57 [61: 65: 69: 73] sts.
Beg with row 1, work in patt as given for back, shaping sides by inc 1 st at each end of 10th and 3 foll 10th rows, taking inc sts into patt. 65 [69: 73: 77: 81] sts.
Cont straight until sleeve meas 12 cm, ending with RS facing for next row.
Cast off.

MAKING UP
Press as described on the information page.
Join right shoulder seam using back stitch, or mattress stitch if preferred.
Neckband
With RS facing and using 3¾mm (US 5) needles, pick up and knit 20 [20: 24: 24: 28] sts down left side of front neck, K across 29 sts on front holder, pick up and knit 20 [20: 24: 24: 28] sts up right side of front neck, and 7 sts down right side of back neck, K across 41 [41: 43: 43: 45] sts on back holder, then pick up and knit 7 sts up left side of back neck. 124 [124: 134: 134: 144] sts.
Work in g st for 2 rows, ending with **WS** facing for next row.
Cast off knitwise (on **WS**).
Join left shoulder and neckband seam. Mark points along side seam edges 18 [19: 20: 21: 22] cm either side of shoulder seams to denote base of armhole openings. See information page for finishing instructions, setting in sleeves using the straight cast-off method.

Honeycomb
RUTH GREEN
Main image page 73

YARN

	S	M	L	XL	XXL

To fit bust
81-86 91-97 102-107 112-117 122-127 cm
32-34 36-38 40-42 44-46 48-50 in
Handknit Cotton
10 11 12 13 15 x 50gm
(photographed in Florence 350)

NEEDLES
1 pair 4mm (no 8) (US 6) needles
1 pair 4½mm (no 7) (US 7) needles

FASTENINGS - 8 x 2195115 13mm
millward snap fasteners. Please see information page for contact details.

TENSION
19 sts and 28 rows to 10 cm measured over patt using 4½mm (US 7) needles.

BACK
Using 4mm (US 6) needles cast on 81 [91: 103: 113: 127] sts.
Row 1 (RS): K1 tbl, *P1 tbl, K1 tbl, rep from * to end.
Row 2: P1 tbl, *K1 tbl, P1 tbl, rep from * to end.
These 2 rows form rib.
Cont in rib, inc 1 st at each end of 5th and 4 foll 6th rows. 91 [101: 113: 123: 137] sts.
Work 3 rows, ending with RS facing for next row.
Change to 4½mm (US 7) needles.
Now work in patt as folls:
Row 1 (RS): K2 [1: 1: 6: 1], yfwd, sl 1, K2tog, psso, yfwd, *K3, yfwd, sl 1, K2tog, psso, yfwd, rep from * to last 2 [1: 1: 6: 1] sts, K2 [1: 1: 6: 1].
Row 2: Purl.

Row 3: K5 [4: 4: 3: 4], yfwd, sl 1, K2tog, psso, yfwd, *K3, yfwd, sl 1, K2tog, psso, yfwd, rep from * to last 5 [4: 4: 3: 4] sts, K5 [4: 4: 3: 4].
Row 4: Purl.
These 4 rows form patt.
Cont in patt until back meas 21 [22: 23: 24: 25] cm, ending with RS facing for next row.
Shape armholes
Keeping patt correct, cast off 4 sts at beg of next 2 rows. 83 [93: 105: 115: 129] sts.
Dec 1 st at each end of next and foll 4 alt rows. 73 [83: 95: 105: 119] sts.
Cont straight until armhole meas 21 [22: 23: 24: 25] cm, ending with RS facing for next row.
Shape back neck
Next row (RS): Patt 23 [28: 33: 38: 44] sts and turn, leaving rem sts on a holder.

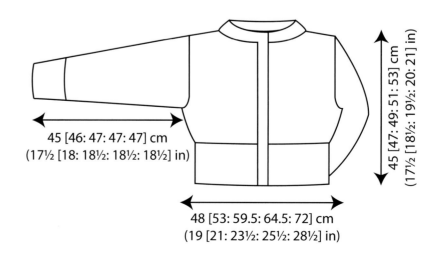

45 [46: 47: 47: 47] cm
(17½ [18: 18½: 18½: 18½] in)

48 [53: 59.5: 64.5: 72] cm
(19 [21: 23½: 25½: 28½] in)

45 [47: 49: 51: 53] cm
(17½ [18½: 19½: 20: 21] in)

Work each side of neck separately.
Dec 1 st at neck edge of next row, ending with RS facing for next row. 22 [27: 32: 37: 43] sts.
Shape shoulder
Cast off 4 [5: 6: 8: 9] sts at beg of next and foll 2 [1: 0: 2: 1] alt rows, then - [6: 7: -: 10] sts at beg of foll - [1: 2: -: 1] alt row **and at same time** dec 1 st at neck edge of next 5 rows.
Work 1 row.
Cast off rem 5 [6: 7: 8: 10] sts.
With RS facing, slip centre 27 [27: 29: 29: 31] sts onto a holder, rejoin yarn to rem sts, patt to end. 23 [28: 33: 38: 44] sts.
Complete to match first side, reversing shapings.

LEFT FRONT
Using 4mm (US 6) needles cast on 46 [52: 58: 62: 70] sts.
Row 1 (RS): K1 tbl, *P1 tbl, K1 tbl, rep from * to last st, K1.
Row 2: K1, P1 tbl, *K1 tbl, P1 tbl, rep from * to end.
These 2 rows form rib.
Cont in rib, inc 1 st at beg of 5th and 4 foll 6th rows. 51 [57: 63: 67: 75] sts.
Work 2 rows, ending with **WS** facing for next row.
Row 34 (WS): Rib 9 sts and slip these 9 sts onto a holder, M1, rib to last 1 [0: 0: 1: 0] st, (inc in last st) 1 [0: 0: 1: 0] times.
44 [49: 55: 60: 67] sts.
Change to 4¹/2mm (US 7) needles.
Now work in patt as folls:
Row 1 (RS): K2 [1: 1: 6: 1], *yfwd, sl 1, K2tog, psso, yfwd, K3, rep from * to end.
Row 2: Purl.
Row 3: K5 [4: 4: 3: 4], *yfwd, sl 1, K2tog, psso, yfwd, K3, rep from * to last 3 sts, yfwd, sl 1, K1, psso, K1.
Row 4: Purl.
These 4 rows form patt.
Cont in patt until left front matches back to beg of armhole shaping, ending with RS facing for next row.
Shape armhole
Keeping patt correct, cast off 4 sts at beg of next row. 40 [45: 51: 56: 63] sts.
Work 1 row.
Dec 1 st at armhole edge of next and foll 4 alt rows. 35 [40: 46: 51: 58] sts.
Cont straight until 10 [10: 12: 12: 14] rows less have been worked than on back to beg of shoulder shaping, ending with RS facing for next row.
Shape front neck
Next row (RS): Patt 25 [30: 36: 41: 48] sts and turn, leaving rem 10 sts on a holder (for neckband).
Keeping patt correct, dec 1 st at neck edge of next 6 rows, then on foll 1 [1: 2: 2: 3] alt rows. 18 [23: 28: 33: 39] sts.
Work 1 row, ending with RS facing for next row.
Shape shoulder
Cast off 4 [5: 6: 8: 9] sts at beg of next and foll 2 [1: 0: 2: 1] alt rows, then - [6: 7: -: 10] sts at

beg of foll - [1: 2: -: 1] alt row **and at same time** dec 1 st at neck edge of next row.
Work 1 row.
Cast off rem 5 [6: 7: 8: 10] sts.

RIGHT FRONT
Using 4mm (US 6) needles cast on 46 [52: 58: 62: 70] sts.
Row 1 (RS): K1, K1 tbl, *P1 tbl, K1 tbl, rep from * to end.
Row 2: P1 tbl, *K1 tbl, P1 tbl, rep from * to last st, K1.
These 2 rows form rib.
Cont in rib, inc 1 st at end of 5th and 4 foll 6th rows. 51 [57: 63: 67: 75] sts.
Work 2 rows, ending with **WS** facing for next row.
Row 34 (WS): (Inc in first st) 1 [0: 0: 1: 0] times, rib to last 9 sts, M1 and turn, leaving rem 9 sts on a holder. 44 [49: 55: 60: 67] sts.
Change to 4¹/2mm (US 7) needles.
Now work in patt as folls:
Row 1 (RS): *K3, yfwd, sl 1, K2tog, psso, yfwd, rep from * to last 2 [1: 1: 6: 1] sts, K2 [1: 1: 6: 1].
Row 2: Purl.
Row 3: K1, K2tog, yfwd, *K3, yfwd, sl 1, K2tog, psso, yfwd, rep from * to last 5 [4: 4: 3: 4] sts, K5 [4: 4: 3: 4].
Row 4: Purl.
These 4 rows form patt.
Complete to match left front, reversing shapings and working first row of neck shaping as folls:
Shape front neck
Next row (RS): Break yarn. Slip first 10 sts onto a holder (for neckband), rejoin yarn and patt to end. 25 [30: 36: 41: 48] sts.

SLEEVES
Using 4mm (US 6) needles cast on 39 [41: 43: 43: 45] sts.
Work in rib as given for back, shaping sides by inc 1 st at each end of 5th and 3 [5: 5: 5: 5] foll 4th rows, then on 1 [0: 0: 0: 0] foll 6th row. 49 [53: 55: 55: 57] sts.
Work 5 [3: 3: 3: 3] rows, ending with RS facing for next row.
Change to 4¹/2mm (US 7) needles.
Now work in patt as folls:
Row 1 (RS): (Inc in first st) 1 [0: 1: 1: 1] times, K4 [1: 1: 1: 2], yfwd, sl 1, K2tog, psso, yfwd, *K3, yfwd, sl 1, K2tog, psso, yfwd, rep from * to last 5 [1: 2: 2: 3] sts, K4 [1: 1: 1: 2], (inc in last st) 1 [0: 1: 1: 1] times.
51 [53: 57: 57: 59] sts.
Row 2: Purl.
Row 3: (Inc in first st) 0 [1: 0: 0: 0] times, K3 [3: 1: 1: 1], (K2tog, yfwd, K3) 0 [0: 1: 1: 0] times, yfwd, sl 1, K2tog, psso, yfwd, *K3, yfwd, sl 1, K2tog, psso, yfwd, rep from * to last 3 [4: 6: 6: 1] sts, (K3, yfwd, sl 1, K1, psso) 0 [0: 1: 1: 0] times, K3 [3: 1: 1: 1], (inc in last st) 0 [1: 0: 0: 0] times. 51 [55: 57: 57: 59] sts.
Row 4: Purl.
These 4 rows form patt and cont sleeve shaping.

Cont in patt, inc 1 st at each end of 3rd [5th: 3rd: next: next] and every foll 6th [6th: 6th: 4th: 4th] row to 79 [83: 87: 69: 77] sts, then on every foll - [-: -: 6th: 6th] row until there are - [-: -: 91: 95] sts, taking inc sts into patt.
Cont straight until sleeve meas 45 [46: 47: 47: 47] cm, ending with RS facing for next row.
Shape top
Keeping patt correct, cast off 4 sts at beg of next 2 rows. 71 [75: 79: 83: 87] sts.
Dec 1 st at each end of next and foll 3 alt rows, then on foll row, ending with RS facing for next row.
Cast off rem 61 [65: 69: 73: 77] sts.

MAKING UP
Press as described on the information page.
Join both shoulder seams using back stitch, or mattress stitch if preferred.
Left front band
Slip 9 sts from left front holder onto 4mm (US 6) needles and rejoin yarn with RS facing.
Row 1 (RS): K1, (K1 tbl, P1 tbl) 3 times, K1 tbl, K1.
Row 2: K1, (P1 tbl, K1 tbl) 3 times, P1 tbl, K1.
These 2 rows form rib.
Cont in rib until band, when slightly stretched, fits up left front opening edge to beg of front neck shaping, ending with RS facing for next row.
Break yarn and leave sts on a holder.
Neatly slip stitch band in place.
Right front band
Slip 9 sts from right front holder onto 4mm (US 6) needles and rejoin yarn with **WS** facing.
Beg with row 2, work in rib as given for left front band until this band, when slightly stretched, fits up right front opening edge to beg of front neck shaping, ending with RS facing for next row.
Do NOT break yarn.
Neatly slip stitch band in place.
Neckband
With RS facing and using 4mm (US 6) needles, rib across first 8 sts of right front band, K tog last st of right front band with first st left on right front holder, K across rem 9 sts on holder, pick up and knit 14 [14: 16: 16: 18] sts up right side of front neck, and 7 sts down right side of back neck, K across 27 [27: 29: 29: 31] sts on back holder, then pick up and knit 7 sts up left side of back neck, and 14 [14: 16: 16: 18] sts down left side of front neck, K across first 9 sts on left front holder, K tog last st on holder with first st of left front band, then rib across rem 8 sts of left front band.
105 [105: 111: 111: 117] sts.
Keeping first and last st of every row worked as a K st, now work in rib across all sts as set by front band sts until neckband meas 3 cm from pick-up row, ending with RS facing for next row.
Cast off in rib.
See information page for finishing instructions, setting in sleeves using the shallow set-in method and attaching stud fasteners to fasten front bands.

BANOFFI
LISA RICHARDSON
Main image page 68

YARN

	S	M	L	XL	XXL	
To fit bust						
	81-86	91-97	102-107	112-117	122-127	cm
	32-34	36-38	40-42	44-46	48-50	in

Panama and Siena 4ply

A Pan Begonia 306
    5   6   6   7   8   x 50gm
B Pan Aster 310
    5   6   6   7   8   x 50gm
C Pan Straw 313
    5   6   6   7   8   x 50gm
D Sie Madras 675
    5   6   6   7   8   x 50gm

NEEDLES

1 pair 6½mm (no 3) (US 10½) needles
One 12mm (US 17) needle

TENSION

10 sts and 13 rows to 10 cm measured over patt
using a combination of one 6½mm (US 10½)
and one 12mm (US 17) needle and one strand
each of yarns A, B, C and D held together
(4 strands in total).

BACK

Using 6½mm (US 10½) needles and one
strand each of yarns A, B, C and D held
together (4 strands in total) cast on 91 [97: 107:
117: 131] sts.
Row 1 (RS): K1, *P1, K1, rep from * to end.
Row 2: P1, *K1, P1, rep from * to end.
These 2 rows form rib.
Work in rib for a further 6 rows, ending with
RS facing for next row.
Row 9 (RS): *(K2tog) 3 times, K1*, rep from
* to * 2 [1: 1: 1: 2] times more, **(K2tog)
twice, K1, rep from ** 9 [13: 15: 17: 17] times
more, rep from * to * 2 [1: 1: 1: 2] times more,
(K2tog) 3 times. 53 [57: 63: 69: 77] sts.
Now work in patt as folls:
Row 1 (WS): Using a 12mm (US 17) needle,
knit.
Row 2: Using a 6½mm (US 10½) needle,
purl.
These 2 rows form patt.
Cont in patt until back meas 62 [64: 66: 68:
70] cm, ending with RS facing for next row.

Shape shoulders and back neck
Next row (RS): Cast off 4 [4: 5: 6: 7] sts, P
until there are 10 [12: 13: 15: 17] sts on right
needle and turn, leaving rem sts on a holder.
Work each side of neck separately.
Dec 1 st at neck edge of next 3 rows, ending
with RS facing for next row, **and at same
time** cast off 4 [4: 5: 6: 7] sts at beg of 2nd row.
Cast off rem 3 [5: 5: 6: 7] sts.
With RS facing, slip centre 25 [25: 27: 27: 29] sts
onto a holder, rejoin yarn to rem sts, P to end.
Complete to match first side, reversing
shapings.

FRONT
Work as given for back until 6 [6: 8: 8: 10] rows
less have been worked than on back to beg of
shoulder shaping, ending with RS facing for
next row.
Shape front neck
Next row (RS): P16 [18: 21: 24: 28] and turn,
leaving rem sts on a holder.
Work each side of neck separately.
Keeping patt correct, dec 1 st at neck edge of
next 4 rows, then on foll 0 [0: 1: 1: 2] alt rows.
12 [14: 16: 19: 22] sts.
Work 1 row, ending with RS facing for next
row.
Shape shoulder
Cast off 4 [4: 5: 6: 7] sts at beg of next and foll
alt row **and at same time** dec 1 st at neck
edge of next row.
Work 1 row.
Cast off rem 3 [5: 5: 6: 7] sts.
With RS facing, slip centre 21 sts onto a
holder, rejoin yarn to rem sts, P to end.
Complete to match first side, reversing shapings.

SLEEVES
Using 6½mm (US 10½) needles and one
strand each of yarns A, B, C and D held
together (4 strands in total) cast on 41 [43: 45:
45: 47] sts.

Work in rib as given for back for 8 rows,
ending with RS facing for next row.
Row 9 (RS): (K2tog) 3 [1: 3: 3: 1] times,
*K1, (K2tog) twice, rep from * 6 [7: 6: 6: 8]
times more, K0 [1: 0: 0: 0], (K2tog) 0 [0: 2: 2: 0]
times. 24 [26: 26: 26: 28] sts.
Beg with patt row 1, now work in patt as given
for back, shaping sides by inc 1 st at each end
of 2nd and foll 1 [1: 2: 4: 4] alt rows, then on
every foll 4th row until there are 46 [48: 50:
52: 54] sts.
Cont straight until sleeve meas 40 [41: 42: 42:
42] cm, ending with RS facing for next row.
Cast off.

MAKING UP
Press as described on the information page.
Join right shoulder seam using back stitch, or
mattress stitch if preferred.
Neckband
With RS facing, 6½mm (US 10½) needles and
one strand each of yarns A, B, C and D held
together (4 strands in total), pick up and knit
10 [10: 13: 13: 17] sts down left side of front
neck, K across 21 sts on front holder as folls:
*(K1, M1) twice, K1, rep from * 6 times more,
pick up and knit 10 [10: 13: 13: 17] sts up right
side of front neck, and 5 sts down right side of
back neck, K across 25 [25: 27: 27: 29] sts on
back holder as folls: K0 [0: 0: 0: 1], **(K1, M1)
twice, K1, rep from ** 7 [7: 8: 8: 8] times more,
K1 [1: 0: 0: 1], then pick up and knit 6 sts up
left side of back neck.
107 [107: 117: 117: 127] sts.
Beg with row 2, work in rib as given for back
for 7 rows, ending with RS facing for next row.
Cast off in rib.
Join left shoulder and neckband seam. Mark points
along side seam edges of back and front 23 [24: 25:
26: 27] cm either side of shoulder seams to denote
base of armhole openings. See information page
for finishing instructions, setting in sleeves using the
straight cast-off method.

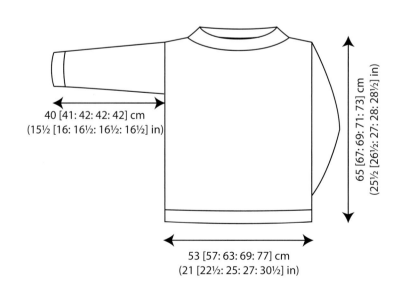

40 [41: 42: 42: 42] cm
(15½ [16: 16½: 16½: 16½] in)

65 [67: 69: 71: 73] cm
(25½ [26½: 27: 28: 28½] in)

53 [57: 63: 69: 77] cm
(21 [22½: 25: 27: 30½] in)

BUBBLEGUM
MARIE WALLIN
Main image page 71

YARN

	S	M	L	XL	XXL	
To fit bust						
	81-86	91-97	102-107	112-117	122-127	cm
	32-34	36-38	40-42	44-46	48-50	in

Panama

A	Lotus 309						
	4	4	4	5	5	x 50gm
B	Blue Fog 317						
	5	6	7	7	8	x 50gm

NEEDLES
1 pair 2¼mm (no 13) (US 1) needles
1 pair 3mm (no 11) (US 2/3) needles

TENSION
28 sts and 38 rows to 10 cm measured over st st using 3mm (US 2/3) needles.

BODY STRIPE SEQUENCE
Rows 1 to 10: Using yarn B.
Rows 11 to 20: Using yarn A.
Rep these 20 rows 7 [7: 8: 8: 8] times more, then rows 1 to 10 again – 17 [17: 19: 19: 19] stripes completed in total.
Break off yarn B and complete work using yarn A **only**.

BACK
Using 2¼mm (US 1) needles and yarn A cast on 121 [135: 151: 169: 187] sts.
Row 1 (RS): K1, *P1, K1, rep from * to end.
Row 2: P1, *K1, P1, rep from * to end.
These 2 rows form rib.
Work in rib for a further 8 rows, ending with RS facing for next row.
Change to 3mm (US 2/3) needles.
Beg with stripe row 1 and a K row, work in st st in body stripe sequence (see above) throughout as folls:
Dec 1 st at each end of 7th and 5 foll 6th rows. 109 [123: 139: 157: 175] sts.
Work 17 [17: 19: 19: 21] rows, ending with RS facing for next row.
Inc 1 st at each end of next and 5 foll 10th rows. 121 [135: 151: 169: 187] sts.
Cont straight until back meas 35 [36: 37: 38: 39] cm, ending with RS facing for next row.
Shape armholes
Keeping stripes correct, cast off 6 [7: 8: 9: 10] sts at beg of next 2 rows.
109 [121: 135: 151: 167] sts.

Dec 1 st at each end of next 5 [7: 9: 11: 13] rows, then on foll 5 [6: 7: 8: 10] alt rows. 89 [95: 103: 113: 121] sts.
Cont straight until armhole meas 17 [18: 19: 20: 21] cm, ending with RS facing for next row. (**Note**: Remember that after 17 [17: 19: 19: 19] stripes, work is completed using yarn A **only**.)
Shape back neck
Next row (RS): K17 [20: 23: 28: 31] and turn, leaving rem sts on a holder.
Work each side of neck separately.
Dec 1 st at neck edge of next 3 rows, ending with RS facing for next row.
14 [17: 20: 25: 28] sts.
Shape shoulder
Cast off 4 [5: 6: 7: 8] sts at beg of next and foll alt row **and at same time** dec 1 st at neck edge of next 3 rows.
Work 1 row.
Cast off rem 3 [4: 5: 8: 9] sts.
With RS facing, slip centre 55 [55: 57: 57: 59] sts onto a holder, rejoin yarn to rem sts, K to end.
Complete to match first side, reversing shapings.

FRONT
Work as given for back until 12 [12: 14: 14: 16] rows less have been worked than on back to beg of shoulder shaping, ending with RS facing for next row.
Shape front neck
Next row (RS): K20 [23: 27: 32: 36] and turn, leaving rem sts on a holder.
Work each side of neck separately.
Dec 1 st at neck edge of next 8 rows, then on foll 1 [1: 2: 2: 3] alt rows.
11 [14: 17: 22: 25] sts.
Work 1 row, ending with RS facing for next row.
Shape shoulder
Cast off 4 [5: 6: 7: 8] sts at beg of next and foll alt row.
Work 1 row.
Cast off rem 3 [4: 5: 8: 9] sts.
With RS facing, slip centre 49 sts onto a holder, rejoin yarn to rem sts, K to end.
Complete to match first side, reversing shapings.

SLEEVE STRIPE SEQUENCE
Rows 1 to 3: Using yarn A.
Rows 4 to 18: Using yarn B.
These 18 rows form sleeve stripe sequence and are repeated throughout.

SLEEVES
Using 2¼mm (US 1) needles and yarn B cast on 57 [59: 61: 61: 63] sts.
Work in rib as given for back for 4 cm, ending with RS facing for next row.
Change to 3mm (US 2/3) needles.
Beg with stripe row 1 and a K row, work in st st in sleeve stripe sequence (see above) throughout as folls:
Inc 1 st at each end of 5th and every foll 6th row to 73 [79: 85: 101: 111] sts, then on 11 [10: 9: 3: 0] foll 8th rows. 95 [99: 103: 107: 111] sts.
Cont straight until sleeve meas 45 [46: 47: 47: 47] cm, ending with RS facing for next row.
Shape top
Keeping stripes correct, cast off 6 [7: 8: 9: 10] sts at beg of next 2 rows. 83 [85: 87: 89: 91] sts.
Dec 1 st at each end of next 5 rows, then on every foll alt row until 45 sts rem, then on foll 9 rows, ending with RS facing for next row.
27 sts.
Cast off 4 sts at beg of next 2 rows.
Cast off rem 19 sts.

MAKING UP
Press as described on the information page.
Join right shoulder seam using back stitch, or mattress stitch if preferred.
Neckband
With RS facing, using 2¼mm (US 1) needles and yarn A, pick up and knit 12 [12: 14: 14: 16] sts down left side of front neck, K across 49 sts on front holder, pick up and knit 12 [12: 14: 14: 16] sts up right side of front neck, and 7 sts down right side of back neck, K across 55 [55: 57: 57: 59] sts on back holder, then pick up and knit 8 sts up left side of back neck.
143 [143: 149: 149: 155] sts.
Beg with row 2, work in rib as given for back for 3 rows, ending with RS facing for next row.
Cast off in rib.
See information page for finishing instructions, setting in sleeves using the set-in method.

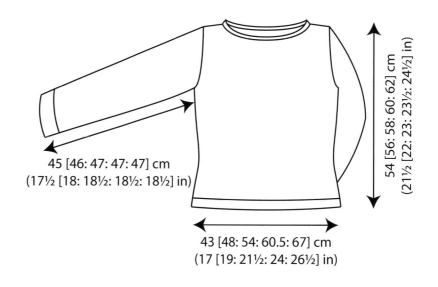

45 [46: 47: 47: 47] cm
(17½ [18: 18½: 18½: 18½] in)

54 [56: 58: 60: 62] cm
(21½ [22: 23: 23½: 24½] in)

43 [48: 54: 60.5: 67] cm
(17 [19: 21½: 24: 26½] in)

CAPPUCCINO
SARAH HATTON
Main image page 74

● ● ●

YARN

	S	M	L	XL	XXL
To fit bust					
	81-86	91-97	102-107	112-117	122-127 cm
	32-34	36-38	40-42	44-46	48-50 in

Panama

7	8	9	9	11	x 50gm

(photographed in Icing 316)

NEEDLES
1 pair 2¾mm (no 12) (US 2) needles
1 pair 3¼mm (no 10) (US 3) needles

TENSION
27 sts and 36 rows to 10 cm measured over patt when slightly stretched using 3¼mm (US 3) needles.

Pattern note: The patt for the body sections consists of 3 separate sections of rib. The centre section between the markers remains constant throughout. The side sections of "sloping" rib are formed by decreasing one st at ends of rows, and balancing this decrease by increasing one st next to the marker. These increased sts should be taken into the rib patt as set by the side sections. All st counts given for the armhole shaping do **NOT** take into account these patt increases and decreases. Therefore it is important to remember to work **both** the patt dec **and** the shaping dec on RS rows where relevant.

BACK
Using 3¼mm (US 3) needles cast on 118 [132: 148: 160: 184] sts.
Row 1 (RS): K2 [3: 2: 3: 3], P0 [2: 1: 2: 2], *K2, P2, rep from * to last 4 [3: 5: 3: 3] sts, K4 [3: 2: 3: 3], (P1, K2) 0 [0: 1: 0: 0] times.
Row 2: P2 [3: 2: 3: 3], K0 [2: 1: 2: 2], *P2, K2, rep from * to last 4 [3: 5: 3: 3] sts, P4 [3: 2: 3: 3], (K1, P2) 0 [0: 1: 0: 0] times.
These 2 rows form rib.
Counting in from both ends of last row, place markers after 34th [41st: 47th: 53rd: 65th] st – there should be 50 [50: 54: 54: 54] sts between markers at centre of row.
Row 3 (RS): K1, K2tog tbl, rib to marker, yrn, slip marker onto right needle, rib to next marker, slip marker onto right needle, yrn, rib to last 3 sts, K2tog, K1.
Row 4: P2, (rib to marker, slip marker onto right needle) twice, rib to last 2 sts, P2.

Last 2 rows form patt. (See pattern note.)
Cont in patt until back meas 12 [13: 13: 14: 14] cm, ending with RS facing for next row.
Change to 2¾mm (US 2) needles.
Work 14 rows, ending with RS facing for next row.
Change to 3¼mm (US 3) needles.
Cont straight until back meas 32 [33: 34: 35: 36] cm, ending with RS facing for next row.
Shape armholes
Keeping patt correct, cast off 5 [6: 7: 8: 9] sts at beg of next 2 rows.
108 [120: 134: 144: 166] sts. (See pattern note.)
Dec 1 st at each end of next 5 [7: 9: 11: 13] rows, then on foll 3 [4: 5: 4: 9] alt rows.
92 [98: 106: 114: 122] sts.★★
Cont straight until armhole meas 19 [20: 21: 22: 23] cm, ending with RS facing for next row.
Shape back neck
Next row (RS): Patt 30 [33: 35: 39: 43] sts and turn, leaving rem sts on a holder.
Work each side of neck separately.
Keeping patt correct, dec 1 st at neck edge of next 3 rows, ending with RS facing for next row. 27 [30: 32: 36: 40] sts.
Shape shoulder
Cast off 8 [9: 10: 11: 12] sts at beg of next and foll alt row **and at same time** dec 1 st at neck edge of next 3 rows.
Work 1 row.
Cast off rem 8 [9: 9: 11: 13] sts.
With RS facing, slip centre 32 [32: 36: 36: 36] sts onto a holder, rejoin yarn to rem sts, patt to end.
Complete to match first side, reversing shapings.

FRONT
Work as given for back to ★★.
Cont straight until armhole meas 6 [7: 8: 9: 10] cm, ending with RS facing for next row.
Shape front neck
Next row (RS): Patt 23 [26: 28: 32: 36] sts, K1 and turn, leaving rem sts on a holder. 24 [27: 29: 33: 37] sts.
Work each side of neck separately.
Next row (WS): K1, patt to end.
This row sets the sts - neck edge st worked as a K st on every row with all other sts still in patt.
Cont as set until front matches back to beg of shoulder shaping, ending with RS facing for

next row.
Shape shoulder
Cast off 8 [9: 10: 11: 12] sts at beg of next and foll alt row.
Work 1 row.
Cast off rem 8 [9: 9: 11: 13] sts.
With RS facing, rejoin yarn to rem sts, cast off centre 44 [44: 48: 48: 48] sts – one st on right needle, patt to end.
Complete to match first side, reversing shapings.

SLEEVES
Using 3¼mm (US 3) needles cast on 64 [66: 68: 68: 70] sts.
Row 1 (RS): P1 [0: 1: 1: 0], K2, *P2, K2, rep from * to last 1 [0: 1: 1: 0] sts, P1 [0: 1: 1: 0].
Row 2: K1 [0: 1: 1: 0], P2, *K2, P2, rep from * to last 1 [0: 1: 1: 0] sts, K1 [0: 1: 1: 0].
These 2 rows form rib.
Cont in rib, shaping sides by inc 1 st at each end of 3rd [3rd: 3rd: next: next] and every foll 6th [6th: 6th: 6th: 4th] row to 74 [80: 88: 102: 78] sts, then every foll 8th [8th: 8th: –: 6th] row until there are 90 [94: 98: –: 106] sts, taking inc sts into rib.
Cont straight until sleeve meas 31 [32: 33: 33: 33] cm, ending with RS facing for next row.
Shape top
Keeping rib correct, cast off 5 [6: 7: 8: 9] sts at beg of next 2 rows. 80 [82: 84: 86: 88] sts.
Dec 1 st at each end of next 5 rows, then on every foll alt row until 45 sts rem, then on foll 11 rows, ending with RS facing for next row.
Cast off rem 23 sts.

MAKING UP
Press as described on the information page.
Back neck edging
With RS facing and using 2¾mm (US 2) needles, pick up and knit 6 sts down right side of back neck, K across 32 [32: 36: 36: 36] sts on back holder, then pick up and knit 6 sts up left side of back neck. 44 [44: 48: 48: 48] sts.
Cast off knitwise (on **WS**).
Join both shoulder seams using back stitch, or mattress stitch if preferred.
See information page for finishing instructions, setting in sleeves using the set-in method.

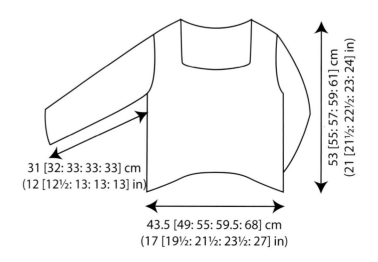

31 [32: 33: 33: 33] cm
(12 [12½: 13: 13: 13] in)

53 [55: 57: 59: 61] cm
(21 [21½: 22½: 23: 24] in)

43.5 [49: 55: 59.5: 68] cm
(17 [19½: 21½: 23½: 27] in)

COOKIES & CREAM
RUTH GREEN

Main image page 72

YARN

S   M   L   XL   XXL
To fit bust
81-86 91-97 102-107112-117 122-127 cm
32-34 36-38 40-42   44-46   48-50 in
Creative Linen
 5   5   6   6   7   x100gm
(photographed in Apple 629)

NEEDLES

1 pair 3³/4mm (no 9) (US 5) needles
1 pair 4¹/2mm (no 7) (US 7) needles

TENSION

19 sts and 25 rows to 10 cm measured over lace
patt using 4¹/2mm (US 7) needles.

Pattern note: When working lace patt, take
care to ensure each dec of patt is matched by
an inc. If there are insufficient sts to work both,
work end sts of rows in st st.

BACK

Using 3³/4mm (US 5) needles cast on 131 [141:
151: 161: 181] sts.
Work in g st for 14 rows, ending with RS
facing for next row.
Change to 4¹/2mm (US 7) needles.
Now work in lace patt as folls:
Row 1 (RS): K1, ★(yfwd, sl 1, K1, psso) twice,
K1, (K2tog, yfwd) twice, K1, rep from ★ to
end.
Row 2: Purl.
Row 3: K1, ★K1, yfwd, sl 1, K1, psso, yfwd, sl
1, K2tog, psso, yfwd, K2tog, yfwd, K2, rep from
★ to end.
Row 4: Purl.
These 4 rows form lace patt.
Cont in lace patt until back meas 14 cm,
ending with RS facing for next row.
Now work in ridge patt as folls:
Rows 1 to 3: Knit.
Row 4 (WS): ★P2tog, yrn, rep from ★ to last
st, P1.
Rows 5 to 7: Knit.
Row 8: Purl.
These 8 rows form ridge patt.
Cont in ridge patt for a further 32 rows, ending
with RS facing for next row.
Hem border is now complete.
Now work in lace patt until back meas
46.5 [48.5: 50.5: 52.5: 54.5] cm, ending with
RS facing for next row.

Shape back neck

Next row (RS): Patt 45 [50: 54: 59: 68] sts
and turn, leaving rem sts on a holder.
Work each side of neck separately.
Dec 1 st at neck edge of next 3 rows, ending
with RS facing for next row.
42 [47: 51: 56: 65] sts.

Shape shoulder

Cast off 13 [15: 16: 18: 21] sts at beg of next
and foll alt row **and at same time** dec 1 st at
neck edge of next 3 rows.
Work 1 row.
Cast off rem 13 [14: 16: 17: 20] sts.
With RS facing, slip centre 41 [41: 43: 43: 45] sts
onto a holder, rejoin yarn to rem sts, patt
to end.
Complete to match first side, reversing
shapings.

FRONT

Work as given for back until 12 [12: 14: 14: 16]
rows less have been worked than on back to
beg of shoulder shaping, ending with RS facing
for next row.

Shape front neck

Next row (RS): Patt 48 [53: 58: 63: 73] sts
and turn, leaving rem sts on a holder.
Work each side of neck separately.
Dec 1 st at neck edge of next 8 rows, then on
foll 1 [1: 2: 2: 3] alt rows.
39 [44: 48: 53: 62] sts.
Work 1 row, ending with RS facing for
next row.

Shape shoulder

Cast off 13 [15: 16: 18: 21] sts at beg of next
and foll alt row.
Work 1 row.
Cast off rem 13 [14: 16: 17: 20] sts.
With RS facing, slip centre 35 sts onto a
holder, rejoin yarn to rem sts, patt to end.
Complete to match first side, reversing
shapings.

SLEEVES

Using 3³/4mm (US 5) needles cast on 45 [47:
49: 51: 53] sts.
Work in g st for 14 rows, ending with RS
facing for next row.

Change to 4¹/2mm (US 7) needles.
Now work in lace patt as folls:
Row 1 (RS): K0 [1: 0: 1: 2], (K2tog, yfwd)
1 [1: 2: 2: 2] times, K1, ★(yfwd, sl 1, K1, psso)
twice, K1, (K2tog, yfwd) twice, K1, rep from
★ to last 2 [3: 4: 5: 6] sts, (yfwd, sl 1, K1, psso)
1 [1: 2: 2: 2] times, K0 [1: 0: 1: 2].
Row 2: Purl.
Row 3: K3 [0: 1: 0: 1], (K2tog, yfwd) 0 [1: 1: 2:
2] times, K0 [2: 2: 2: 2], ★K1, yfwd, sl 1, K1,
psso, yfwd, sl 1, K2tog, psso, yfwd, K2tog, yfwd,
K2, rep from ★ to last 2 [3: 4: 5: 6] sts, K0 [1: 1:
1: 1], (yfwd, sl 1, K1, psso) 0 [1: 1: 2: 2] times,
K2 [0: 1: 0: 1].
Row 4: Purl.
These 4 rows form lace patt.
Cont in patt, shaping sides by inc 1 st at each
end of next and 4 [4: 4: 3: 2] foll 4th rows, then
on foll 12 [13: 14: 16: 18] alt rows, taking inc
sts into patt. 79 [83: 87: 91: 95] sts.
Work 1 row, ending with RS facing for next
row. (Sleeve should meas approx 21.5 [22.5:
23.5: 23.5: 23.5] cm.)
Cast off.

MAKING UP

Press as described on the information page.
Join right shoulder seam using back stitch, or
mattress stitch if preferred.
Neckband
With RS facing and using 3³/4mm (US 5)
needles, pick up and knit 12 [12: 14: 14: 16] sts
down left side of front neck, K across 35 sts on
front holder, pick up and knit 12 [12: 14: 14:
16] sts up right side of front neck, and 7 sts
down right side of back neck, K across 41 [41:
43: 43: 45] sts on back holder, then pick up and
knit 7 sts up left side of back neck.
114 [114: 120: 120: 126] sts.
Work in g st for 12 rows, ending with **WS**
facing for next row.
Cast off knitwise (on **WS**).
Join left shoulder and neckband seam. Mark
points along side seam edges 22 [23: 24: 25:
26] cm either side of shoulder seams to denote
base of armhole openings. See information
page for finishing instructions, setting in sleeves
using the straight cast-off method.

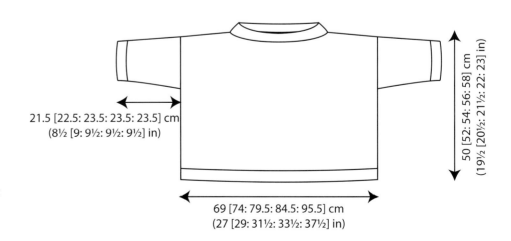

21.5 [22.5: 23.5: 23.5: 23.5] cm
(8½ [9: 9½: 9½: 9½] in)

50 [52: 54: 56: 58] cm
(19½ [20½: 21½: 22: 23] in)

69 [74: 79.5: 84.5: 95.5] cm
(27 [29: 31½: 33½: 37½] in)

PISTACHIO
JULIA FRANK

Main image page 75

●●

YARN

	S	M	L	XL	XXL
To fit bust
81-86 91-97 102-107 112-117 122-127 cm
32-34 36-38 40-42 44-46 48-50 in

Summerspun

8 9 10 12 13 x 50gm
(photographed in Blackfriars 121)

NEEDLES

1 pair 4mm (no 8) (US 6) needles
3¾mm (no 9) (US 5) circular needle, 80 cm long
4mm (no 8) (US 6) circular needle, 80 cm long
Set of 4 double-pointed 3¾mm (no 9) (US 5) needles
Set of 4 double-pointed 4mm (no 8) (US 6) needles
4.00mm (no 8) (US G6) crochet hook

TENSION

22 sts and 30 rows to 10 cm measured over st st using 4mm (US 6) needles.

BODY (worked in one piece to armholes)
Using 3¾mm (US 5) circular needle cast on 208 [232: 256: 284: 316] sts.
Taking care not to twist cast-on edge and working in rounds, cont as folls:
Round 1 (RS): K1, ★P2, K2, rep from ★ to last 3 sts, P2, K1.
This round forms rib.
Work in rib for a further 7 rounds.
Round 9: (M1, rib 104 [116: 128: 142: 158]) twice. 210 [234: 258: 286: 318] sts.
Change to 4mm (US 6) circular needle.
Round 10: K43 [49: 55: 62: 70], P4, K1, cast off next 9 sts (one st on right needle) placing marker on centre cast-off st, P4, K to end.
Round 11: K43 [49: 55: 62: 70], P4, K1, turn and cast on **10** sts, turn, K1, P4, K to end. 211 [235: 259: 287: 319] sts.
Now work in patt as folls:
Next round: K43 [49: 55: 62: 70], P4, K1, P10, K1, P4, K to end.
Last round forms patt.
Cont in patt until body meas 26 [27: 28: 29: 30] cm.
Divide for armholes
Next round (RS): Patt 106 [118: 130: 144: 160] sts and slip these sts onto a holder for front, K to end.
Work on this last set of 105 [117: 129: 143:

159] sts only for back.
Now working in **rows** of st st (beg with a P row), change to straight 4mm (US 6) needles and cont as folls:
Cont straight until armhole meas 20 [21: 22: 23: 24] cm from dividing row, ending with RS facing for next row.
Shape shoulders and back neck
Next row (RS): Cast off 7 [9: 10: 12: 13] sts, K until there are 27 [31: 35: 40: 46] sts on right needle and turn, leaving rem sts on a holder.
Work each side of neck separately.
Dec 1 st at neck edge of next 4 rows, ending with **WS** facing for next row, **and at same time** cast off 7 [9: 10: 12: 14] sts at beg of 2nd row, then 8 [9: 10: 12: 14] sts at beg of foll alt row.
Work 1 row.
Cast off rem 8 [9: 11: 12: 14] sts.
With RS facing, slip centre 37 [37: 39: 39: 41] sts onto a holder, rejoin yarn to rem sts, K to end.
Complete to match first side, reversing shapings.
Shape front
Rejoin yarn to 106 [118: 130: 144: 160] sts on first holder with **WS** facing.
Now working in **rows** and using straight 4mm (US 6) needles, cont as folls:
Next row (WS): P43 [49: 55: 62: 70], K4, P1, K10, P1, K4, P43 [49: 55: 62: 70].
Next row: K43 [49: 55: 62: 70], P4, K1, P10, K1, P4, K43 [49: 55: 62: 70].
These 2 rows form patt.
Cont straight until 31 [31: 33: 33: 35] rows less have been worked than on back to beg of shoulder shaping, ending with **WS** facing for next row.
Shape front neck
Next row (WS): Patt 48 [54: 60: 67: 75] sts and slip these sts onto another holder (for right side of neck), patt 10 sts and drop these 10 sts off needle, allowing them to unravel down to cast-on sts at top of rib, patt to end.
Work each side of neck separately.
Next row (RS): K42 [48: 54: 61: 69] and turn, leaving rem 6 sts on another holder (for neckband).
Dec 1 st at neck edge of next 6 rows, then on foll 3 [3: 4: 4: 5] alt rows, then on 2 foll 4th rows, then on foll 6th row.
30 [36: 41: 48: 55] sts.

Work 3 rows, ending with RS facing for next row.
Shape shoulder
Cast off 7 [9: 10: 12: 13] sts at beg of next and foll 1 [2: 2: 2: 0] alt rows, then 8 [–: –: –: 14] sts at beg of foll 1 [–: –: –: 2] alt rows.
Work 1 row.
Cast off rem 8 [9: 11: 12: 14] sts.
With RS facing, return to sts left on holder for right side of neck, slip first 6 sts onto another holder (for neckband), rejoin yarn to rem sts, K to end. 42 [48: 54: 61: 69] sts.
Complete to match first side, reversing shapings.

SLEEVES

Using double-pointed 3¾mm (US 5) needles cast on 64 [68: 68: 68: 72] sts.
Distribute sts evenly over 3 of the 4 needles and, taking care not to twist cast-on edge and using 4th needle, work in rounds as folls:
Work in rib as given for body for 8 rounds.
Round 9: (K1, M1) 1 [0: 1: 1: 0] times, rib to last 1 [0: 1: 1: 0] st, (M1, K1) 1 [0: 1: 1: 0] times. 66 [68: 70: 70: 72] sts.
Change to double-pointed 4mm (US 6) needles.
Now working in st st (K every round), cont as folls:
Work 6 [4: 4: 4: 2] rounds.
Next round: K1, M1, K to last st, M1, K1.
Working all increases as set by last round, inc 1 st at each end of 8th [6th: 6th: 6th: 4th] and every foll 8th [8th: 6th: 6th: 4th] round to 84 [88: 80: 96: 78] sts, then on every foll – [–: 8th: –: 6th] round until there are – [–: 92: –: 100] sts.
Cont straight until sleeve meas 32 [33: 34: 34: 34] cm.
Cast off.

MAKING UP

Press as described on the information page.
Join both shoulder seams using back stitch, or mattress stitch if preferred.
Front decoration
Using 4.00mm (US G6) crochet hook, insert hook into marked st at centre of cast-off sts at top of front rib, pick up first 6 "bars" on unravelled yarn and draw these 6 strands of yarn through st on hook, ★pick up next 6 "bars" of unravelled yarn and draw these

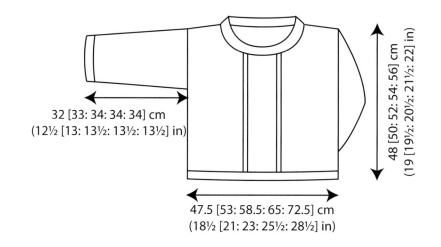

32 [33: 34: 34: 34] cm
(12½ [13: 13½: 13½: 13½] in)

47.5 [53: 58.5: 65: 72.5] cm
(18½ [21: 23: 25½: 28½] in)

48 [50: 52: 54: 56] cm
(19 [19½: 20½: 21½: 22] in)

strands through loop on hook, rep from ★ to neck edge, noting that last rep may have less than 6 "bars" to draw through loop on hook. At top of unravelled sts, slip st on hook onto a safety pin.

Neckband
With RS facing and using double-pointed 3¾mm (US 5) needles, pick up and knit 30

[30: 33: 33: 34] sts down left side of front neck, K across 6 sts on left front holder, turn and cast on 4 sts, turn and K st on safety pin, turn and cast on 4 sts, turn and K across 6 sts on right front holder, pick up and knit 30 [30: 33: 33: 34] sts up right side of front neck, and 5 sts down right side of back neck, K across 37 [37: 39: 39: 41] sts on back holder, then pick up and

knit 5 sts up left side of back neck. 128 [128: 136: 136: 140] sts. Work in rib as given for body for 6 rounds. Cast off in rib. See information page for finishing instructions, setting in sleeves using the straight cast-off method.

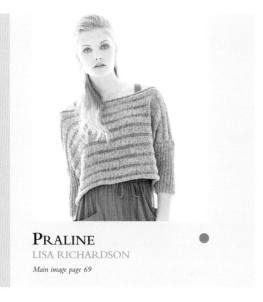

PRALINE
LISA RICHARDSON
Main image page 69

YARN

S	M	L	XL	XXL

To fit bust
81–86 91–97 102–107 112–117 122–127 cm
32–34 36–38 40–42 44–46 48–50 in

Summerspun

7	7	8	9	10	x 50gm

(photographed in Covent Garden 114)

NEEDLES
1 pair 3¼mm (no 10) (US 3) needles
1 pair 4mm (no 8) (US 6) needles

TENSION
18 sts and 30 rows to 10 cm measured over body patt once sts are unravelled, 22 sts and 30 rows to 10 cm measured over st st, both using 4mm (US 6) needles. 33 sts and 34 rows to 10 cm measured over sleeve rib patt when slightly stretched using 3¼mm (US 3) needles.

BODY (worked sideways in one piece)
Using 4mm (US 6) needles cast on 129 [137: 145: 151: 159] sts.
Place marker on centre st – this is shoulder point.
Row 1 (RS): K7 [5: 3: 6: 4], yfwd, K2tog, ★K4, yfwd, K2tog, rep from ★ to last 6 [4: 2: 5: 3] sts, K6 [4: 2: 5: 3].
Row 2: K1, P to last st, K1.
Row 3: Knit.
Last 2 rows set the sts – first and last st of every row worked as a K st with all other sts in st st.
Cont as now set until body meas 17 [19.5: 22: 25: 28] cm, ending with RS facing for next row.

Divide for neck opening
Next row (RS): K64 [68: 72: 75: 79] and turn, leaving rem sts on a holder.
Work each side of neck separately.
Next row (WS): K1, P to last st, K1.
This row sets the sts – first and last st of every row worked as a K st with all other sts still in st st.
Cont as now set until work meas 30 [30: 31: 31: 32] cm **from dividing row**, ending with **WS** facing for next row.
Break yarn and leave sts on a holder.
With RS facing, rejoin yarn to rem sts, K2tog, K to end. 64 [68: 72: 75: 79] sts.
Next row (WS): K1, P to last st, K1.
This row sets the sts – first and last st of every row worked as a K st with all other sts still in st st.
Cont as now set until work meas 30 [30: 31: 31: 32] cm **from dividing row**, ending with **WS** facing for next row.
Join sections
Next row (WS): K1, P to last st of second section (on needles), inc in last st, then P to last st of first section (on holder), K1.
129 [137: 145: 151: 159] sts.
Cont in patt as set (with first and last st of every row worked as a K st and all other sts in st st) until work meas 17 [19.5: 22: 25: 28] cm **from joining row**, ending with **WS** facing for next row. (Work should meas 64 [69: 75: 81: 88] cm from cast-on edge.)
Next row (WS): K1, P5 [3: 1: 4: 2], inc in next st, drop next st off left needle and unravel

this st down to row 1, ★P4, inc in next st, drop next st off left needle and unravel this st down to row 1, rep from ★ to last 7 [5: 3: 6: 4] sts, P6 [4: 2: 5: 3], K1.
Cast off all 129 [137: 145: 151: 159] sts, placing marker on centre st – this is shoulder point.

SLEEVES
Using 3¼mm (US 3) needles cast on 86 [88: 90: 90: 92] sts.
Row 1 (RS): P0 [1: 0: 0: 1], K2, ★P2, K2, rep from ★ to last 0 [1: 0: 0: 1] st, P0 [1: 0: 0: 1].
Row 2: K0 [1: 0: 0: 1], P2, ★K2, P2, rep from ★ to last 0 [1: 0: 0: 1] st, K0 [1: 0: 0: 1].
These 2 rows form rib patt.
Cont in rib patt, shaping sides by inc 1 st at each end of 7th [5th: 5th: 3rd: 3rd] and every foll 6th [6th: 6th: 4th: 4th] row to 106 [108: 104: 126: 124] sts, then on every foll – [4th: 4th: –: alt] row until there are – [112: 118: –: 132] sts, taking inc sts into rib patt.
Work 5 [3: 3: 1: 1] rows, ending with RS facing for next row. (Sleeve should meas approx 20 [21: 22: 22: 22] cm.)
Cast off in patt.

MAKING UP
Press as described on the information page.
Mark points along side seam (cast-on and cast-off) edges 17 [18: 19: 20: 21] cm either side of shoulder point markers to denote base of armhole openings. See information page for finishing instructions, setting in sleeves using the straight cast-off method.

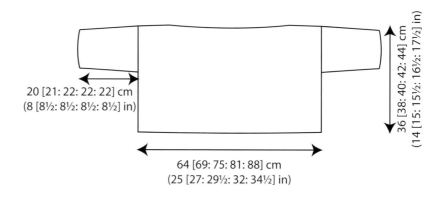

20 [21: 22: 22: 22] cm
(8 [8½: 8½: 8½: 8½] in)

36 [38: 40: 42: 44] cm
(14 [15: 15½: 16½: 17½] in)

64 [69: 75: 81: 88] cm
(25 [27: 29½: 32: 34½] in)

MARSHMALLOW

JULIA FRANK

Main image page 65 & 66

YARN

	S	M	L	XL	XXL	
To fit bust						
	81-86	91-97	102-107	112-117	122-127	cm
	32-34	36-38	40-42	44-46	48-50	in

Kidsilk Haze and Handknit Cotton

A KSH Pearl 590						
	3	3	3	4	4	x 25gm
B HKC Linen 205						
	1	1	2	2	2	x 50gm

NEEDLES

1 pair 6mm (no 4) (US 10) needles

6mm (no 4) (US 10) circular needle, 80 cm long

Set of 4 double-pointed 6mm (no 4) (US 10) needles

2 double-pointed 4½mm (no 7) (US 7) needles

EXTRAS - Oddment of scrap yarn (for cast-on edges)

TENSION

13 sts and 15 rows to 10 cm measured over st st using 6mm (US 10) needles and Kidsilk Haze.

BODY (worked in one piece to armholes)

Using 6mm (US 10) circular needle and scrap yarn cast on 112 [124: 140: 156: 176] sts.

Taking care not to twist cast-on edge and working in rounds, cont as folls:

Knit 2 rounds.

Break off scrap yarn and join in yarn A.

Now work in **rounds** of st st (K every round) until body meas 33 [34: 35: 36: 37] cm **from scrap yarn**.

Divide for armholes

Next round (RS): Cast off 2 sts, K until there are 52 [58: 66: 74: 84] sts on right needle and slip these sts onto a holder for front, cast off next 4 sts, K until there are 52 [58: 66: 74: 84] sts on right needle, cast off rem 2 sts.

Break yarn.

Now working in **rows** of st st (beg with a P row), change to straight 6mm (US 10) needles and cont as folls:

Shape back

Rejoin yarn to last set of 52 [58: 66: 74: 84] sts with **WS** facing and work 1 row.

Dec 1 st at each end of next and foll 2 alt rows. 46 [52: 60: 68: 78] sts.

Cont straight until armhole meas 18 [19: 20:

21: 22] cm from dividing row, ending with RS facing for next row.

Shape shoulders and back neck

Next row (RS): Cast off 3 [4: 5: 7: 8] sts, K until there are 10 [12: 14: 16: 19] sts on right needle and turn, leaving rem sts on a holder.

Work each side of neck separately.

Dec 1 st at neck edge of next 3 rows, ending with RS facing for next row, **and at same time** cast off 3 [4: 5: 7: 8] sts at beg of 2nd row.

Cast off rem 4 [5: 6: 6: 8] sts.

With RS facing, slip centre 20 [20: 22: 22: 24] sts onto a holder, rejoin yarn to rem sts, K to end.

Complete to match first side, reversing shapings.

Shape front

Rejoin yarn to 52 [58: 66: 74: 84] sts on first holder with **WS** facing and work 1 row.

Dec 1 st at each end of next and foll 2 alt rows. 46 [52: 60: 68: 78] sts.

Cont straight until 14 [14: 16: 16: 18] rows less have been worked than on back to beg of shoulder shaping, ending with RS facing for next row.

Shape front neck

Next row (RS): K18 [21: 25: 29: 34] and turn, leaving rem sts on a holder.

Work each side of neck separately.

Dec 1 st at neck edge of next 6 rows, then on foll 1 [1: 2: 2: 3] alt rows, then on foll 4th row. 10 [13: 16: 20: 24] sts.

Work 1 row, ending with RS facing for next row.

Shape shoulder

Cast off 3 [4: 5: 7: 8] sts at beg of next and foll alt row.

Work 1 row.

Cast off rem 4 [5: 6: 6: 8] sts.

With RS facing, slip centre 10 sts onto a holder, rejoin yarn to rem sts, K to end.

Complete to match first side, reversing shapings.

SLEEVES

Using double-pointed 6mm (US 10) needles and scrap yarn cast on 26 [28: 30: 30: 32] sts.

Distribute sts evenly over 3 of the 4 needles and, taking care not to twist cast-on edge and using 4th needle, work in rounds of st st as folls:

Knit 2 rounds.

Break off scrap yarn and join in yarn A.

Work 4 [4: 4: 2: 2] rounds.

Next round: K1, M1, K to last st, M1, K1.

Working all increases as set by last round, inc 1 st at each end of 6th [6th: 6th: 4th: 4th] and every foll 6th round to 40 [40: 48: 52: 54] sts, then on every foll 8th [8th: 8th: –: –] round until there are 44 [46: 50: –: –] sts.

Cont straight until sleeve meas 44 [45: 46: 46: 46] cm **from scrap yarn**.

Shape top

Next round (RS): Cast off 2 sts, K to last 2 sts, cast off last 2 sts. 40 [42: 46: 48: 50] sts.

Break yarn.

Now working in **rows** of st st (beg with a P row), cont as folls:

Rejoin yarn with **WS** facing and work 1 row.

Dec 1 st at each end of next and foll alt row, then on foll row, ending with RS facing for next row.

Cast off rem 34 [36: 40: 42: 44] sts.

MAKING UP

Press as described on the information page. Join both shoulder seams using back stitch, or mattress stitch if preferred.

Neckband

With RS facing, using double-pointed 6mm (US 10) needles and yarn A, pick up and knit 14 [14: 16: 16: 18] sts down left side of front neck, K across 10 sts on front holder, pick up and knit 14 [14: 16: 16: 18] sts up right side of front neck, and 4 sts down right side of back neck, K across 20 [20: 22: 22: 24] sts on back holder, then pick up and knit 4 sts up left side of back neck. 66 [66: 72: 72: 78] sts.

Break off yarn A.

★★Join in yarn B.

Using 4½mm (US 7) double-pointed needles, now work cast-off edging as folls:

Next row (RS): Cast on 3 sts, K2, sl 1, K first st of previous round, psso, ★without turning slip these 3 sts to opposite end of needle and bring yarn to opposite end of work pulling it quite tightly across **WS** of work, K2, sl 1, K next st of previous round, psso, rep from ★ until all sts of previous round have been used up.

Cast off.

Join cast-on and cast-off ends of edging.**★★**

See information page for finishing instructions, setting in sleeves using the shallow set-in method.

Hem edging

Carefully slip all 112 [124: 140: 156: 176] sts of

45 [46: 47: 47: 47] cm
(17½ [18: 18½: 18½: 18½] in)

43 [47.5: 54: 60: 67.5] cm
(17 [18½: 21½: 23½: 26½] in)

54 [56: 58: 60: 62] cm
(21½ [22: 23: 23½: 24½] in)

first round in yarn A onto 6mm (US 10) circular needle and unravel scrap yarn of cast-on edge.
Complete as for neckband from ★★ to ★★, noting that you are working into sts of first round of body worked in yarn A, not previous round.

Cuff edgings (both alike)
Carefully slip all 26 [28: 30: 30: 32] sts of first round in yarn A onto double-pointed 6mm (US 10) needles and unravel scrap yarn of cast-on edge.

Complete as for neckband from ★★ to ★★, noting that you are working into sts of first round of sleeve worked in yarn A, not previous round.

Decoration
Using double-pointed 4½mm (US 7) needles and yarn B cast on 3 sts.
Row 1 (RS): K3, ★without turning slip these 3 sts to opposite end of needle and bring yarn to opposite end of work pulling it quite tightly across **WS** of work, K these 3 sts again, rep from ★ until strip is approx 75 [80: 80: 85: 85] cm long.

Slip sts onto a safety pin and break yarn, leaving a long length (to adjust length of strip if required).
Make another 5 strips in same way.
Using photograph as a guide, neatly sew these strips in place onto front to form cable effect. Once strips are in place, slip sts back onto needles and either unravel strip back to correct length or knit further rows as required. Once strip is correct length, cast off and secure end of strip in position.

VIDAL
JOSH BENNETT
Main image page 40 & 41

●●

YARN

XS	S	M	L	XL	XXL	2XL	
To fit chest							
97	102	107	112	117	122	127	cm
38	40	42	44	46	48	50	in
Creative Linen							
A Stormy 635							
4	4	4	5	5	5	5	x 100gm
B Foggy 624							
3	3	3	3	4	4	4	x 100gm

NEEDLES
1 pair 3¾mm (no 9) (US 5) needles
1 pair 4½mm (no 7) (US 7) needles

TENSION
21 sts and 28 rows to 10 cm measured over st st using 4½mm (US 7) needles.

BACK
Using 3¾mm (US 5) needles and yarn A cast on 102 [106: 114: 118: 122: 130: 138] sts.
Row 1 (RS): K2, ★P2, K2, rep from ★ to end.
Row 2: P2, ★K2, P2, rep from ★ to end.
These 2 rows form rib.
Cont in rib until back meas 10 cm, dec [inc: dec: inc: inc: inc: dec] 1 st at end of last row and ending with RS facing for next row.
101 [107: 113: 119: 123: 131: 137] sts.
Change to 4½mm (US 7) needles.★★
Beg with a K row, now work in striped st st throughout as folls:
Rows 1 to 6: Using yarn A.

Rows 7 to 12: Using yarn B.
These 12 rows form striped st st.
Cont in striped st st for a further 72 [74: 76: 70: 72: 72: 76] rows, ending after 6 [2: 4: 4: 6: 6: 4] rows using yarn B [A: A: B: B: B: A] and with RS facing for next row. (Back should meas approx 40 [41: 41: 39: 40: 40: 41] cm.)
Shape armholes
Keeping stripes correct, cast off 5 sts at beg of next 2 rows.
91 [97: 103: 109: 113: 121: 127] sts.
Dec 1 st at each end of next 3 rows, then on foll 5 alt rows. 75 [81: 87: 93: 97: 105: 111] sts.
Work 35 [41: 47: 53: 57: 57: 61] rows, ending after 2 [4: 6: 6: 6: 6: 2] rows using yarn A [B: A: A: B: B: B] and with RS facing for next row. (Armhole should meas approx 18 [20: 22: 24: 26: 26: 27] cm.)
Shape back neck and shoulders
Next row (RS): K24 [26: 29: 31: 33: 36: 39] and turn, leaving rem sts on a holder.
Work each side of neck separately.
Keeping stripes correct, dec 1 st at neck edge of next 4 rows, ending with **WS** facing for next row, **and at same time** cast off 7 [7: 8: 9: 10: 11: 12] sts at beg of 2nd and foll alt row.
Work 1 row.
Cast off rem 6 [8: 9: 9: 9: 10: 11] sts.

With RS facing, slip centre 27 [29: 29: 31: 31: 33: 33] sts onto a holder, rejoin appropriate yarn to rem sts, K to end.
Complete to match first side, reversing shapings.

FRONT
Work as given for back to ★★.
Beg and ending rows as indicated and using the **intarsia** technique as described on the information page, cont in patt from chart, which is worked entirely in st st beg with a K row, as folls:
Cont straight until chart row 84 [86: 88: 82: 84: 84: 88] has been completed, ending with RS facing for next row. (Front should meas approx 40 [41: 41: 39: 40: 40: 41] cm.)
Shape armholes
Keeping patt correct, cast off 5 sts at beg of next 2 rows.
91 [97: 103: 109: 113: 121: 127] sts.
Dec 1 st at each end of next 3 rows, then on foll 5 alt rows. 75 [81: 87: 93: 97: 105: 111] sts.
Cont straight until chart row 118 [126: 134: 132: 138: 136: 144] has been completed, ending with RS facing for next row.
Shape front neck
Next row (RS): Patt 28 [30: 33: 36: 38: 42:

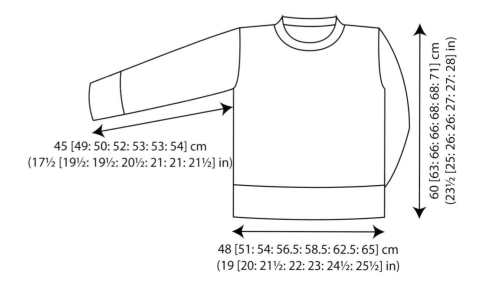

45 [49: 50: 52: 53: 53: 54] cm
(17½ [19½: 19½: 20½: 21: 21: 21½] in)

48 [51: 54: 56.5: 58.5: 62.5: 65] cm
(19 [20: 21½: 22: 23: 24½: 25½] in)

60 [63: 66: 66: 68: 68: 71] cm
(23½ [25: 26: 26: 27: 27: 28] in)

45] sts and turn, leaving rem sts on a holder.
Work each side of neck separately.
Keeping patt correct, dec 1 st at neck edge of
next 4 rows, then on foll 3 [3: 3: 4: 4: 5: 5] alt
rows, then on foll 4th row.
20 [22: 25: 27: 29: 32: 35] sts.
Work 3 rows, ending after chart row 136 [144:
152: 152: 158: 158: 166] and with RS facing
for next row.

Shape shoulder

Cast off 7 [7: 8: 9: 10: 11: 12] sts at beg of next
and foll alt row.
Work 1 row.
Cast off rem 6 [8: 9: 9: 9: 10: 11] sts.
With RS facing, slip centre 19 [21: 21: 21: 21:
21: 21] sts onto a holder, rejoin appropriate
yarn to rem sts, patt to end.
Complete to match first side, reversing
shapings.

SLEEVES

Using 3¾mm (US 5) needles and yarn A cast
on 46 [50: 50: 54: 54: 58: 58] sts.
Work in rib as given for back for 10 cm, inc
[dec: inc: dec: inc: dec: inc] 1 st at end of last
row and ending with RS facing for next row.
47 [49: 51: 53: 55: 57: 59] sts.
Change to 4½mm (US 7) needles.
Beg with 2 [6: 6: 6: 6: 6: 6] rows using yarn B
[A: A: A: A: A: A] and a K row, now work in
striped st st as given for back throughout as
folls:
Inc 1 st at each end of 3rd and every foll 4th
row to 65 [61: 61: 69: 75: 71: 69] sts, then on
every foll 6th row until there are 81 [85: 89: 93:
97: 97: 99] sts.
Cont straight until sleeve meas approx 45 [49:
50: 52: 53: 53: 54] cm, ending after same stripe
row as on back to beg of armhole shaping and
with RS facing for next row.

Shape top

Keeping stripes correct, cast off 5 sts at beg of
next 2 rows. 71 [75: 79: 83: 87: 87: 89] sts.
Dec 1 st at each end of next 5 rows, then on
every foll alt row until 51 sts rem, then on foll
9 rows, ending with RS facing for next row.
33 sts.
Cast off 5 sts at beg of next 2 rows.
Cast off rem 23 sts.

MAKING UP

Press as described on the information page.
Join right shoulder seam using back stitch, or
mattress stitch if preferred.

Neckband

With RS facing, using 3¾mm (US 5) needles
and yarn A, pick up and knit 23 [23: 23: 24: 24:
27: 27] sts down left side of front neck, K across
19 [21: 21: 21: 21: 21: 21] sts on front holder,
pick up and knit 23 [23: 23: 24: 24: 27: 27] sts
up right side of front neck, and 5 sts down
right side of back neck, K across 27 [29: 29: 31:
31: 33: 33] sts on back holder, then pick up and
knit 5 sts up left side of back neck.
102 [106: 106: 110: 110: 118: 118] sts.
Beg with row 2, work in rib as given for back
for 7 rows, ending with RS facing for next row.
Cast off in rib.
See information page for finishing instructions,
setting in sleeves using the set-in method.

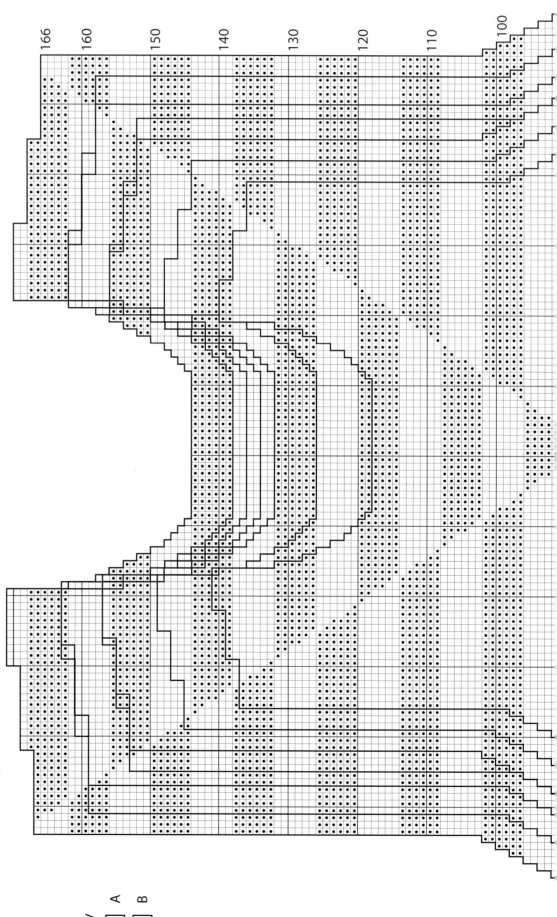

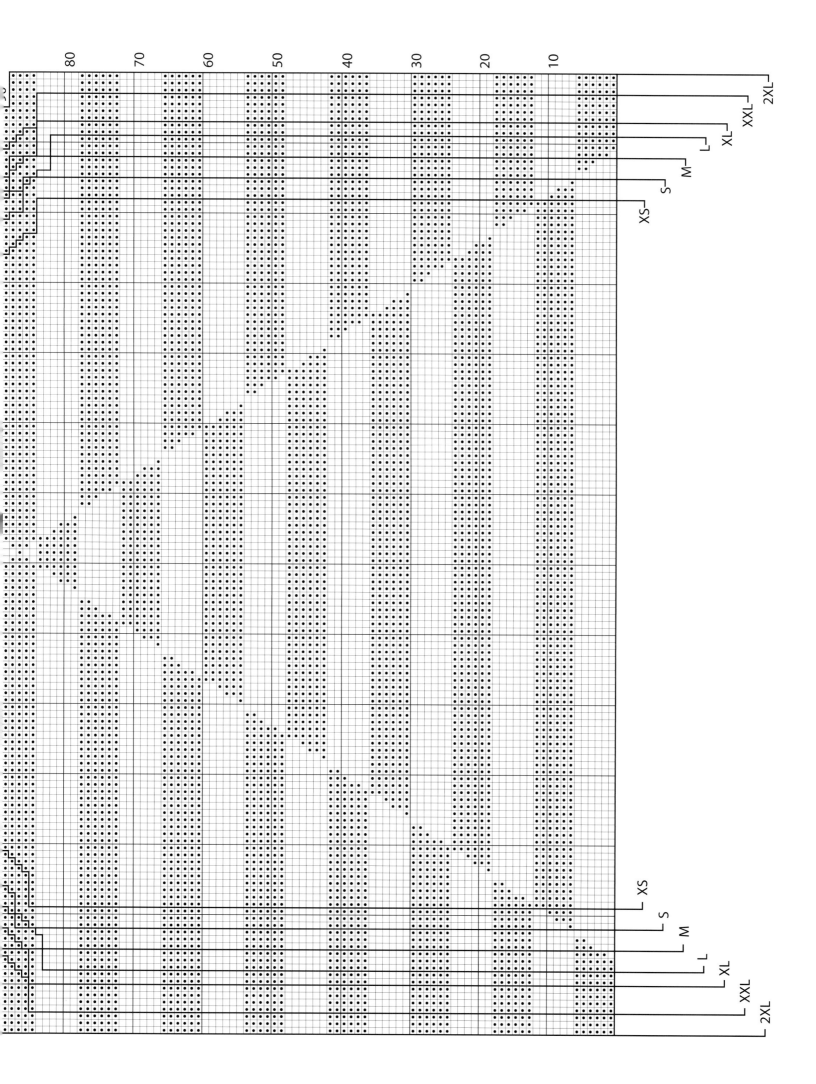

TUTTI FRUTTI

MARIE WALLIN

Main image page 76 & 77

YARN

S	M	L	XL	XXL	

To fit bust

81-86 91-97 102-107 112-117 122-127 cm

32-34 36-38 40-42 44-46 48-50 in

Summerspun

11   13   14   16   17   x 50gm

(photographed in Nottinghill 125)

CROCHET HOOK

3.00mm (no 11) (US C2) crochet hook

6.00mm (no 4) (US J10) crochet hook

TENSION

13½ sts and 6½ rows to 10 cm measured over patt using 6.00mm (US J10) crochet hook and yarn DOUBLE.

CROCHET ABBREVIATIONS

ch = chain; **dc** = double crochet; **dtr** = double treble; **htr** = half treble; **sp(s)** = space(s); **ss** = slip stitch; **tr** = treble; **ttr** = triple treble.

BACK and FRONT (both alike)

Using 3.00mm (US C2) crochet hook and yarn SINGLE make 79 [87: 95: 103: 111] ch.

Row 1 (RS): 1 dc into 2nd ch from hook, 1 dc into each ch to end, turn.

78 [86: 94: 102: 110] sts.

Row 2: 1 ch (does NOT count as st), 1 dc into each dc to end, turn.

Rep last row until work meas 16 cm, ending with **WS** facing for next row.

Next row (WS): 1 ch (does NOT count as st), 1 dc into each of first 3 [2: 6: 5: 4] dc, 2 dc into next dc, (1 dc into each of next 6 [7: 7: 8:

9] dc, 2 dc into next dc) 10 times, 1 dc into each of last 4 [3: 7: 6: 5] dc, turn.

89 [97: 105: 113: 121] sts.

Change to 6.00mm (US J10) hook and join in second strand of yarn.

Using yarn DOUBLE, cont as folls:

Next row (RS): 1 ch (does NOT count as st), 1 dc into first dc, *1 htr into next dc, 1 tr into next dc, 1 dtr into next dc, 1 ttr into next dc, 1 dtr into next dc, 1 tr into next dc, 1 htr into next dc, 1 dc into next dc, rep from * to end, turn. 11 [12: 13: 14: 15] patt reps.

Now work in patt as folls:

Row 1 (WS): 6 ch (counts as 1 tr and 3 ch), miss first 4 sts, *1 tr into next ttr, 3 ch, miss 3 sts, 1 tr into next dc**, 3 ch, miss 3 sts, rep from * to end, ending last rep at **, turn.

Row 2: 5 ch (counts as 1 ttr), miss tr at base of 5 ch, *(1 dtr, 1 tr and 1 htr) into next ch sp, 1 dc into next tr, (1 htr, 1 tr and 1 dtr) into next ch sp, 1 ttr into next tr, rep from * to end, working ttr at end of last rep into 3rd of 6 ch at beg of previous row, turn.

Row 3: 6 ch (counts as 1 tr and 3 ch), miss first 4 sts, *1 tr into next dc, 3 ch, miss 3 sts**, 1 tr into next ttr, 3 ch, miss 3 sts, rep from * to end, ending last rep at **, 1 tr into top of 5 ch at beg of previous row, turn.

Row 4: 1 ch (does NOT count as st), 1 dc into tr at base of 1 ch, *(1 htr, 1 tr and 1 dtr) into next ch sp, 1 ttr into next tr, (1 dtr, 1 tr and 1 htr) into next ch sp, 1 dc into next tr, rep from * to end, working dc at end of last rep into 3rd of 6 ch at beg of previous row, turn.

These 4 rows form patt.

Cont in patt until work meas approx 54 [56: 58: 60: 62] cm, ending after patt row 2 or 4. Fasten off.

MAKING UP

Press as described on the information page. Join both shoulder seams using back stitch, or mattress stitch if preferred and leaving 28 [28: 29: 29: 30] cm opening at centre (for neck edge).

Neck edging

With RS facing, using 3.00mm (US C2) crochet hook and yarn SINGLE, attach yarn at neck edge of left shoulder seam, 1 ch (does NOT count as st), work 1 round of dc evenly around entire neck edge, ending with ss to first dc, turn.

Next round (RS): 1 ch (does NOT count as st), 1 dc into each dc to end, ss to first dc.

Fasten off.

Mark points along side seam edges 28 [29: 30: 31: 32] cm either side of shoulder seams to denote base of armhole openings. Join side seams below armhole openings.

Armhole edgings (both alike)

With RS facing, using 3.00mm (US C2) crochet hook and yarn SINGLE, attach yarn at top of side seam, 1 ch (does NOT count as st), work 1 round of dc evenly around entire armhole opening edge, ending with ss to first dc, turn.

Next round (RS): 1 ch (does NOT count as st), 1 dc into each dc to end, ss to first dc.

Fasten off.

See information page for finishing instructions.

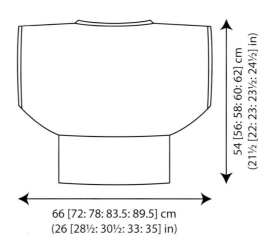

54 [56: 58: 60: 62] cm
(21½ [22: 23: 23½: 24½] in)

66 [72: 78: 83.5: 89.5] cm
(26 [28½: 30½: 33: 35] in)

INFORMATION

TENSION

Obtaining the correct tension is perhaps the single factor which can make the difference between a successful garment and a disastrous one. It controls both the shape and size of an article, so any variation, however slight, can distort the finished garment. Different designers feature in our books and it is **their** tension, given at the **start** of each pattern, which you must match. We recommend that you knit a square in pattern and/or stocking stitch (depending on the pattern instructions) of perhaps 5 - 10 more stitches and 5 - 10 more rows than those given in the tension note. Mark out the central 10cm square with pins. If you have too many stitches to 10cm try again using thicker needles, if you have too few stitches to 10cm try again using finer needles. Once you have achieved the correct tension your garment will be knitted to the measurements indicated in the size diagram shown at the end of the pattern.

CHART NOTE

Many of the patterns in the book are worked from charts. Each square on a chart represents a stitch and each line of squares a row of knitting. Each colour used is given a different letter and these are shown in the **materials** section, or in the **key** alongside the chart of each pattern. When working from the charts, read odd rows (K) from right to left and even rows (P) from left to right, unless otherwise stated. When working lace from a chart it is important to note that all but the largest size may have to alter the first and last few stitches in order not to lose or gain stitches over the row.

WORKING A LACE PATTERN

When working a lace pattern it is important to remember that if you are unable to work both the increase and corresponding decrease and vica versa, the stitches should be worked in stocking stitch.

KNITTING WITH COLOUR

There are two main methods of working colour into a knitted fabric: **Intarsia** and **Fairisle** techniques. The first method produces a single thickness of fabric and is usually used where a colour is only required in a particular area of a row and does not form a repeating pattern across the row, as in the fairisle technique.

Fairisle type knitting: When two or three colours are worked repeatedly across a row, strand the yarn **not** in use loosely behind the stitches being worked. If you are working with more than two colours, treat the "floating" yarns as if they were one yarn and always spread the stitches to their correct width to keep them elastic. It is advisable not to carry the stranded or "floating" yarns over more than three stitches at a time, but to weave them under and over the colour you are working. The "floating" yarns are therefore caught at the back of the work.

Intarsia: The simplest way to do this is to cut short lengths of yarn for each motif or block of colour used in a row. Then joining in the various colours at the appropriate point on the row, link one colour to the next by twisting them around each other where they meet on the wrong side to avoid gaps. All ends can then either be darned along the colour join lines, as each motif is completed or then can be "knitted-in" to the fabric of the knitting as each colour is worked into the pattern. This is done in much the same way as "weaving- in" yarns when working the Fairisle technique and does save time darning-in ends. It is essential that the tension is noted for intarsia as this may vary from the stocking stitch if both are used in the same pattern.

FINISHING INSTRUCTIONS

After working for hours knitting a garment, it seems a great pity that many garments are spoiled because such little care is taken in the pressing and finishing process. Follow the text below for a truly professional-looking garment.

PRESSING

Block out each piece of knitting and following the instructions on the ball band press the garment pieces, omitting the ribs. Tip: Take special care to press the edges, as this will make sewing up both easier and neater. If the ball band indicates that the fabric is not to be pressed, then covering the blocked out fabric with a damp white cotton cloth and leaving it to stand will have the desired effect. Darn in all ends neatly along the selvage edge or a colour join, as appropriate.

STITCHING

When stitching the pieces together, remember to match areas of colour and texture very carefully where they meet. Use a seam stitch such as back stitch or mattress stitch for all main knitting seams and join all ribs and neckband with mattress stitch, unless otherwise stated.

CONSTRUCTION

Having completed the pattern instructions, join left shoulder and neckband seams as detailed above. Sew the top of the sleeve to the body of the garment using the method detailed in the pattern, referring to the appropriate guide:

Straight cast-off sleeves: Place centre of cast-off edge of sleeve to shoulder seam. Sew top of sleeve to body, using markers as guidelines where applicable.

Square set-in sleeves: Place centre of cast-off edge of sleeve to shoulder seam. Set sleeve head into armhole, the straight sides at top of sleeve to form a neat right-angle to cast-off sts at armhole on back and front.

Shallow set-in sleeves: Place centre of cast off edge of sleeve to shoulder seam. Match decreases at beg of armhole shaping to decreases at top of sleeve. Sew sleeve head into armhole, easing in shapings.

Set-in sleeves: Place centre of cast-off edge of sleeve to shoulder seam. Set in sleeve, easing sleeve head into armhole.

Join side and sleeve seams.

Slip stitch pocket edgings and linings into place. Sew on buttons to correspond with buttonholes. Ribbed welts and neckbands and any areas of garter stitch should not be pressed.

ABBREVIATIONS

K	knit
P	purl
st(s)	stitch(es)
inc	increas(e)(ing)
dec	decreas(e)(ing)
st st	stocking stitch (1 row K , 1 row P)
g st	garter stitch (K every row)
beg	begin(ning)
foll	following
rem	remain(ing)
rev st st	reverse stocking stitch (1 row K , 1 row P)
rep	repeat
alt	alternate
cont	continue
patt	pattern
tog	together
mm	millimetres
cm	centimetres
in(s)	inch(es)
RS	right side
WS	wrong side
sl 1	slip one stitch
psso	pass slipped stitch over
p2sso	pass 2 slipped stitches over
tbl	through back of loop
M1	make one stitch by picking up horizontal loop before next stitch and knitting into back of it
M1P	make one stitch by picking up horizontal loop before next stitch and purling into back of it
yfwd	yarn forward
yrn	yarn round needle
meas	measures
0	no stitches, times or rows
-	no stitches, times or rows for that size
yon	yarn over needle
yfrn	yarn forward round needle
wyib	with yarn at back

CROCHET TERMS

UK crochet terms and abbreviations have been used throughout. The list below gives the US equivalent where they vary.

ABBREV.	UK	US
dc (sc)	double crochet	(single crochet)
htr (hdc)	half treble	(half double crochet)
tr (dc)	treble	(double crochet)
dtr (tr)	double treble	(treble)

EXPERIENCE RATING

 = Easy, straight forward knitting

 = Suitable for the average knitter

 = For the more experienced knitter

BUTTONS, BEADS AND RIBBONS USED IN THIS MAGAZINE ARE SOURCED FROM:

Coats Crafts UK, Green Lane Mill, Holmfirth, West Yorkshire HD9 2DX.
www.knitrowan.com
www.coatscrafts.co.uk
Tel: +44 (0)1484 681881
Email: mail@knitrowan.com

Bedecked Limited, 5 Castle Street, Hay-on-Wye, Hereford, HR3 5DF.
www.bedecked.co.uk
Shop tel: +44 (0)1497 822769
Email: thegirls@bedecked.co.uk

Debbie Abrahams
Tel: +44 (0)115 9161524
Mobile: 07900 066376
Email: beads@debbieabrahams.com

Rowan recommends:

WASH CARE INFORMATION

You may have noticed over the last season that the wash care symbols on our ball bands and shade cards have changed. This is to bring the symbols we use up to date and hopefully help you to care for your knitting and crochet more easily. Below are the symbols you are likely to see and a brief explanation of each.

MACHINE WASH SYMBOLS

Machine Wash, Cold | Machine Wash, Cold, Gentle | Machine Wash, Warm | Machine Wash, Warm, Gentle

HAND WASH SYMBOLS

Do Not Wash | Hand Wash, Normal | Hand Wash, Cold | Hand Wash, Warm

DRY CLEAN SYMBOLS

Do Not Dry Clean | Dry Clean | Dry Clean, in Certain Solvents, Consult Cleaner | Dry Clean, Any Solvent

IRONING SYMBOLS

Do Not Iron | Iron Low Heat | Iron Medium Heat

DO NOT BLEACH SYMBOL

Do Not Bleach

DRYING SYMBOLS

Do Not Tumble Dry | Tumble Dry, Gentle, Low Heat | Dry Flat in Shade | Dry Flat | Do Not Wring

Rowan Overseas Stockists

For more information on overseas stockists and Mail Order details please contact the Rowan distributor / agent listed under each country.
'ROWAN AT ....' stockists, which are in **bold**, carry a large range of Rowan Yarns.

AUSTRALIA

VIC	*MELBOURNE*	*Australian Country Spinners Pty Ltd (Distributor)*	*Level 7, 409 St. Kilda Road*	*sales@auspinners.com.au*	*3004*	*(03) 9380 3830*	
NSW	Avalon Beach	Avalon Fabrics & Crafts	Shop 4, 24 Avalon Parade	info@avalonfabrics.com	2107	(02) 99182978	
NSW	Balmain	Calico and Ivy Balmain	10 Birchgrove Road	info@calicoandivy.com	2041	(02) 9555 9909	
NSW	Beecroft	Yarns & Gifts	Shop 8a 16-24 Hannah St	yarns_and_gifts@optusnet.com.au	2119	(02) 8407 9512	
NSW	Bowral	Wool Addiction	The Penders, Shop 3, 20 Station Street	jill@wooladdiction.com.au	2576	(02) 4862 4799	
NSW	Hornsby	Hornsby Wool & Craft Nook	Shop 3-3A, 25-31 Florence St	hornsbywoolcraft@optusnet.com	2077	(02) 9482 4924	
NSW	Katoomba	Katoomba Knitting & Needle Craft	Shop 5 Town Centre Arcade, Katoomba Street	katoombaknitting@gmail.com	2780	(02) 4782 6137	
NSW	Loftus	Jules Craft Shoppe	Shop 3/69, National Avenue	judy@julescraftshoppe.com.au	2237	(02) 9542 3298	
NSW	Mosman	Mosman Needlecraft	Shop 3, 529 Military Road	mosmanneedlecraft@bigpond.com	2088	(02) 9969 5105	
NSW	Pennant Hills	Sue's Cherryhills	Shop 7, 354 Pennant Hills Road	pczerny@unwired.com.au	2120	(02) 94840212	
NSW	Penrith	The Wool Inn	Shop 14 N & K Centre, 450 High Street	anitab@the_wool_inn.com.au	2750	(02) 4732 2201	
NSW	Phillip	Stitch N Time	Unit 2, 55 Colby Court	robynmiranda@bigpond.com	2607	(02) 6282 8383	
NSW	Smeaton Grange	Tijuana Alpacas	Unit 1 / 8 Blackmore Road	sharon@tijuana-alpaca.com.au	2567	(02) 4647 1155	
NSW	St Ives	Mahala Knits	39 Eucalyptus Close	mahalaknits@hotmail.com	2075	(02) 8407 9512	
NSW	Sydney	Tapestry Craft	50 York Street	email@tapestrycraft.com.au	2000	(02) 929 8588	
NSW	Turramurra	Turramurra Drapery	1319 Pacific Highway	sue-croston2003@yahoo.com.au	2074	(02) 9449 5843	
NSW	Woolombi	Woolombi Wool Store	2883 Woolombi Rd	woolombiwoolstore@bigpond.com	2325	(02) 4998 8154	
QLD	Buderim	Nimble Stitches	Shop 1, 65 Burnett St	traed7@bigpond.com	4556	(07) 5476 6495	
QLD	Sherwood	Threads And More	Shop 7, 637 Sherwood Road, cnr Oxley Road	accounts@threadsandmore.com.au	4075	(07) 3379 6699	
VIC	Albert Park	Wool Baa	124 Bridport Street	sales@woolbaa.com	3206	(03) 9690 6633	www.woolbaa.com
VIC	Geelong	Twisted Threads	106 Ryrie Street	mandy@twistedthreads.com.au	3220	(03) 5221 0099	
VIC	Healesville	Crumbz	P.O BOX 1714	kayt@crumbz.com.au	3777	0412389192	
VIC	Kyneton	Pick Up Stitches Pty Ltd	46 Piper Street	pickupstitches@bigpond.com	3444	(03) 5422 6614	
VIC	Malvern	Wondoflex Yarn Craft Centre	1353 Malvern Road	marilyn@wondoflex.com.au	3144	(03) 9822 6231	
VIC	Mansfield	Country Folk	P O BOX 233	lafolk@bigpond.com	3724	(03) 5775 2044	
VIC	**MELBOURNE**	**Sunspun**	**185 Canterbury Road, Canterbury**	**shop@sunspun.com.au**	**3126**	**(03) 9830 1609**	**www.sunspun.com.au**
VIC	Mount Eliza	Windmills & Roses	36-38 Ranelagh Drive	windmillsandroses@bigpond.com	3930	(03) 9787 4949	
VIC	Oakleigh	Craftee Cottage	52-54 Atherton Road	info@crafteecottage.com.au	3166	(03) 9568 3606	
VIC	Panton Hill	Wool On The Hill	56 Bakehouse Rd	kaitlan.o@bigpond.com	3759	(03) 9719 7282	
VIC	Sassafras	Sassafras Wool Store	Shop 2, 372 Mt. Dandenong Tourist Road	sassafraswoolstore@bigpond.com	3787	(03) 9755 2510	
VIC	Surrey Hills	Wool Shop	486 Whitehorse Road		3127	(03) 9836 9614	
VIC	Wandin North	Catharinas Country Collection	382 Warburton Highway	sales@cccpatchwork.com.au	3139	(03) 5964 3592	
VIC	Williamstown	Stitchery Blue	1 / 91 Ferguson Street	stitcheryblue@bigpond.com	3016	0412 634 296	
VIC	Melbourne	Clegs	60 Elizabeth St	clegsbrunswick@clegs.com.au	3000	(03) 9654 7677	www.clegs.com.au
WA	Claremont	Remember Me	28 Freshwater Parade	qr.barrie@bigpond.com.au	6010	(08) 9385 3478	
WA	Innaloo	The Wool Shack	5A Langley Place	emma@the woolshack.com.au	6918	(08) 94466344	
WA	Mosman Park	Calico and Ivy	1 Glyde Street	info@calicoandivy.com,	6012	(08) 9383 3794	
WA	Wembley	Woolly Latteis	46-48 Grantham Street	info@woolylattes.com	6014	(08) 9287 1492	

AUSTRIA

Baden	Stick + Strick	Hauptplatz 8	susanne.hasieber@stickundstrick.at	2500	0043/2252/49570	www.stickundstrick.at
Kitzbuehel	Kitzbuehel Handarbeiten	Im Gries Nr. 23		6370	0043/535672646	
Kolsass	Wolle + Staune (Sabine Kahn)	Auweg 2a	kahn@wolleundstaune.at	6114		www.wolleundstaune.at
Lustenau	**Zum Schwarzen Schaf**	**Roseggerstraße 13**	**wolle@zumschwarzenschaf.at**	**6890**	**0043/5577/62967**	**www.zumschwarzenschaf.at**
Schruns	KNOPF & WOLLE	Silbertaler Straße 2	gabi@juen.biz	6780	05556-74410	
Wien	Laniato - das Wiener Wollcafe	Beatrixgasse 4		1030	0043/69915249911	www.laniato.com
Wien	Stick + Strick	Simmeringer Haupstrasse 86	susanne.hasieber@stickundstrick.at	1110	0043/1/7494268	www.stickundstrick.at
Wien	Wollboutique Pinguin	Alserstrasse 21		1080	0043/1/4080010	
Wien	Wolle fuer Mode Fleischmann	Neubaugasse 59/3		1070	0043/1/5233394	
Wien	**Zwei Glatt Zwei Verkehrt**	**Josefstädter Str. 14**	**wolle@zweiglattzweiverkehrt.at**	**1080**	**0043/1/4035736**	**www.zweiglattzweiverkehrt.at**
Mödling	Krawany GmbH	Hauptstrasse 83	handarbeit@krawany.com	2340	0043/2236 41500 15	

BELGIUM

Aalter	Angelas Wolboetiek	Stationstraat 40	angela.vercruysse@telenet.be	9880	09 / 374 27 28	
Aarschot	Kreatrend plus	Martelarenstraat 17	het.vlijtig.bijtje@skynet.be	3200	016.49 00 16	www.hetvlijtigbijtje.be
Antwerpen	**Lana**	**Anselmostraat 92**	**info@lana-antwerpen.be**	**2018**	**03/ 238 70 17**	**www.lana-antwerpen.be**
Arlon	Brin De Soi	Rue des Faubourg 19	brindesoi@skynet.be	6700	063/ 445 680	
Brussel	Art et Fil	25, Rue du Baillie		1000	02/ 647 64 51	
Brussel	**Be creative by schleiper**	**63 Rue de l'Etang**		**1040**	**02.541.05.12**	**www.becreativebyschleiper.com / www.millemillersdemailles.fr**
Brussel	Warianne bvba	Vanderkinderestraat 401	ariane.vangijsel@mac.com	1180	0475 94 05 33	
Chênée	Rêve de quilts	Rue d'Embourg 29	quiltsdream@skynet.be	4032	0475 66 76 61	www.revedequilts.be
Eeklo	Hobbyfarm	Pastoor Bontestraat, 37	hobbyfarm@pandora.be	9900	09/3786664	www.hobbyfarm.be
Gent	**Stoffenidee**	**Burgstraat 38A**	**stoffenidee@skynet.be**	**9000**	**09/233.37.48**	**www.stoffenidee.net**
Geraardsbergen	Maxime's Hobby	Guilleminlaan 237	info@maximeshobby.com	9500	054/411145	www.maximeshobby.com
Hamme	Guy's Naaicentrum	Roodkruisstraat 98	info@guysnaaicentrum.be	9220	052/ 47 18 05	www.guysnaaicentrum.be
Jemeppe	Boite a fils	Rue Joseph Wettinck, 40		4101	04/2338710	
Keerbergen	Linnenmandje	Mechelsebaan 3	linnenmand@hotmail.com	3140	015 515 753	
Kortrijk	Alle steken op een rij	Grote Kring 14	info@allestekenopeenrij	8500	0477 49 70 18	www.allestekenopeenrij.be
Kraainem	Atelier de la passion	Avenue des Tarins 24		1950	02 731 85 83	
Leper	Origami	Jules Capronstraat 10	nicolie.origami@scarlet.be	8900	057/216022	www.hobbyshop-origami@skynet.be
Leuven	**t Wolwinkeltje**	**Parijsstraat 25**	**deforcerosemie@hotmail.com**	**3000**	**016 22 75 48**	**www.twolwinkeltje.be**
Lokeren	De Wolkamer	Gentsesteenweg 477	therese.coens@telenet.be	9160	09/355 20 55	
Mechelen	Huis Inge Goderis	O.L.V. straat 131-133	info@dehandwerkwinkel.be	2800	015.41.40.54	www.dehandwerkwinkel.be
Oostende	Paulette	Torhoutsesteenweg 479		8400	059 43 04 95	
Ronse	Creasis VOF	Zonnestraat 24	creasis@telenet.be	9600	0495 70 81 90	www.creasis.be
Sint Truiden	Govaerts Van Mechelen	Van Mechelen, Markt 61		3800	011/682288	www.govaerts-mercerie.info
Torhout	Lana Exclusief	Oostendestraat 88A	retrans@skynet.be	8820	050/213632	www.lana-exclusief.be
Tournai	Paprika Cotton	Rue Saint-Martin 62		7500	069/235383	www.paprikacotton.be
Virton	La Compagnie des Laines	Grand Rue 38	lacompagniedeslaines@live.be	6760	063 67 78 00	www.lacompagniedeslaines.be
Westerlo	Atelier Salgarollo	Koning Leopoldlaan 16	kristel.salgarollo@telenet.be	2260	014 264 393	www.salgarollo.be
Wilsele	D.Yarns	P Van Langendoncklaan 17	d_van_nueten@hotmail.com	3012	(016) 20 13 81	

CANADA

South Carolina	*Greer*	*Westminster Fibers (Distributor)*	*8 Shelter Drive*		*29650*	*(800) 445-9276*	*www.westminsterfibers.com*
Alberta	**Calgary**	**Pudding Yarns**	**1516-6th St, SW**		**T2R 0Z8**	**403 244 2996**	
Alberta	**Edmonton**	**River City Yarns**	**16956-111 Avenue**	**barb@rivercityyarns.com**	**T5M 4C9**	**780 477-9276**	
British Columbia	Langley	88 Stitches	602-21183 88 Avenue		V1M 2G5	604 888-6689	
British Columbia	**North Vancouver**	**Urban Yarns, 4437 West 10th Ave**	**urbanyarns@telus.net**		**V6R 2H8**	**604 228 1122**	**www.urbanyarns.ca**
British Columbia	**North Vancouver**	**Urban Yarns, 3111 Highland Boulevard**	**knitting@urbanyarns.ca**		**V7R 2X5**	**604 984 2214**	**www.urbanyarns.ca**
British Columbia	Port Moody	Black Sheep Yarns	88 Grant Street		V3H 0B6	778 355-9665	
British Columbia	Richmond	Wool and Wicker	120-12051 Second Avenue	dianedebray@shaw.ca	V7E 3L6	604 275-1239	
British Columbia	Vancouver	Three Bags Full	4458 Main St		V5V 3R3	604 874 9665	
British Columbia	**Victoria**	**The Beehive Wool**	**1700 Douglas Street**	**beehivewoolshop@telus.net**	**V8W 2G7**	**250 385 2727**	
British Columbia	Victoria	Boutique de Laine	2534 Estevan Avenue		V8R 2S7	250 592-9616	
Ontario	**Ancaster**	**The Needle Emporium**	**420 Wilson St. East**		**L9G 2C3**	**800 667-9167**	**www.needleemporium.com**
Ontario	**Orleans**	**Wool N Things**	**1439 Youville Drive, # 20**	**gisele@woolnthings.com**	**K1C 4M8**	**613-841-8680**	**www.woolnthings.com**
Ontario	**Toronto**	**Romni Wools Ltd**	**658 Queen St West**		**M6J 1E5**	**416 703 0202**	
Quebec	**Montreal**	**Effiloche**	**6260 Saint Hubert**	**ginette@effiloche.com**	**H2S 2M2**	**514-276-2547**	**www.effiloche.com**
Quebec	Montreal	Espace Tricot	6054 Monkland Ave		H4A 1H1	514 486-5648	
Quebec	**Montreal**	**Mouline Fine Yarns**	**2657 Notre-Dame West**	**svetlana@moulineyarns.com**	**H3J 1N9**	**514-935-4401**	**www.moulineyarns.com**
Quebec	**Salabery de Valleyfield**	**Amite & Passion**	**18 Nicholson**		**J6T 4M3**	**450-370-1001**	
Saskatchewan	Humboldt	Haus of Stitches	626 Main Street , PO Box 2458		S0K 2A0	306 682-0772	www.hausofstitches.com

CHINA

China	*Shanghai*	*Coats Shanghai Limited (Distributor)*	*9 BaoSheng Rd, Songjiang Industrial Zone*	*victor.li@coats.com*		*+86 13816681825*	
China	**Shanghai**	**Good Friend Crafts Store**	**No.408 Fuzhou Rd**	**jessechang@vip.163.com**	**200002**	**+86-21-63739785;63739786;63739787**	**www.coatscraftschina.com**
China	Shanghai	Shanghai Yujun CO. LTD	Room 701 Wangjiao Plaza, No.175 Yan'an Road(E)	jessechang@vip.163.com	200002	+86-21-63739785;63739786;63739787	www.coatscraftschina.com

DENMARK

Dalsjöfors	*Distributor: Coats Expotex AB*	*Stationsvägen 2*		*S-516 21*	*45 35 86 90 49*	
Ålborg	**Design Vaerkstedet**	**Boulevarden 9**		**9000**	**45 98 12 07 13**	
Århus	**City Stoffer**	**Park Alle 9**		**8000**	**45 86 19 03 93**	**www.citystoffer.dk**
Århus	**Inger's**	**Volden 19**	**design.club@mail.dk**	**8000**	**45 86 19 40 44**	**www.design-club-dk**
Blåvand	**Ho Strik**	**Hovej 21**	**info@hostrik.dk**	**6857**	**45 75 27 54 03**	**www.hostrik.dk**
Ebeltoft	Birn & Bagger	Jernbanegade 10	info@bbgarnstrik.dk	8400	45 86 34 11 51	
Farum	Fingerbollet	Farum Hovedgade 85	fingerboellet@gmail.com	3520	45 44 95 70 01	
Farup	Quiltefant	Spurvevej 1	camilla@quiltefant.dk	8990	45 96 68 00 28	www.quiltefant.dk
Gilleleje	Gilleje Stof og Garn	Stationsvej 1		3250	45 48 30 31 10	
Grindsted	Cirkelline	Borgerade 14	anette.may@mail.tele.dk	7200	45 75 32 32 99	www.cirkelinegarn.dk
Helsinge	Uldgalleriet	Østergade 2	gitte@uldgalleriet.dk	3200	45 48 79 71 36	
Hornslet	Filt	Tingvej 7B	fischer-filt@mail.dk	8543	45 86 97 51 33	www.fischer-filt.dk
Horsens	**Strikkekunsten**	**Søndergade 41 B**	**kontakt@strikkekunsten.dk**	**8700**	**45 75 65 16 54**	**www.strikkekunsten.dk**
Hørsholm	Engle Stof	Usserød Kongevej 10 A	englestof@mail.dk	2970	45 45 86 33 78	
Kgs. Lyngby	**Uldstedet**	**Gl. Jernbanevej 7**	**uldstedet@get2net.dk**	**2800**	**45 45 88 10 88**	**www.uldstedet.dk**
København	**Sommerfuglen**	**Vandkunsten 3, Kbh.K**	**mail@sommerfuglen.dk**	**1467**	**45 33 32 82 90**	**www.sommerfuglen.dk**
København	Uldstedet	Fiolstræde 13, Kbh.K	uldstedet@get2net.dk	1171	45 33 91 17 71	www.uldstedet.dk
Kolding	Martha	Søndergade 4	martha-garn@webspeed.dk	6600		
Nyborg	Ulrikka	Nørregade 13	ulrikkagarn@yahoo.dk	5800	45 65 30 22 80	www.ulrikkagarn.dk
Randers	Uldma	Rosengade 2	salg@uldma.dk	8900	45 86 46 64 66	www.uldma.dk
Ribe	Ribes Broderi & Garn	Dagmarsgade 4	symaskineland@symaskineland.dk	6760		
Roskilde	**Garnhøkeren**	**Karen Olsdatterstræde 9**		**4000**	**45 46 37 20 63**	
Silkeborg	Onskegarn	Nygade 12	onskegarn@onskegarn.dk	8600	86825707	www.oskegarn.dk
Skanderborg	**Stof & Sy**	**Adelgade 123**	**info@stofogsy.dk**	**8660**	**45 86 52 02 45**	**www.stofogsy.dk**
Slangerup	**Paradisets Bamser**	**Kvinderupvej 17**		**3550**	**45 47 33 58 66**	**www.butikparadiset.dk**
Svendborg	Ulrikka	Gerritsgade 2	ulrikkagarn@yahoo.dk	5700	45 62 22 21 17	www.ulrikkagarn.dk
Tarm	Uldgården	Fjerbaekvej 12,Vodstrup	uldgaarden@uldgaarden.dk	6880	45 97 37 42 71	www.uldgaarden.dk
Thisted	**Strikkefeen**	**J.P Jacobsens Plads 5**	**strikkefeen@hotmail.com**	**7700**	**97921233**	**www.strikkefeenthisted.dk**
Varde	Cotton Wear	Smedegade 9	cccsejunge@hotmail.com	6800	45 75 22 33 00	www.cottonwear.dk
Vejle	**Garn & Design Arne S. Hansen**	**Vestergade 45**	**garn-design@mail.dk**	**7100**	**45 75 82 02 49**	**www.garn-design.dk**
Viborg	Mathilde	St. Sct. Mikkelsgade 37		8800	45 86 61 50 22	

EIRE

Co Cathair	Galway	Island Yarn Ltd	1 Middle Street			00 353 91 566972	
Co Clare	Tulla	Saolre	Tulla Stables Studio			353876496040	
Co Dublin	**Blackrock**	**Winnies Wool Wagon**	**3 Woodbine Park**			**00353 87 2439801**	
Co Dublin	Dublin	Springwools Ltd	The Olde Sawmills, Walkinstown	sales@springwools.com	12	353 1 450 9134	www.springwools.com
Co Dublin	**Dublin**	**This is knit LTD**	**Powerscourt, Town house Centre**		**2**	**35316709981**	
Co Galway	**Galway**	**Pippa Blue**	**1 Middle Street**			**35391566972**	
Co Kerry	Killarney	Spin a Yarn LTD	43 New street				
Co Kildare	**Naas**	**Treasure**	**42 South Main Street**			**353879574959**	
Co Wicklow	Bray	The Wool Shop	71 Main Street			3531 2760029	
Co Wicklow	**Roundwood**	**The yarn Room**	**Moneystown**			**0404045696**	

FAERO ISLANDS

Klaksvik	Fa B´nin	N.P. Gøta 20, Postrum 282		F-700	00298 455210	
Torshavn	Igloo SP/F Spuni	Sverresgøta 19, Postbox 181		F-110	00298 315264	

FINLAND

Kerava	*Coats Opti Crafts Oy (Distributor)*	*Huhtimontie 6*		*FI-04200*	*358 9 274871*	
Espoo	Menita Outlet	Ylakartanontie 26		02360	358 9 2567536	
Helsinki	Fiinaneule	Annankatu 20		00120	358 9 47890065	www.fiinaneule.fi
Helsinki	Oy Menita Ab	Korkeavuorenkatu 20		00120	358 44 2698045	
Helsinki	Tikata	Itäkatu 11	info@tikata.fi	00930	358 50 3063662	www.tikata.fi
Joensuu	Joensuun Kasityovakka	Kauppakatu 30	myynti@kasityovakka.fi	80100	358 400 602 908	www.kasityovakka.fi
Kirkkonummi	Mamman Tupa	Toritie 3		02400	358 45 2311470	
Kuopio	Kuopion Nauha ja Nappi	Vuorikatu 23		70100	358 17 2165756	
Oulu	Menita Oy	Isokatu 54		90100	358 50 5666527	
Päntäne	Tapio E Nevanpää	Oikotie 4	info@tapionkauppa.net	61980	358400362416	www.lankatalo.net
Sastamala	Silmu & Solmu	Marttilankatu 16	info@silmusolmu.fi	38200	358 50 407 5758	www.silmusolmu.fi
Tampere	Lankaidea T-Skirt	Aleksanterinkatu 37	shop@lankaidea.fi	33100	358 3 4475 720	www.lankaidea.fi

FRANCE

Angers	Maison Marot	12 rue Champeronniere		49100	02 41 88 37 66	
BesanÁon	La Boite a Laine	15 Rue Xavier Marnier		25000	06 07 23 25 37	
Bordeaux	**La Lainerie**	**22 rue des Ayres**	**la.lainerie@orange.fr**	**33000**	**05 56 81 43 92**	**www.lalainerie.com**
Bourgoin-Jallieu	Coclicote	8 rue de Stalingrad	murielduche@orange.fr	38300	04 74 28 41 94	
BrianÁon	L'Atelier de la laine	2 Rue Pasteur	nathphilip@email.com	05100	04 92 20 45 60	
Colmar	**Ambiance Laine**	**5 Rue Des Pretres**	**info@ambiance-laine.fr**	**68000**	**03 89 41 87 71**	**www.ambiance-laine.fr**
Dijon	**Planete Laines**	**20 rue du Chateau**		**21000**	**03 80 30 37 96**	**www.planete-laine.com**
Joigny	**Lady Laine**	**47 bis rue Gambetta**	**ladylaine.joigny@wanadoo.fr**	**89300**	**03 86 62 21 21**	**www.ladylaine.fr**
La Varenne St. Hilaire	Lili Coquelicot	124 avenue Pierre Semart	contact@lilicoquelicot.fr	94210	01 47 06 71 63	
Le Plessis Robinson	La Mercerie Carrée	8 place Francois Spoerry	contact@la-mercerie-carree.fr	92350	01 46 32 61 74	www.la-mercerie-carree.fr
Levallois-Perret	Laines en Vogue	36 rue Gabriel Peri		923000	01 47 57 58 64	www.millemilliersdemailles.fr
Montpellier	Anne Ouvrages	28 rue Paul Brousse	anneouvrages@bbox.fr	34000	04 67 92 50 92	
Montpellier	Avant Aprés	29 rue Foch	avant.apres0219@orange.fr	34000	04 99 06 95 35	
Nancy	**2 Aiguilles dans la CafetiËre**	**5 rue Gustave Simon**		**54000**	**03 83 39 46 70**	
Orléans	**Au fil d'Emma**	**79 Boulevard A. Martin**		**45000**	**09 50 14 85 84**	**www.aufildemma.com**
Osmoy	**So ! Fil**	**6 chemin du moutier**	**tricothe.sofil@gmail.com**	**78910**	**01 34 87 29 15**	**www.tricothe.jimdo.com**
Paris (7)	**Le Bon Marche**	**115 rue du Bac**		**75007**	**01 44 39 80 00**	
Paris (9)	Le Comptoir	26 rue Cadet		75009	01 42 46 20 72	www.lecomptoir.canalblog.com/
Poitiers	La Mercerie	9 rue Lebascles		86000	05 49 52 59 22	www.lamercerie.commerces-poitiers.fr
Rennes	LTM	11 rue Poullain Duparc		35000	02 99 78 20 60	
Thonon les Bains	Au vieux rouet	7 rue Ferdinand Dubouloz	auvieuxrouet@orange.fr	74200	04 50 71 07 33	
Toulouse	**Fifi Jolipois**	**11 rue Cujas**	**contact@fifijolipois.com**	**31000**	**05 62 30 80 09**	**www.perles-et-bijoux.com**
Tours	La Boîte à Laine	37, rue du Grand Marché	laboitealaine@orange.fr	37000	02 47 37 76 47	

GERMANY

Ammersbek	Angelika Lehmann	Schwarzerweg 21		22949	04532/4641	
Arnstein	Jutta Heurung	Marktstr. 5		97450	0163/1621785	
Aschaffenburg	Nähwelt Machemer	Lorbeerweg 2	anjapunt@naehwelt-machemer.de	63741	06021/3713650	www.naehwelt-machemer.de
Au a. Inn	Helga Holzner	Steinbach 1	bachmair-helga@t-online.de	83546	08073-916666	
Augsburg	Augsburger Restehaus	Vorderer Lech 39		86150	0821 - 519019	
Backnang	**Wollstube Wollin**	**Schillerstr. 19**	**info@wolle-backnang.com**	**71522**	**07191/902828**	**www.wolle-backnang.com**
Bad Bruckenau	Inge Vogel	Ludwigstr. 42		97769	0974 14034	
Bad D,rkheim	Atelier Blum	Römerstr. 23	post@atelier-blum.de	67098	06322-4094950	www.atelier-blum.de
Bad Laer	Gäbel	Mozartstr. 12		49196	54248939	
Bad Mergenteim	Bianca Bendraouia,	Frommengasse 3	wollig_warm@yahoo.de	97980	07931/5430374	
Bad Nauheim	Stickdesign& Kunst Susanne Nellinger	Karlstr. 17a	kontakt@nelsu.de	61231	06032-1500	www.nelsu.de
Bad Neuenahr-Ahrweiler	Dat Lädche,	Niederhutstr. 17	dat-laedche_adams@t-online.de	53474	02641/4464	
Bad Soden	Beate Schilb	Hasselstr. 19	beate.schilb@wollkreativ.de	65812	06196/644113	
Bamberg	**Friedericke Pfund**	**Promenadestr. 18**	**wollstudio@fritzi.pfund.de**	**96047**	**0951-202173**	**www.home.t-online.de/home/fritzi.pfund**
Bayreuth	**Strickart**	**Kirchplatz 7**	**strickwerk@gmx.de**	**95444**	**0921/5304870**	**www.strickart-cafe.de**
Berlin	Birgit K,ttner	Teltower Damm 34		14169	030-8026500	
Berlin	Claudia Thees	Bahnhofstr. 3		12555	030 /6562697	
Berlin	Holz & Wolle	Warnem,nder Str. 29		14199	030/83222762	
Berlin	Jolanta Schulze	Aflmannstr. 40		12587	030-65484239	
Berlin	Kerstin Hering	Helene-Weigl-Platz 13		12681	030 66 30 80 55	
Berlin	Loops	Wörther Str. 19		10405	030/44054934	
Biberach	Regina Kreuzer-Krause	Gymnasiumstr. 14		88400	07351/1889980	
Biebertal-Rodheim	Scherer, Barbara,	Hauptstr. 62		35444	06409-8080330	
Bielefeld	Kercan	Friedrich-Ebert-Strasse 2		33602	0521/60296	
Bielefeld	WollZauber	Vilsendorferstr. 45		33739	05206/2992	
Bocholt	Marieluise Schlichte	Nordstr. 49		46399	02871/2373661	
Bochum	Danijela Semmler	Viktoriastr. 18		44787	0234/8937990	
Bonn-Duisdorf	Petra Klein	Rochusstr. 245	kontakt@atelier-rosenbaum.de	53123	0228-39047787	www.atelier-rosenbaum.de
Braunschweig	Susanne Wenke	Sch,tzenstr. 37	info@stil-bluete.net	38100	0177/3447082	www.stil-bluete.net
Bremen	Wollstube A. Heyn	Br,ggeweg 40-42		28309	0421/413869	
Burscheid	Bergische Schnatterh,tte	B,rgermeister_Schmidt-Str. 6-8		51399	02174 - 892101	
Chemnitz	Zwilllingsnadel	Neumarkt 2	info@zwillingsnadel.de	9111	0371-3331866	www.zwillingsnadel.de
Coburg	**Kristina Hackert**	**Steinweg. 32**	**kristina.hackert@umgarnt.de**	**96450**	**095617958133**	
Creuzburg	Lenhard	Adelbert-K,hmstädt-Strafle 2	info@wollmaus-wolle.de	99831	036926-9411	
Dachau	Barbara Reischl	Konrad-Adenauer-Str. 20	info@cotton-club-dachau.com	85221	08131-736859	www.cotton-club-dachau.com
Dannenberg	Annette Gierow	Lange Str. 32		29451	05861/976050	
Detmold	Handarbeitsgeschäft M,ller	Krummestr. 19	info@handarbeitenmueller.de	32756	05231/28216	www.handarbeitenmueller.de
Dinslaken	Andrea Magedanz	Marschallstr. 9		46539	02064 - 827980	www.quiltzauberei.de
Dornhan	Regina Temelkoski	Roflgartenstr. 14		72175	07455/2785	
Dreieich	Seelbach	Alte Schulgasse 2	anja.seelbach@googlemail.com	63303	0163-6785902	
Dresden	**Strick und Faden**	**Rothenburger Str. 14**	**nachstrickundfaden@web.de**	**1099**	**0351/8104086**	
D,sseldorf	Woll Duo	Scharnhorststr. 16		40477	0211/467776	
Emmering	Bodendörfer & Heggberg	Kirchplatz 7	dunja@luise-online.net	82275	08141-3634839	www.luise-online.net
Erlangen	Emanuel Keller	Hauptstr. 115	shop@wollkontor-erlangen.de	91054	09131/204327	www.wollkontor-erlangen.de
Ernsdorf	Rebecca Mothes	Provincialstr. 153	woll-faszination@gmx.de	66806	06831-508504	
Fallingbostel	Dagmar Ohlsen	Walsroder Str. 5		29683	05162/909320	
Fallingbostel	Dagmar Ohlsen	Walsroder Str. 5		29683	05162/909320	
Felsberg	Wollstube	Untergasse 30		34587	05662-3741	
Frankfurt	Lana	Grofle Bockenheimer Str.35		60313	069/281758	
Frankfurt	Wolle-Boutique	Eckenheimer Landstr. 34		60318	069/59792080	
Frankfurt	**am Main**	**Maschenwerke, Marburger Str. 4**	**info@maschenwerke.de**	**60487**	**069-71 58 89 80**	**www.maschenwerke.de**
Freiburg	**Welt der Handarbeit**	**Salzstr.37-39**	**info@welt-der-handarbeit.com**	**79098**	**0761/2172135**	
Freising	Kirsten B,rgel	Obere Hauptstr. 37	info@kimoco.de	85354	08161-140269	www.kimoco.de
Freudenberg	Gabriele Rosler	Mittelstrasse 2	roesler.gabriele@t-online.de	57258	02734/436999	
Friedrichsdorf	Claudia Hahn	Hugenottenstr. 85a	info@wolleundwolle.de	61381	06172/72498	
Garmisch-Partenkirchen	Edith Vogel,	Ludwigstr. 81		82467	88212200	
Gauting	**Bonifaktur**	**Grubm,hlerfeldstr. 25**	**mgraeb@aol.com**	**82131**	**089-89357858**	**www.bonifaktur.de**
Gedern	Bettina's Wollstube	Herrenweg 6		63688	06045-952266	
Gifhorn	Schmedt, Heidelore	Steinweg 60		38518	0537-153260	
Grafschaft	Wollschmiede	Zum Josefshäuschen 7	b.gutzmer@wollschmiede-holzweiler.de	53501	02641-916222	www.wollschmiede-holzweiler.de
Haan	Andrea Schleicher	Turnstr. 2		42781	02129 - 3797966	
Hamburg	Hamburg Alsterhaus	Jungfernstieg 16-20		20354		
Hamburg	Hand-Werk	Papenhuder Strasse 24		22087	040/2798254	
Hamburg	Pur-Pur-Wolle	Heuflweg 41b,	info@purpurwolle.de	20255	040/4904579	www.purpurwolle.de
Hamburg	Wollboutique	Wandsbeker Chaussee 315	service@wollboutique.de	22089	040/2007620	
Hamburg	Wollvik	Ratsm,hlendamm 26	wollvik@web.de	22335	040/41543767	
Hanau	Annette Schnabl	Bangertstr.7	Wollparadies-Hanau@web.de	63450	61815072732	
Hannover	Zeier-Möller Sophie	Sallstr. 81		30171	0511/3009622	
Heilbronn	Wollke	Am Kieselmarkt 2	wollke@t-online.de	74072	07131/629357	
Heppenheim	Alpaka	Friedrichstr. 23	hennes.schaab@web.de	64646	06252/2889	
Herne	Verstrickt und Zugenäht	Mont-Cenis-Str. 1		44623	02323/9595839	
Herzberg	Ursula Deppe-Krieger	Heidstr. 23		37412	0552 172861	
Hilden	Ellen Klaft	Worrington Platz 28		40721	02103-298249	
Hohenhameln-Soflnar	**Next Systems,**	**Kleine Sackstr. 2**	**info@wollfactory.de**	**31249**	**05128/4091366**	**www.wollfactory.de**
Homburg	Filatum	Saarbr,cker Str.3	Ibeyersdorf@t-online.de	66424	06841/171300	
Hoyerhagen	Waltraud Elsner	Haupstr. 44	blumenstube-hoyerhagen@gmx.de	27318	0425 13478	
Ibbenb,ren	Pottmeier	Unterer Markt 4		49477	05451/936417	
Ingelheim am Rhein	Wolle-im-Hof, Schulstrafle 8	astridkirch@gmx.de		55218	0173/6714610	www.wolle-im-hof.de
Kamp-Lintfort	Elfi's Wollwelt	Mörser Strasse 270		47475	02842/10 226	
Kandel	Sybille Riehm	Waldstr. 10	mail@nadel-adel.de	76870	07275 729064	
Kappeln	Ulrike Jödecke	Schmiedestr. 14		24376	04642 / 987766	
Karlsruhe	Gabriele Bodesohn	Marienstr. 55	g.bodesohn@web.de	76137	0721/7597840	
Kassel	Christina Geyer	Friedrich-Ebert-Str. 147	info@fil-garn-wolle.de	34117	0561/710029	www.fil-garn-wolle.de
Kelkheim	Kelkheimer Masche	Höchster Str. 8,		65779	06195/975678	
Kiel	Dörte Dietrich	Damaschkeweg 50a		24113	0431/2405493	www.wollwerkstatt-kiel.de
Kirchheim	Ulrike Beck-Kley	Schuhstr. 5		73230	0702 145275	
Kirchlengern	Corinna Schumacher	L,bbecker Str 5		32278	05223-9859721	
Koblenz	Birgit Reich	An der Liebfrauenkirche 11	dasi-tuepfelchenkoblenz@web.de	56068	0261-9733224	
Köln	Maschenkunst	Christophstr. 9-11	info@maschenkunst.de	50670	0221/2783489	www.maschenkunst.de
Köln	Rapp	Goltsteinstr. 96		50568	0221-16906088	
Landshut	**Barbara Zeilhofer**	**Kirchgasse 247**		**84028**	**0871/2764217**	
Langenau	Burmeister u. Steck	Bahnhofstr. 3	wollelangenau@aol.com	89129	07345-5393	
Langgöns	Patch-Work-Statt	Breitgasse 12	simone-junker@gmx.de	35428	06403-940665	www.patchworkstatt.de
Leutkirch	Brigitta Schwarz-Frehner	Marktstr. 30	info@diezweigstelle.de	88299	07561-9834566	
Limburgerhof	Fabrizio, Mira	Speyererstr. 111	mirafabrizio@aol.de	67117	06236-428387	
Lingen	Daniela Feike	Göthestr. 27	info@emslaedchen.de	49811	0591/75631	www.emslaedchen.de
Mainz	Andrea Seufert	Fuststr. 2	wolle-seufert@t-online.de	55166	06131-2407196	
Marburg	Saskia Krieger	Frauenbergstr. 13	wolle-laedchen@t-online.de	35039	06421-34230	

GERMANY (cont)

Meckenheim	Filonenko, Svetlana	Neuer Markt 23		53340	02225-887969	
Melle	Freya Hoffknecht	An der Kirche 3		49326	05428/927877	
Michelstadt	Haberkorn	Neutorstr. 5	haberkorn.doris@gmx.de	64720	06061-965891674	www.nobelschaf.de
M,nchen	**Brigitte Kreische**	**Nordendstr. 17**	**info@strickeria-muenchen.de**	**80799**	**089/88904532**	**www.strickeria-muenchen.net**
M,nster	Lacatus	Hörster Strasse 56	info@maschenrausch.com	48143	0049521/3846293	
Neum,nster	Anja Kuptz	Grandsee 20		24536	04321 / 528969	
Nidderau	Wolle Ambiente	Friedberger Str. 17		61130	06187-906162	
Norderney	Patchwork-St,bchen	Jann-Berghaus-Str.13		26548	04932/927160	
N,rnberg	Anita Hammel	Weinmarkt 10	mail@tollewolle.de	90403	0911-209497	www.tollewolle.de
N,rnberg	Katharina Stumpf	Zerzabelshofer Hauptstr. 4	kontakt@wollwerkstatt-woll-lust.de	90480	0177-4973353	
Oberursel	Daniela Queifler	Rathausplatz 6	info@wolllaus.de	61440	06171/586555	
Oldenburg	Simone Wörl	Lindenallee 56		26122	0441/39021818	
Oppenheim	A. Seufert	Sant-Ambrosius-Ring 31	wolle-seufert@t-online.de	55276	06133/2131	
Osnabr,ck	Woll-Perle	Hakenstr. 3		49074	0541/258561	
Paderborn	Nicole Kersek-Meilwes	K,rassierweg 8		33104	05254-10126	
Plauen	Heike Bromnitz	Stresemannstr. 6		08523	03741 221316	www.naehstuebl-bromnitz.de
Potsdam	Rosmarie Adler	Friedrich-Ebert-Str. 27		14467	0331-2800609	
Ratingen	Wollkörbchen (Frau Szczygielski)	Turmstr. 30		40878	02102-80844	
Regensburg	Birgit Birner	Am Fuchsengang 2	Strickeria@gmx.net	93047	0941-58612300	www.strickeria.net
Reutlingen	Wolle und Mehr	Metzgerstr. 64		72764	07121/310488	
Salzhausen	Wollart Ute Rudat	Eyendorfer Str. 3		21376	04172-969123	
Schl,chtern	Dagmar Marburger	Obertorstr.8	marburgerwollstube@web.de	36381	06661-1337	
Siegen	Stecknadel	Rathausser. 2	creativ@stecknadel.info	57078	027189002667	http://www.stecknadel.info
Soest	Der Faden	Potsdamer Platz 1		59494	02921/3192277	
Solingen	Sabine Ziel	Gr,newalderstr. 1		42657	0212-2437886	
Stadtlohn	**Wolle und Design**	**Görkeskamp 6**	**info@wolleunddesign.de**	**48703**	**02563/98208**	**www.wolleunddesign.de**
Stuttgart	Isabelle Roche	Sophienstr. 24		70178	0711 2265758	
Suhl	Steffi Hengelhaupt	Friedrich-König-Str. 5		98527	03681-723704	
Sulzbach a.d.Murr	Flour-Bretschneider Schettler,	Haller Str. 1	m.schetter-flour@vonhand.info	71560	07193-6492	www.vorhand.info
Titisee-Neustadt	Ingeborg Steiert	Scheuerlenstr. 24		79822	07651/7218	
Troisdorf	Olga Wanner	Kölner Str. 83		53840	02241-72974	
Ulm	**Wolle & Ideen**	**Pfauengasse 17**	**Heike@Redlinghaus.de**	**89073**	**0731/619491**	**www.wolleundideen.de**
Undorf	Roswitha Baierl	Hofmarkstr. 38	rosis_wollstube@yahoo.de	93152	09404-6410341	
Voerde	Anne Straus - Laube	Buelow Str. 28		46562	0281/43731	
Waghäusl-Wiesental	Petra Holzer,	Mannheimer Str. 7		68753	07254-7799741	www.Bastelstubediesunddas.de
Weiden	Strickeria	T,rlgasse 5	strickeria-weiden@arcor.de	92637	0961/40194152	
Weimar	Steffi Hengelhaupt	Eisfeld 3		99423	03643/901748	
Weinheim	Heide Fabian	Giselherstr. 19	heides-wollwerkstatt@t-online.de	69469	06201/256910	
Wenden	Barbarah Klur	Severinusstr. 2		57482	02762/490291	
Wetter-Volmarstein	Christiane A. Struck,	Osterfeldstrasse 11		58300	02335/8451940	
Wiesbaden	**Fil a Fil Der Woll-Laden**	**Rathausstr. 61**		**65203**	**0611-66969**	
Wiesbaden	fil-a-fil Der Woll-Laden	Grabenstr. 9	h.valaee@tbooker.com	65183	0611-36082102	
Winsen/ Aller	Markus Schroter	Celler Str. 11		29308	0514 35336	
Wolfsburg	Quell, Margot	Bahnhofstr. 20a		38442	0536-261108	
Wörrstadt	Gabriele Plamann	Friedrich-Ebert-Str.38	fam-plamann@t-online.de	55286	06734-960474	
W,lfrath	Heike Reich	Wilhelmstr. 177		42489	02058/8952798	
Wuppertal	Strick und Stick	Auer Schulstrasse 5	d.teege-schitthelm@hotmail.de	42103	0202/4292104	
Zetel	Marion Schäfer	Feldhörn 70		26340	04453 - 3971	

HOLLAND

Almere-Haven	Het Spoeltje	Meerstraat 52	handwerkzaak@hetspoeltje.nl	1353 AZ	036-5216817	www.hetspoeltje.nl
Amersfoort	Elitt VOF	Koestraat 16	info@elitt.nl	3811 HK	0334650010	
Amersfoort	H.W. Mur	Langestraat 13	info@hwmur.nl	3811 AA	033 461 7837	www.hwmur.nl
Amstelveen	Averecht	Groenhof 163	info@averecht.eu	1186 EZ	06 29010554	
Amsterdam	**de Afstap (Lonnie Bussink)**	**Oude Leliestraat 12**	**info@afstap.nl**	**1015 AW**	**020-6231445**	**www.afstap.nl**
Bergen	**Finlandia**	**Kleine Dorpsstraat 26**	**info@finlandia.nl**	**1861 KN**	**0725 894642**	**www.finlandiaimport.nl**
Dalen	Breiweb	Hoofdstraat 44	info@breiweb.nl	7751 GD	052 4551597	www.breiweb.nl
Eindhoven	**Breimode Brigitte**	**Ouverture 212**	**info@brigitte-handwerken.nl**	**5629 PX**	**040-2435576**	**www.brigitte-handwerken.nl**
Etten-Leur	De Wolboetiek	Bisschopsmolenstraat 169		4876 AL	076-5022597	www.wolboetiek.nl
Haarlem	**WOL V.O.F.**	**Wilhekminastraat 51**	**barte892@planet.nl**	**2011VL**	**06.518 951 75**	**www.wol-online.nl**
Heerlen	Ut Bolke	Benzenraderweg 92	info@utbolke.nl	6417 SV	045 /571 64 51	www.utbolke.nl
Helmond	Het Breiatelier	Groot Schulen 10	marleen@dutchknittingdesign.com	5706 KJ	0492549756	www.breipakket.nl
Hoorn	FA Schouten	Grote Noord, 120	info@schoutenhandwerken.nl	1621 KM	031/229215682	www.schoutenhandwerken.nl
Horst	t Schipperke	schoolstraat 6	schippertjehorst@hotnet.n	5961 EH	077 3981 975	www.schippertjehorst.com
Joure	Ajoure	Pastorielaan 2	www.ajoure.nl	8501 EZ	051/3413344	www.ajoure.nl
Kampen	Pingouin wol & handwerken	Oudestraat 20	pingouinkampen@uwnet.nl	8261 CP	038-3322811	
Koewacht	Wolboerderij Blij Bezuiden	Het Zand 61	info@wolboerderij.nl	4576 CB	114361402	www.wolboerderij.nl
Leeuwarden	Wereldwol	de Lauwers 2	info@wereldwol.nl	8939 BW	058/2881301	www.wereldwol.nl
Leiden	**Ribbels**	**Pieterskerk-Choorsteeg 18**	**annelies.danton@ribbels.nl**	**2311 TR**	**071 5133126**	**www.ribbels.nl**
Nieuwpoort	**De Schapekop**	**Hoogstraat 30**	**info@deschapekop.nl**	**2965 AL**	**0184-602678**	**www.deschapekop.nl**
Oldenzaal	Lohuis	Steenstraat 26	t.lohuis@planet.nl	7571 BK	05415-12626	www.lohuis-tijhuis.nl
Ridderkerk	Alpaca Milestone	Tarwestraat 1	info@alpacamilestones.nl	2989 AV	0786822444	
Rotterdam	Lydialaine	Goudsesingel 231 A	info@lydialaine.nl	3031 EK	010/4136697	www.lydialaine.nl
Sittard	**Wollstreet**	**Rijksweg Noord 61**	**info@wollstreet.nl**	**6131 CJ**	**0464-586330**	**www.wollstreet.nl**
Someren	Het Weverke	Molenstraat 24	info@weverke-someren.nl	5711EW	0493-492092	www.weverke-someren.nl
Utrecht	**Modilaine**	**Lijnmarkt 22**	**info@modelaine.nl**	**3511 KH**	**030-2328911**	**www.modilaine.nl**
Voorburg	De Breikorf	Koningin Julianalaan 274	info@debreikorf.nl	2274 JR	070 3871286	www.breikorf.nl
Woudsend	Hannah Tricotage	Carmelieterstraat, 6	hannahdh@zonet.nl	8551 RJ	031/514592343	
Zuidlaren	**Ryahuis**	**Telefoonstraat 26**	**info@ryahuis.nl**	**9471 EN**	**050-4092618**	**www.ryahuis.nl**

HONG KONG

	East Unity Company Ltd.	Unit B2, 7/F., Block B, Kailey Industrial Centre, 12 Fung Yip Street, Chai Wan		eastunityco@yahoo.com.hk		(852)2869 7110

ICELAND

Reykjavik	Rowan At Storkurinn	Laugavegur 59	storkurinn@storkurinn.is	101	551 8258	www.storkurinn.is
Reykjavik	**Storkurinn**	**Laugavegur 59**	**storkurinn@storkurinn.is**	**101**	**+354-5518258**	**www.storkurinn.is**

ITALY

MI	*Milano*	*Coats Cucirini srl (Distributor)*	*Viale Sarca n∞ 223*	*20126*	*0039 02636151*
AG	Menfi	Turturici Rosalba	VIA Santi Bivona 16	92013	
AG	Racalmuto	Agnello Maria Grazia	VIA Regina Margherita 7	92020	
AL	Casale Monferrato	La Bottega Della Lana	Via Bruna 4	15033	
AT	Asti	La Bottega Di Evelina	VIA Gioberti 62	14100	0141595579
BG	Clusone	Baretti SNC	Piazza uccelli 2O	24023	034621404
BG	Bergamo	Savoir Faire Di Secomandi Ugo	Via Corridoni 26M	24124	035361092
BG	Ponte Nossa	Il Filo Di Arianna-Dondoni Giovanni	Via Europa 119	24028	035 704334
BL	Cortina D'Ampezzo	La Cooperativa Di Cortina S.C.	Corso Italia 40	32043	0436861245
BO	Bologna	Casa della lana	Via augusto righi 19	40126	051227731
BO	Castel San Pietro	Molinari	VIA Matteotti 116	40024	051 6958688
BO	Imola	2 Colonne	VIA Emilia 61	40026	054225854
BO	Rastignano	Il Mondo Di Alice	Via A. Costa 45/G	40067	
BS	Castenedolo	Cdb Mercerie Di Casarotti A.	Via Brescia 65/67 C/O Cityper	25014	030 2131204
BS	Edolo	Fantasie Di Poli & C. Snc	Via Porro 42	25048	036471931
BS	Provaglio D'Iseo	L'Agoraio	VIA Fiume 8	25050	0306154578
BZ	Merano	Wolle Anita	VIA Galilei Str 10	39012	0473237025
BZ	Prato Allo Stelvio	Berger Gerda	Via Principale 59	39026	
CN	Cuneo	Mina Snc Di Garro Alberto & C.	Via Peveragno 4	12100	0171603941
CO	Como	La Merceria IMAC	VIA P.Carcano 15	22100	031260163
CO	Mozzate	Filofollia	VIA Rosselli 24	22076	0331831488
CR	Cremona	Mangiarotti Monica	Via Lamo 2	26100	
FC	Cesena	L'Ago E il Ditale	VIA Albertini 35	47023	0547610552
GE	Genova	Fonte Della Lana	Galata 27 R	16121	010562594
LE	Lecce	Aracne Di Negro Paola	Viale Giacomo Leopardi 41	73100	
LU	Lucca	L'Arcolaio	Piazza Cittadella 11	55100	0583580248
MI	Arese	Mapa SNC	Pzza 5 Giornate 6/D	20020	029383921
MI	Busnago	Il Filo Di Arianna	VIA Italia 157	20040	
MI	Milano	La Botteguccia Di Guzzon Elena	Via Lodovico Il Moro 129	20142	02 36554752
MI	Milano	Plana Merceria SNC	VIA Plana 43	20155	0233002241
MI	Milano	Tricots	Piazza Sienna 8	20146	024075777
MI	Paderno dugnano	Bigatti lana	VIA Roma 30/A	20037	
MN	Castiglione Delle Stiviere	Punti & Spunti Di Menta E. E A. Snc	Via Mazzini 14	46043	
MN	Mantova	Il Filo Di Usvardi Franca	Via Aldo Moro 10	46100	0376321637
MO	Carpi	Sala Lorena	Via Duomo 19	41012	059 8397656
MO	Modena	Diritto e rovescio	Largo s. Francesco 144	41121	0594555316
MS	Avenza	Maria Vittoria	VIA Campo D'Appio 12	54033	058552943
PA	Palermo	La Merceria Di Onofrio Srl	Via Sammartino 4 C/D	90141	0916852473
PD	Camposampiero	Boton e buseta s.a.s.	Via G.pascoli 2/B	35012	0495790302
PD	Este	Fanin lucia ''nonsolomerceria'	VIA G. Marconi 15	35042	0429602513
PD	Monselice	Rangon Chiara	VIA Zanellato 14	35043	042974417
PD	Noventa Padovana	Celin Marilena "1° Laboratorio"	Via Valmarana 49/C	35027	0498959126
PD	Padova	AKI SAS	Piazza dei signori 19	35139	049663818
PG	Gualdo Tadino	Bergamasco S.N.C. Di Radici P.	Via Roberto Calai 22	06023	075913254
PI	Pisa	Brico chic	VIA Delle belle torri 50	56127	
PR	Parma	Zuccheri SNC	VIA Mazzini 10/A	43121	0521281262
PV	Casorate Primo	Il Gomitolo D'Oro	VIA Salici 6	27022	
PV	Casteggio	Non Solo Lana Di Sensale Giacomina	Via Emilia 14	27045	0383 82386
PV	Pavia	Boutique Lana Ciotti Donatella	Via Mascheroni 18	27100	038223675
RE	Reggio Emilia	Iori & Pattacini S.A.S	Via Farini 1 Q	42100	0522432362
RE	Scandiano	Il Filo Di Arianna	VIA Garibaldi 9/C	42019	0522984736
RM	Roma	Capuani mariantonietta	Piazza della torretta 22	*00186	06 6871215
SI	Poggibonsi	Sul Filo Di Lana	Largo Gramsci 14	53036	0577 982110
SO	Regoledo di cosio valtellino	Emporio di lazzari federico	VIA Statale 8	23013	0342638150
SP	La spezia	Cerretti E C. SNC	Corso cavour 178	19122	0187735108
TN	Ledro - Mezzolago	Il Gomitolo	VIA Ptice 17	38060	
TN	Mezzolombardo	Punto Maglia & Cucito	C.SO Mazzini 36/A	38017	0461 603263
TO	Torino	La Compagnia Del Cotone	VIA Mazzini 44	10123	0118178381
TO	Torino	Wool Crossing Di Giudice Federica	Via Buniva 9	10124	011 2630927
TS	Trieste	Fonda Silva Sas	VIA Delle Torri 2	34122	040771717
TV	Treviso	Al Trionfo Tessuti & Confezioni	Piazza San Leonardo 7	31100	0422 547221
TV	Vedelago	Barrichello SAS	VIA montegrappa 28	31050	0423 700167
UD	Cervignano Del Friuli	Gama Snc	Via Xxiv Maggio 19/1	33052	0431 32753
UD	Udine	Elisa cesselli	VIA Savorgnana 18	33100	0432 295633
VB	Domodossola	Il Gomitolo	VIA Galletti 28	28845	

ITALY (cont)

VE	Jesolo Paese	Ago & filo	VIA Piave Vecchio 1/B		30016	0421952282	
VE	Portogruaro	Lane E Filati Graziella	VIA Mazzini 9		30026	042174808	
VE	Venezia	Pertile Marianna Macripe	Cannaregio 2629		30121	041 8228247	
VI	Thiene	Borgo Gisella 'La Stoffa'	Via Fogazzaro 66		36016	0445366150	
VR	Parona	Falcetto S.N.C. Di Righetti Laura E	Via Degli Arusnati 3		37025	045941091	
VR	Verona	Dritto e rovescio snc	Via rosa morando 32 a		37131		

JAPAN

Chiba	Chiba	Mitsukoshi Department Store	6F Mitsukoshi Bild., 2-6-1 Fujimi Cyuouku		260-8631	81-043-221-0515	
Hiroshima	Hiroshima	Puppy Hiroshima	8-16 kamihacchoubori, nakaku		730-0012	81-082-222-0537	
Hukuoka	Kitakyusyu	Izutsuya Department Store	2-4 igashiko , Kokurakitaku		803-0802	81-093-522-2729	
Hyogo	Kobe	Union Wool	1-30-22 Kitanagasadori, Chuouku	union@smile.ocn.ne.jp	650-0012	81-078-331-8854	
Japan	Osaka	room amie	3-11-8-109Yamate-cho, Suita-city	info@roomamie.jp	564-0073	06-6821-3717	http://roomamie.jp
Osaka	Osaka	Hankyu Department Store	8-7 kakudacho, Kitaku		530-8350	81-06-6313-8938	
Osaka	Osaka	Masuzakiya	4-5-4 Kawaramachi, Chuouku		541-0048	81-06-6222-1110	
Tokyo	Tokyo	Mitsubaya	1-1-1 Minamiaoyama, Minatoku		107-0062	81-03-3404-1677	
Tokyo	Tokyo	Mitsukoshi Department Store	Hobby & Craft Salon 8F Mitsukoshi New Bild., 1-4-1 Nihonbashi Chuouku		103-8001	81-03-3273-6500	
Tokyo	Tokyo	Puppy Shimokitazawa	2-26-4 Kitazawa, Setagayaku		155-0031	81-03-3468-0581	

KOREA

Seoul	*Seocho-Gu*	*Coats Korea Co. Lt (Distributor)*	*5F Telcom B/D, 935-40 Bangbae-Dong*	*rozenpark@coats.com*	*137-844*	*82-2-521-6262*	*www.coats.com*
Seoul	Jongno-Gu	Danju	1F, 65-4 Samcheongro 110-230	jade@danju.co.kr	110-200	82-2-720-1127	www.danju.co.kr
Seoul	Jongno-Gu	My Knit Studio	3F, 144 Kwanhoon-Dong	myknit@mykint.com	110-300	82-2-722-0006	www.myknit.com

LEBANON

	Beirut	y.knot	Saifi Village, Mkhalissiya Street 162	y.knot@cyberia.net.lb		(961) 1 992211	

LUXEMBOURG

Luxembourg	ESCH s/ALZETTE	Ouvrages Elisabeth	Rue S. Bolivar 29	hansen_elisabeth@yahoo.de	4037	00352 26 53 27 86	
Luxembourg	Luxembourg	Bastel Kiste	Rue Du Fort Elisabeth 17-19	mail@bastelkiste.lu	1463	00352/40 05 06	www.bastelkiste.lu

MEXICO

Mexico	Monterrey	Estambres Crochet SA de CV	Aaron Saenz 1891-7, PO Box Santamaria		64650	+52 (81) 8335-3870	
Mexico City	Cd. Satelite	Crochet Satelite	Pafnuncio Padilla 47			+52 (55) 5374-3167	
Mexico City	Col. Jardines del Pedregal		Crochet Pedregal, Plaza Santa Teresa, Periferico Sur		4020	+52 (55) 5652-0694	
Mexico City	Col. Polanco	Crochet Masaryk	Pasaje Polanco, Masaryk		360	+52 (55) 5280-5385	
Monterrey	Col. Cumbres	Crochet Cumbres	Plaza Milenium, Paseo de los Leones		2968	+52 (81) 1167-0992	
Monterrey	Col. Del Valle	Crochet Valle	Plaza Las Palmas, Gomez Morin		911-7	+52 (81) 8335-2980	

NEW ZEALAND

Christchurch	*Belfast*	*ACS New Zealand (Distributor)*	*1 March Place*			*64-3-323-6665*	
Auckland		Alterknitives	PO Box 47961			(64 9) 376 0337	
Aukland		Wild & Woolly	38 Victoria Road	wildandwoollyyarns@gmail.com		09 445 3255	
Christchurch		Knit World	189 Peterborough St			03 379 2300	
Nelson		Creations Unlimited	118 Hardy Street	creations@jasnelson.co.nz		03 548 4297	
Northland	Kaiwaka	The Apple Basket	1914 State Highway 1	applebasketquilts@xtra.co.nz		09 4312 443	
Northland		Twinset and Pearls	Elizabeth Street	twinsetandpearls@clear.net.nz		09 425 7246	
Taupo		Fabryx	Unit 5a, 29 Totara Street			07 376 7494	
Tauranga		Tauranga Knitting Centre	8/152 11th Avenue	tgaknitcentre@hotmail.com		07 571 8892	
Wellington	Cuba Mall	Knit World	Shop 210b, Left Bank			04 385 1918	

NORWAY

Bergen	*Ulset*	*Coats Knappehuset AS*	*Pb 100*		*5873*	*0047 55 53 93 00*	
Arendal		Blad Trad	Harebakksenteret,	blatrad@online.no	4846	37 03 64 33	
Bryne		**Idestova a/s Bryne**	**Arne Garborgs veg 15**	**anny@idestova.no**	**4370**	**99 29 30 03**	**www.idestova.no**
Dombås		Tusenogen Tråd	Dombås Senter		2660	61 24 16 50	
Drammen		Ulla Garn & Broderi	Sankt Olavsgate 2	butikk@ullgarn.no	3018	32 89 00 58	www.ullagarn.no
Ejve		Garn & Lysstua A/S	Nils Hegelandsveg		4735	37 93 06 46	
Grimstad		**Broderihjørnet Huslidstua**	**Storgata 32**	**Husflidstua@live.no**	**4876**	**37 04 89 14**	
Heimdal		Quiltegården A/S	Heimdalsvn. 3a	siw@quiltegaarden.com	7080	(+047) 72 58 67 37	
Horten		Flittig Lise Horten	Apotekergaten 16	flittiglise@c2i.net	3187	33 04 60 55	
Jessheim		**Ull og Saker**	**Jessheim Storsenter**	**post@ullogsaker.no**	**2050**	**(+047) 63973474**	
Kongsberg		**Strikkestua Kongsberg**	**Kongsberg**	**tkolseth@online.no**	**3616**	**32 73 23 12**	
Kragero		Strikk Inom	Sannidalsv. 196		3770	35 98 03 40	www.strikkinom.no
Kristiansand		**Langfeldt Garn**	**H.Wergwlandsgt. 21-23**		**4612**	**38 02 20 29**	
Laksevåg		Pinsvin Design	Lyngboveien 160	kontakt@pinnsvinsdesign.no	5164	92370912	www.pinnsvindesign.no
Nittedal	Mosenteret	H.P. Kjærvik		hpkj@online.no	1482	(+047) 90 13 24 30	
Oslo		Ariadne Garn	Lilleakervn 16		0283	22 73 06 20	
Oslo		Linderud Garn og Hobby	Linderud Senter		0594	22 64 49 94	
Oslo		Nøstet Mitt	Tveita Senter		0671	22 75 50 65	
Oslo		Nøstet Mitt	Lambertseter Senter		1150	23 38 22 20	
Oslo		**Nøstet Mitt**	**Storo Senter**	**henille@gmail.no**	**0485**	**(+47) 48 06 66 63**	
Oslo		Nye Sømsenteret A/S	Akersgt. 8	oslo@somsenteret.no	0158	(+47) 22 41 35 69	
Oslo		Strikkeriet	Stilla Senter	iren@strikkeriet.no	0491	22 95 78 13	www.strikkeriet.no
Oslo		**Tjorven Garn og Gaver**	**Valkyriegt. 17**	**tina@tjorven.no**	**0366**	**22 69 33 60**	**www.tjorven.no**
Sandnes		Kreaaktiv	Kvadrat Kjøpesenter	kreaktiv-kvadrat@quiltebutikken.com	4301	51960155	
Sarpsborg		Sarpsborg Garn og Broderi	Jernbanegaten 13	post@sarpsborg.no	1706	69 15 27 60	
Ski		Trine Sv og Strikk	Idretsveien 6	post@trinestrikk.no	3018	64 87 25 68	
Skien		Strikkepinnen Skien	Ulefossveien 26	opgons@online.no	3730	35 52 72 21	
Tromsø		Bundingen	Heilovn 4	bundingen@bundingen.no	9015	(+047) 95835525	
Trondheim		**Quiltegården A/S**	**Dronningensgt. 23**	**siw@quiltegaarden.com**	**7012**	**(+047) 73 52 98 08**	
Vestby		Bryggerhuset	Nordbyvn 2	eombudstvedt@gmail.com	1540	(+47) 64 95 08 57	
	Asker	Garnstua Asker	Knud Askersvei		1383	66 78 19 86	www.garnstua.no
	Bergen	**Norwegian Spirit**	**Seiersbjerget 4**	**anne@norwegian-spirit.com**	**5022**	**48123799**	**www.norwegian-spirit.com**
	Lillehammer	Uldvaren	Lillehammer	post@uldvaren.no	2609	(+47) 61250844	
	Moss	Strikkedilla Moss a/s	Th.Petersonsgate 12	kontakt@strikkedilla-moss.no	1530	(+47) 69255282	
	Oslo	Bentes Boutique	Gjovikgt. 1		0470	22 18 26 39	
	Sandvika	Stoffhjørnet	Engervannsveien 39	maia__55@hotmail.com	1337	(+47) 40241556	
	Ski	**Trine Sy og Strikk**	**Idretsveien 6**	**post@trinestrikk.no**	**1400**	**64872568**	

PORTUGAL

Portugal	*Vila Nova de Gaia*	*Coats & Clark (Distributor)*	*Quinta de Cravel, Apartado 444*		*4431-968*	*223770700*	*www.coatscrafts.com.pt*
Portugal	Funchal	Eduardo G. Luiz & Fª (Coats & Clark agent in Madeira)	Av. De Zarco, 22, Cx. Postal 155		9002	291201990	
Portugal	Ponta Delgada	Eduardo J. Moura (Coats & Clark agent in Azores)	R. Arcanjo Lar, Cave. Apartado 182		9500	296284341	
Portugal	Porto	Ovelha Negra	Rua da ConceiÃ,,o, 100		4050-214	+351 220935847	www.ovelha-negra.com

RUSSIA

	Moscow	*Cityarn*	*Roll Holl, office 312a, Holodil'nyi pereulok, 3*	*info@cityarn.ru*	*115191*	*007 (495) 933-87-98*	*www.cityarn.ru*
	Irkutsk	Tanzanite	Kooperativnyi pereulok, 2	tanza-knit@mail.ru	664011	007 (3952) 72-15-02	www.tanza-knit.ru
	Moscow	Triskeli	Ostankino Red, 2 floor, 24-26, 1-ya Ostankinskaya, 53	triskeli@triskeli.ru	129515	007 (495) 926-88-64	www.triskeli.ru
	Moscow	Triskeli	Taganskaya, 31/22	triskeli@triskeli.ru	109147	007 (926) 779-96-70	www.triskeli.ru

SINGAPORE

Singapore		*Golden Dragon Store (Distributor)*	*101 Upper Cross St. #02-51, Peopleis Park Centre*	*gdscraft@hotmail.com*	*058357*	*(65) 65358454 /65358234*	

SOUTH AFRICA

South Africa	*Johannesburg*	*Arthur Bales Ltd (Distributor)*	*62 Fourth Avenue, Linden*	*arthurb@new.co.za*	*2195*	*(27) 118 882 401*	*www.arthurbales.co.za*

SPAIN

Barcelona		*Coats Fabra, SA (Distributor)*	*Sant Adrià, 20*	*atencion.clientes@coats.com*	*08030*	*(34) 93 290 84 00*	*www.coatscrafts.es*
Álava	Vitoria-Gasteiz	LOG CABIN	C/ Manuel Iradier, Pza. Iglesia del Carmen	logcabin.vitoria@gmail.com	1005	(+34) 945142430	
Barcelona	Badalona	Montserrat Mata	Maria Cristina 11		8912	(34) 93 3832657	
Barcelona	Vilassar De Mar	Iulia Komarova	Enric Granados 153				www.lanadeioulia.com
Barcelona		Club de la Aguja	Ganduxer 72		08021	(34) 93 4143815	
Barcelona		El Corte Inglés Barcelona	Plaza Catalunya 14		8002		
Barcelona		Lanas RodrIguez	Providencia 130		8024	(34) 93 2196970	
Barcelona		MercerIa Santana	Avda. Portal de l'Angel, 26		8002	(34) 933020948	
Barcelona		Oyambre	Pau Claris 145		08009	(34) 93 4872672	
Bilbao		El Corte Inglés Bilbao	Gran Via 9		48001		
Eibar	Guipuzcoa	Artile	Bidebarrieta 18		20600	(34) 94 3207227	www.artilepunto.com
La Coruña		El Corte Inglés Coruña	Ramón y Cajal SN		15006		
La Rioja	Logroño	MJ Patchwork	Duques de Najera, 2		26002	(34) 94 1585222	www.mjpatchwork.com
Madrid	Alcobendas	ISABEL PRIETO	Pº Alcobendas, 10 (C.C. Bulevar)		28109		
Madrid		El club de labores	Infanta Ma Teresa 11	clubdelabores@gmail.com	28016	(+34) 913441068	www.clubdelabores.com
Madrid		El Corte Inglés Madrid Castellana	Raimundo Fernandez Villaverde 79		28003	(34) 91 418 88 00	
Madrid		El Corte Inglés Madrid Preciados	Calle Preciados nº3		28013	(34) 91 3798000	
Madrid		Inke Labores S.L	Don Ramón de la Cruz, 47		28001	(34) 91 5762847	
Palma de Mallorca		El Corte Inglés Palma Mallorca - Roselló	Alexandre Roselló 12 (suc.23)		7002	(34) 971770177	
Pamplona		La Chica de las lanas	San Miguel, 5		31001	(34) 948221684	
Valladolid	Renedo de Esgueva	Tira del ovillo	RosalIa de Castro 32		47170	(34) 686361083	www.tiradelovillo.com
Zaragoza		El Corte Inglés Zaragoza	Pº Sagasta 3		50008		

SWEDEN

	Dalsjöfors	*Coats Expotex AB (Distributor)*	*Stationsvägen 2*		*S-516 21*	*(46) 33 720 79 00*	
	Åhus	PP CO i Åhus	Gamla Skeppsbron 10	kristina@ppco.se	296 31	044-240521	

SWEDEN (cont)

Almunge	Garngalleriet	Mogavägen 25	angeli.holmstedt@telia.com	740 10	0708-490483	
∫lvsjö	ZigZag	Långsjövägen 25	bergqvist.katarina@telia.com	125 30	070-5713309	
Arvika	Garnmoster	Hamngatan 5	info@garnmoster.se	671 31	0570-124 40	www.garnmoster.se
Bollebygd	Nedergården	Stationsvägen 12	nedergardensgarn@telia.com	517 35	(033) 28 94 28	www.nedergardens.com
Boras	Stickat och Klart	Hallbergsgatan 2	kristina.karlson@hotmail.com	503 30	(033) 10 32 38	
Borlänge	Kecathu AB	Målaregatan 12 B	k.thunmarker@telia.com	784 33	0243-221057	
Degerberga	Hemslojdsboden	Tingsvagen 23	lina@hemslojdsboden.com	297 31	(044) 350262	www.hemslojdsboden.com
Goteborg	2 Knit	Bondegatan 7	info@2knit.se	416 65	(031) 199080	www.2knit.se
Goteborg	Strikk	Vallgatan 23	info@strikkdesign.com	411 16	(031) 711 37 99	www.strikkdesign.com
Göteborg	Garnfabriken	Linnegatan 3	johansson-ingalill@hotmail.com	413 04	0704-802772	
Haljarp	Hedenskougs Garnhorna	Olofstorpsvagen 25		261 72	(0418) 430485	
Helsingborg	Tant Thea AB	Möllegränden 15	info@tantthea.se	252 23	(042) 13 51 53	www.tantthea.se
Hörby	Garnverandan	Gamla Torg 5	info@garnverandan.se	242 31	0415-311300	
Hudiksvall	Tyghuset Manuffen	Storgatan 23	manuffen@telia.com	824 30	0650-101 98	
Jönköping	Garnshopen	Klostergatan 64	astrid@astridknitting.se	553 35	0735-200485	www.astridknitting.se
Kristianstad	HelYlle	Ostra Storgatan 51	eva.martinsson@helylle.se	291 31	(044) 353250	www.helylle.se
Linköping	Garnverket	Storgatan 54	johanna@garnverket.se	582 28	013-139509	www.garnverket.com
Ludvika	Syosticka.se	Storgatan 34 A	info@syosticka.se	771 30		
Lund	Slandan	Lilla Fiskaregatan 1	slandan@telia.com	222 22	046 128077	www.slandaninlund.se
Malmo	Irmas Hus	Kalendegatan 13	annkarin@irmashus.se	211 35	(040) 611 08 00	www.irmashus.se
Malmö	Malmö Centralmagasin	Lilla Ostergatan 36	ingela@ystad.se	271 34	0411-552270	
Orebro	Trend Tyg & Garn	Köpmangatan 9	trend-tyg-garn@hotmail.com	702 10	019-103055	
Sigtuna	Knocks	Stora Gatan 35	info@knocks.se	193 30	08-59251010	
Stockholm	Garnverket	Hantverkargatan 14	lena@garnverket.se	112 21	(08) 651 78 08	www.garnverket.com
Stockholm	NK Tyg & Sy	Regeringsgatan 55	sidencarlson@swipnet.se	111 77	08-7628850	
Stockholm	Sticka by Marie Viktoria	Osterlanggatan 20	marievictoria@gmail.com	111 31	(08)21 18 31	www.knitting.se
Stockholm	**Wincentgarner**	**Norrtullsgatan 27**	**butik.wincent@gmail.com**	**113 27**	**(08) 33 70 60**	**www.wincentgarner.se**
Sundsvall	Garnkorgen	Klackvagen 17	info@garnkorgen.se	856 53	(060) 124 501	www.garnkorgen.se
Taby	Trasselgarn & Broderi	Stationsvagen 16	info@trassel.se	187 30	(08) 638 00 59	www.trassel.se
Umea	Hemflit	Kungsgatan 51	eva@hemflit.com	903 26	(090) 77 03 84	www.hemflit.se
Uppsala	Yll & Tyll	Bredgrand 7c	info@yllotyll.com	753 20	(018) 10 51 90	www.yllotyll.com
Vadstena	Vadstena Ull & Garn	Krigsberga 106		592 91	0143-20149	
Vasteras	Upplings Garn	Kungsgatan 2	info@upplings.se	722 11	(021) 13 00 94	
Västerhaninge	Mia's Garn & Färgstudio	Bokstigen 3	mia@miasgarnstudio.se	137 34	08-40011891	
Växjö	Umbra Stickspår	Sandgårdsgatan 12b	info@umbra.nu	352 30	0470-777901	
Vaxsjo	Umbra	Batmanstorget 2	info@umbra.nu	352 80	46470777901	
Vellinge	Vellinge Garnhörna	Ostergatan 4	monaalm@hotmail.com	235 33	040-42 44 05	

SWITZERLAND

Untersiggenthal AG	*Coats Stroppel AG (Distributor)*			*5300*	*00800 26272800*	
Aarau	**Mode + Wolle**	**Graben 30**	**bpeter@mode-wolle.ch**	**5000**	**0041/628246611**	
Aigle	Brin de Laine	Mme Sylviane Mosimann, Rue du Bourg 12		1860	024 466 61 84	
Arlesheim	Lana Moda	Obere Holle 25	tschanz.verena@intergga.ch	4144	0041/61 703 92 59	
Bad Zurzach	Mercerie-Handarbeiten	H. Frick, Hauptstr. 60		5330	056 249 13 10	
Basel	Zum Roten Faden	Steinenring 41		4051	079 919 71 87	
Bern	**WollWirrWare**	**Astrid Balli, Wylestrasse 53**	**info@wollwirrware.ch**	**3014**	**0041/31332 06 33**	**www.wollwirrware.ch**
Biel	Tasche & Masche	Ariane Fischer, Schmiedengasse 13	tasche@tascheundmasche.ch	2502	032 322 26 12	
Buchs	Wollig-Anstalt	Ingrid Näscher, Gr‚naustr. 17		9470	081/ 756 36 19	
Cham	Strickstrack	Knonauerstrasse 19	info@strickstrack.ch	6330	078 764 07 07	
Chur	Wollenhof	Y. Magnin, Bahnhofstr. 20		7000	081 252 13 84	
Erlinsbach	Fadegrad	Cécile Blattner, Hauptstr. 12	info@collection-cecile.ch	5018	062/844 05 40	www.collection-cecile.ch
Fulenbach	Wulle-Egge	Dorfstrasse 19	info@atelier-aebi.ch	4629	062 926 28 53	
GenÈve 28	Elna SA Centre Balexert	Av. Louis-Casai 27		1211	022 884 86 66	
Grabs	RTK Fashion	M‚hlebachstr. 9		9472	079 646 78 81	
Heiden	Bettina Gantenbein	Vorderbrenden 365 , Poststr. 9	be.gantenbein@bluewin.ch	9410		
Hölstein	Wullest‚bli Hölstein	Dora Huber, Hauptstr. 19		4434	061 951 19 53	
Klosters	Mystitch Strickcafe	Aeussere Bahnhofstrasse 1		7250	081 422 62 32	
Lausanne	Boutique la Marcerie	rue Mercerie 3		1003	021 312 07 44	
Lugano	Il Filo di Penelope	Dina Ducoli, Via Trevano 58		6900	079 262 17 04	
Luzern	Naturel	M‚ller A., Habsburgerstr. 33		6003	041/210 65 41	
Muri	Stoff-und Wullehuesli	Markstrasse 17	wullehuesli@bluewin.ch	5630	056 664 41 20	
Pratteln	Zur Masche	M. Brunner, Burggartenstr. 3		4133	061 821 51 11	
Romanshorn	Strick-IN	Aleestrasse 44		8590	071 463 68 18	
Schoeftland	Mercerie	Vontobel Maya, Dorfstrasse 19		5040	062 721 00 80	
Signy-Centre	Passé Présent	Gabriele Fiachetti, Centre Commercial Signy		1274	022 361 18 45	
Sirnach	Wullwerk	Fischingerstr. 26		8370	071 960 06 90	
St. Gallen	Boutique Tonja Mode mit Wolle	Vadianstrasse 22		9000	071 223 12 71	
Steffisburg	Hinkel Pinkel Folmer Winkel	Thunstr. 57	mfolmer@bluewin.ch	3612	033/437 08 80	
Teufen	Presto-Lana	Sammelbuehldtrasse 11		9053	071 335 75 55	
Thun	we love wool	Charlotte Schmid, Obere Hauptgasse 25	charlotteschmid@gmx.ch	3600	033 222 54 46	
Uster	Fallmasche GmbH	Poststrasse 6		8610	044 942 38 58	
Visp	Web and Wollstube	Kantonsstrasse 14	web-wollstube@bluewin.ch	3930	027 946 47 06	
Weinfelden	Wollring	Rathausstrasse 14		8570	071 622 19 27	
Wettingen	Lana LunaÖmehr als Wolle	Landstrasse 28	info@lanaluna.ch	5430	056 430 00 26	
Zofingen	Blum Handarbeiten	Rathausgasse 17		4800	062 751 36 04	
Zurich	Hand-Art	Neumarkt 10		8001	0041/4455757	
Zurich	**Vilfil**	**Kreuzstrasse 39, Beim Kreuzplatz**	**office@vilfil.com**	**8032**	**0041/443839903**	**www.vilfil.com**
Chur	Tartaruga	Reichsgasse 52	mail@tartaruga-design.ch	7000		

TAIWAN

Taiwan, R.O.C.	*Taipei*	*Cactus Quality Co. Ltd (Distributor)*	*7FL-2, No. 140, Sec.2 Roosevelt Rd*	*cqcl@ms17.hinet.net*	*10084*	*00886-2-23656527*	*www.excelcraft.com.tw*

THAILAND

Bangkok		*Global Wide Trading (Distributor)*	*10 Lad Prao Soi 88*	*TheNeedleWorld@yahoo.com / global.wide@yahoo.com*	*10310*	*00 662 933 9019*	

UNITED STATES OF AMERICA

South Carolina	*Greer*	*Westminster Fibers (Distributor)*	*8 Shelter Drive*	*info@westminsterfibers.com*	*29650*	*(800) 445-9276*	*www.westminsterfibers.com*
Florida	**Sarasota**	**A Good Yarn**	**7668 South Tamiami Trail**		**34231**	**941-487-7914**	
Alabama	Birmingham	In The Making	3108 Heights Village		35243	(205) 298 1309	
Alaska	**Anchorage**	**Far North Yarn Co**	**2636 Spenard Road, Ste 6**		**99503**	**(907) 258 5648**	**www.farnorthyarnco.com**
Arizona	**Scottsdale**	**Jessica Knits**	**10401 East McDowell Mountain Ranch Road #7**		**85255**	**(480) 515 4454**	**www.jessicaknits.com**
California	Clio	Wolly Notions	7580 Hwy 89, Suite 18	woollynotions@psln.com	96106	530-836-1680	
California	Eureka	Northcoast Knittery	320 2nd Street	info@northcoastknittery.com	95501	707 442-9276	
California	Long Beach	Alamitos Bay Yarn Company	174 MARINA DRIVE		90803	562-799-8484	www.yarncompany.com
California	**Los Altos**	**Uncommon Threads**	**293 State Street**		**94022**	**650-941-1815**	**www.uncommonthreadsyarn.com**
California	Napa	Yarns on First	1305 First Street	marcieschwartz@gmail.com	94559	707 257-1363	
California	Petaluma	Knitterly	1 Fourth St		94952	707-762-9276	
California	**San Francisco**	**Imagiknit**	**3897 18th Street**	**imagiknit@sbcglobal.net**	**94114**	**415-621-6642**	**www.imagiknit.com**
California	**Santa Barbara**	**Cardigan's**	**3030 State Street, Suite A**	**pams@cardigansknits.com**	**93105-3304**	**805-569-0531**	
California	Santa Cruz	The Golden Fleece Inc.	317 Potrero Street, Suite D		95060	831 426-1425	
California	Santa Monica	Compatto Yarn Salon	2112 Wilshire Blvd		90403	310-453-2130	
Colorado	**Denver**	**Lamb Shoppe**	**3512 E 12th Ave**		**80206**	**(303) 322-2223**	
Colorado	Fort Collins	Lambspun of Colorado	1101 E Lincoln Ave		80524	(800) 558 5262	
Connecticut	Windsor	Creative Fibers LLC	645A Poquonock Avenue, PO Box 69		94559	860 687-9931	
Connecticut	Woodbridge	The Yarn Barn	1666 Litchfield Tpk		06525	(203)389-5117	
Distric of Columbia	**Washington**	**Looped Yarn Works**	**2510 Upton St SW**		**20010**	**202-714-5667**	
Florida	Belleair Bluffs	Flying Needles	2933 W Bay Drive		33770	727-581-8691	
Florida	Coral Gables	The Knitting Garden	2716 Ponce De Leon Blvd.	administrator@theknittinggarden.org	33134	305-774-1060	
Florida	Tampa	Knit 'N' Knibble	4027 S. Dale Mabry Hwy		33611	(813)837-5648	www.knitnknibble.com
Georgia	**Roswell**	**Cast On Cottage**	**Coleman Village, 860 Marietta Hwy**		**30075**	**(770) 998-3483**	**www.castoncottage.com**
Georgia	Woodstock	The Whole Nine Yarns	8226 Main Street		30188	(678) 494-5242	
Illinois	**Downers Grove**	**Knitche Inc**	**5150-B Main St**		**60515**	**(630) 852-5648**	
Illinois	**Galena**	**Fiber Wild**	**304 South Main Street**	**info@fiberwild.com**	**61036**	**815-777-3550**	**www.fiberwild.com**
Illinois	**Northbrook**	**Three Bags Full**	**1927 Cherry lane**		**60062**	**(847) 291-9933**	
Illinois	ST. CHARLES	Wool and Company	107A WEST MAIN ST		60175	630-444-0480	
Indiana	**Bremen**	**Broad Ripple Knits**	**3794 E Third Rd**		**46506**	**(317)255-0540**	
Indiana	**Indianapolis**	**Knit Stop**	**3941 East 82nd Street**		**46240**	**(317) 595-5648**	**www.knit-stop.com**
Indiana	**Indianapolis**	**Mass Avenue Knit Shop**	**862 Virginia Avenue**	**massaveknitship@ameritech.net**	**46203**	**317-638-1833**	
Indiana	**Newburgh**	**The Village Knitter**	**8A West Jennings St.**	**dociaknits@yahoo.com**	**47630**	**812-842-2360**	
Iowa	**West Des Moines**	**Knitted Together**	**7450 Bridgewood Blvd, SUITE #225**	**info@knittedtogether.com**	**50266**	**(515) 222-9276**	
Kansas	**Lawrence**	**The Yarn Barn**	**930 Mass Ave.**		**66044**	**(800) 468-0035**	**www.YarnBarn-ks.com**
Kentucky	Bowling Green	Crafty Hands	2910B Scottsville Road	craftyhands@bellsouth.net	42104	270-846-4865	
Kentucky	Lexington	Magpie	513 East High Street		40502	(859)455-7437	
Louisiana	Lafayette	The Vermilion Bay Yarn Co.	221 Verot School Road, Suite 283	japenningtonla@yahoo.com	70508	337-216-4564	
Maine	**Freeport**	**Grace Robinson & Co**	**208 US Rte 1, Ste 1**		**04032**	**(207) 865-6110**	**www.yarnandneedlepoint.com**
Maine	Glenburn	Essentially Felt Studio & Fine Yarns	865 Pushaw Road	info@essentiallyfelt.com	4401	207-942-0365	
Maryland	**Baltimore**	**Woolworks**	**6117 Falls Rd**		**21209**	**(410) 377-2060**	
Maryland	Bethesda	Knit & Stitch - Bliss	4706 Bethesda Ave		20814	301 652-8688	www.knitandstitch.com
MARYLAND	**LEONARDSTOWN**	**CRAZY FOR EWE,**	**22715 WASHINGTON STREET**		**20650**		
Maryland	**Rockville**	**Royal Yarns**	**404 Barnside Place**	**service@royalyarns.com**	**20850**	**(202)215-230**	**www.royalyarns.com**
Maryland	Rockville	Woolwinders	404 King Farm Blvd		20874	240-632-9276	
Massachusetts	Boston	Windsor Button	35 Temple Place		02111	(617) 482-4969	
Massachusetts	**Lenox**	**Colorful Stitches**	**48 Main St**		**01240**	**(800) 413-6111**	**www.colorful-stitches.com**
Massachusetts	Lexington	Wild & Woolly Studio	7A Meriam St	wwoolly@aol.com	02420	(781) 861-7717	
Massachusetts	**Northampton**	**Webs**	**75 Service Center Road**		**01060**	**(413)584-2225**	**www.yarn.com**
Massachusetts	Salem	Seed Stitch Fine Yarn	21 Front Street		01970	(978)744-5557	
Massachusetts	Winchester	Another Yarn	600 Main Street	distrib@anotheryarn.com	1890	781-570-2134	
Michigan	ADA	Clever Ewe	590 Ada Drive SE		49301	616 682-1545	
Michigan	Macomb	Crafty Lady Trio, Inc.	15401 Hall Road		48044-3840	586-566-8008	
Michigan	Northville	Center Street Knits	111 N Center St		48167	(248)349-6700	
Michigan	**Royal Oak**	**Ewe-nique Knits**	**515 South Lafayette Ave**		**48067**	**248 584-3001**	
Minnesota	Excelsior	Lakeside Yarn	347 Water Street	info@lakesideyarn.com	10024	212-787-5896	
Minnesota	Mahtomedi	Lila and Claudine's	86 Mahtomedi Avenue	lilaandclaudines@qwestoffice.net	55115	651-429-9551	
Minnesota	**Maple Grove**	**Amazing Threads**	**11262 86th Ave**		**55369**	**(763) 391-7700**	
Minnesota	**Mendota Heights**	**3 Kittens Needle Arts**	**750 Main Street, Suite 112**	**laura@3kittensneedlearts.com**	**55118**	**651-457-4969**	
Minnesota	Minneapolis	Needlework Unlimited	4420 Drew Ave S		55410	(612) 925-2454	www.needleworkunlimited.com
Minnesota	**St Paul**	**The Yarnery KMK Crafts**	**840 Grand Ave**		**55105**	**(651) 222-5793**	**www.yanery.com**
Minnesota	Stillwater	Darn Knit Anyway	423 South Main Street, Ste. 423B		55082	612 963-9056	
Minnesota	White Bear Lake	A Sheepy Yarn Shoppe, Inc.,	2185 3rd Street		55110	651 426-5463	
Montana	Billings	Purl Yarn Boutique	1001 Shiloh Crossing Blvd.		59102	406 652-4876	
Nebraska	**Omaha**	**Personal Threads Boutique**	**8600 Cass Street**		**68114**	**402 391-7733**	**www.personalthreads.com**
Nevada	**Reno**	**Jimmy Beans Wool**	**1312 Capital Blvd, Ste 103**		**89502**	**(775) 827-9276**	**www.jimmybeanswool.com**
New Hampshire	**Center Harbor**	**Keepsake Quilting**	**12 Main Street**	**bnadeau@keepsakequilting.com**	**03226-1618**	**603-253-8148**	**www.keepsakequilting.com**
New Jersey	Basking Ridge	Down Cellar	25 South Finley Ave		07920	(908) 766-2300	
New Jersey	Madison	The Blue Purl	92 Green Ave		07940	(973)377-5648	
New York	East Rochester	The Village Yarn & Fiber	350 West Commercial St		14445	(585)586-5470	
New York	Farmingdale	Infinite Yarns Inc.	34 Hemtstead Turnpike 3B		11735	516 293-0010	
New York	**Hampton Bays**	**Hampton Knitting Yarn**	**14 Carter Road**	**kathleen@hamptonknittingyarns.com**	**11946**	**(631)728-4792**	**www.hamptonknittingyarn.com**

New York	Ithaca	Knitting Etc	2255 North Triphammer Rd		14850	(607) 277-1164	
New York	Jamesville	YARN CUPBOARD	6487 East Seneca Turnpike		13087	315 399-5148	
New York	Montauk	Purl by the Sea, Inc.	649 Montauk Hwy		11954	631 668-7875	
New York	New York City	Knitty City	208 W 79th Street		10024	(212) 787-5896	
New York	Sayville	Rumpelstiltskin	22 Main Street		11782	(631)750-1790	
New York	Staten Island	The Naked Sheep	4038 Victory Blvd.	tracy@nakedsheepyarn.com	10314	718-477-9276	
New York	White Plains	Scarsdale Sticks & String	104 Smith Avenue	scarsdaleknits@gmail.com	10605	914-723-5478	
North Carolina	Chapel Hill	Yarns Etc	99 S Elliott Rd, Ste 2		27514	(919) 928-8810	
North Carolina	Raleigh	Great Yarns	1208 Ridge Rd		27607	(919)832-3599	
North Carolina	Swansboro	The Salty Sheep	101-4 Church Street	thesaltysheep@gmail.com	28584	910-325-0018	
Ohio	Cincinnati	HANK YARN LLC	2651 Observatory Avenue,nSuite 101		45208	513 386-9869	
Ohio	Cleveland	Fine Points	12620 Larchmere Blvd		44120	(216) 229-6644	www.shopfinepoints.com
Ohio	Columbus	Knitter's Mercantile	214 Graceland Blvd	jan@knittersmercantile.com	43214	614-888-8551	www.knittersmercantile.com
Ohio	Dublin	TEMPTATIONS	35 South High Street		43017	614-734-0618	
Ohio	Granville	Wisp	224 E. Broadway		43023		
Ohio	Pickerington	Yarn Market	12936 Stonecreek Dr, unit D		43147	(888) 996-9276	www.yarnmarket.com
Oklahoma	Tulsa	Loops	2042 Utica Sq		74114	(918) 742-9276	www.loopsknitting.com
Oklahoma	Tulsa	Loops	8274 South Memorial	south@loopsknitting.com	74133	918-850-6100	
Oregon	Ashland	The Web-Sters	11 North Main St		97520	(800) 482-9801	www.yarnatwebsters.com
Oregon	Beaverton	For Yarn Sake	11679 SW Beaverton		97005	(503)469-9500	
Oregon	Portland	Knit Purl	1101 SW Alder		97205	(503) 227-2999	www.knit-purl.com
Oregon	Portland	Knitting Bee	18305 NW West Union Rd		97229	(503)439-3316	
Pennsylvania	Grove City	Wolf Creek Yarns	112 Blair Street	wolfcreekyarns@zoominternet.net	16127	724-458-5290	
Pennsylvania	Mcmurray	Bloomin Yarns	3323 Washington Rd, Ste 102		15317	(724) 942-1025	
Pennsylvania	New Hope	Twist Knitting & Spinning	6220 Lower York Road		18938	(215) 862-8075	
Pennsylvania	Newtown Square	Slip Knot	3719 W Chester Pike		19073	(610) 359-9070	
Pennsylvania	Philadelphia	Loop (Yarn)	1914 South Street	stitch@spoolsewing.com	19146	215 545-0755	
Pennsylvania	Pittsburgh	Dyed In The Wool	3458 Babcock Blvd		15237	(412)364-0310	
Pennsylvania	Pittsburgh	Knit One	2721 Murray Avenue		15217	412-421-6666	
Pennsylvania	Sewickley	Yarns Unlimited	435 Beaver St		15143	412-741-8895	www.yarnsunlimitedpa.com
South Carolina	Hilton Head Island	The Courtyard	32 Palmetto Bay Rd, Ste 10A		29928	(843) 842 5614	
South Dakota	Sioux Falls	Athena Fibers	3915 South Hawthorne Avenue	athenafibers@gmail.com	57105	605-271-0741	
Tennessee	Brentwood	Bliss Yarn	127 Franklin Rd	dana@blissyarns.com	37027	615-370-8717	www.blissyarns.com
Texas	Austin	Hill Country Weavers	1701 South Congress		78704	(512) 707 7396	www.hillcountryweavers.com
Texas	Austin	Yarnbow	1607 Ranch Rd, 620 North,Ste 800		78734	(512) 535 2332	www.yarnbow.com
Texas	Dallas	Holley's Yarn Shoppe	5211 Forest Lane, Suite 115	info@holleysyarn.com	75244	972-503-5648	www.holleysyarn.com
Texas	Houston	Knitting in the Loop	2805 Bammel Lane		77098	713 942-7881	
Vermont	Essex Junction	Kaleidoscope Yarns	15 Pearl St.	jill@kyarns.com	5452	802 288-9200	
Vermont	Norwich	Northern Nights Yarn Shop	289 Main Street		05055	(802) 649 2000	
Virginia	Alexandria	Fiber Space/Knit a Gogo	102 N Fayette Street	danielle@fiberspace.com	22314	703-664-0344	danielle@fiberspace.com
Virginia	Charlottesville	Laughing Sheep Yarns	188 Zan Road	info@laughingsheepyarns.com	22901	434-973-0331	
Virginia	Charlottesville	The Needle Lady	111 W. Main St		22902	434-296-4625	
Virginia	Richmond	THE YARN LOUNGE	3003 West Cary St,		23221	804 340-2880	
Virginia	Virginia Beach	The Yarn Club	240 Mustang Trail , Suite 8		23452	757-486-5648	
Virginia	Williamsburg	Knitting Sisters	1915 Pocahontas Trail, SUITE #B1	info@knittingsisters.com	23185	(757) 258 5005	
Washington	Bainbridge Island	Churchmouse Yarn and Teas	118 Madrone Lane	info@charlotteyarn.com	98110	704-373-7442	www.churchmouseyarns.com
Washington	Mount Vernon	Wildfibers	706 South First St	sparker@wildfibers.net	98273	360-336-5202	
Washington	Seattle	Little Knits	3221 California Ave SW		98116	(206)935-4072	
Washington	Seattle	The Weaving Works Inc	4717 Brooklyn Ave, N.E.		98105	(888) 524 1221	www.weavingworks.com
Washington	Seattle	Tricoter	3121 East Madison St		98112	(206) 328 6505	www.tricoter.com
Washington	Seattle	Bad Woman Yarns	1815 N. 45th Street, Suite 215		98103	206 547-5384	
Washington	Seattle	The Fiber Gallery	8212 Greenwood Avenue N		98103	206 706-4197	
Washington	Spokane	Paradise Fibers	225 W. Indiana Avenue	accounting@paradisefibers.com	99205	888-320-7746	
Wiscon	Appleton	Iris Fine Yarns	132 E. Wisconsin Ave		54911	(920) 954 9001	
Wisconsin	Brookfield	Cream City Yarn	15565 W. North Avenue		53005	262 923-7014	
Wisconsin	Delafield	Knitch	608 Milwaukee Street		53018	262-646-9392	
Wisconsin	Fox Point	Knitting Knook LLC	8632 N Manor Lane		53217	(414)540-4080	
Wisconsin	Madison	The Knitting Tree	2614 Monroe St		53711	(608)238-0121	
Wisconsin	Milwaukee	RUHAMA'S YARN & NP	420 E Silver Spring Drive		53217	414 332-2660	www.ruhamas.com
Wisconsin	Sturgeon Bay	Spin LLC	108 South Madison Ave		54235	(920) 746 7746	

UNITED KINGDOM

'ROWAN AT ....' stockists carry a large range of Rowan Yarns.

Avon	Bristol	John Lewis	Cribbs Causeway		BS12 5TP	0117 959 1100	
Bedfordshire	Bedford	Tudor Rose Patchwork	Oakley Park, Station Road, Oakley	info@tudorrosepatchwork.co.uk	MK43 7RB	01234 824983	www.tudorrosepatchwork.co.uk
Bedfordshire	Leighton Buzzard	Nutmeg Needlecrafts,	1-4 Peacock Mews	nutmeg-needlecrafts@hotmail.co.uk	LU7 1JH	01525 376456	www.Nutmegneedlecraft.com
Berkshire	Reading	John Lewis	Broad Street		RG7 4AH	01189 575955	
Buckinghamshire	Buckingham	The Nimble Thimble	9 Bridge Street	sales@nimble-thimble.co.uk	MK18 1EL	01280 822236	www.nimble-thimble.co.uk
Buckinghamshire	Great Missenden	Rainbow Silks,	85 High Street	caroline@rainbowsilks.co.uk	HP16 0AL	01494 862111	www.rainbowsilks.co.uk
Buckinghamshire	Milton Keynes	John Lewis	Central Milton Keynes		MK1 1NN	01908 679171	
Cambridge	ELY	Yarn On The Square	22, Market Place		CB7 4NT	01353 661024	
Cambridgeshire	Cambridge	John Lewis	10 Downing Street		CB2 3DS	01223 361292	
Cambridgeshire	Peterborough	John Lewis	Queensgate Centre		PE1 1NL	01733344644	
Cambridgeshire	Whittlesford	Affinity Yarns	PO Box 972		CB22 4WQ	01223 839 476	
Cheshire	Cheadle	John Lewis	Wilmslow Road		SK9 3RN	0161491 4914	
Cheshire	Cheshire	Sew-In of Marple	46 Market Street, Marple		SK6 7AD	0161 427 2529	www.myknittingyarnandwool.co.uk
Cheshire	Chester	Stash	Unit 48, Evanís Business Park, Minerva Ave	stash@celticove.com	CH1 4QL	01244 389310	www.celticove.com
Cheshire	Nantwich	Homemade	3 Mill Street	lizzydrippingsales@btopenworld.com	CW5 5ST	01270 625318	
Cheshire	Northwich	Thimble Town	Unit 1, Blakemeret Centre	thimbletown@hotmail.co.uk	CW8 2EB	01606883232	
Cheshire	Risley	Black Sheep	Glaziers Lane		WA3 4EQ	0 1925764231	www.blacksheepwools.com
Co. Fermanagh	Enniskillen	Boston Quay Craft Shop	Down Street		BT74 7DU	028 6632 3837	
Conwy	Llanrwst	Ar-y-Gweill	24 Station Road	arygweill@aol.com	LL26 0EP	01492641149	
Cornwall	Launceston	The Cornwall Yarn Shop	1 Madford Lane	info@thecornwallyarnshop.co.uk	PL15 9EB	01566 779930	www.thecornwallyarnshop.co.uk
Cornwall	Penzance	Iriss	66 Chapel Street	rowan@iriss.co.uk	TR18 4AD	01736 366568	www.rowan-at-iriss.co.uk
Cornwall	Truro	Truro Fabrics	Lemon Quay	info@trurofabrics.co.uk	TR1 2LW	01872 222130	www.trurofabrics.com
Cornwall	Wadebridge	ArtyCrafts	41Molesworth Street	artycrafts@btconnect.com	PL27 7DH	01208 812274	
Cumbria	Kendal	Williams Wools	3 Kirkland	adrienne@williamswools.co.uk	LA9 5AU	01539 724300	
Cumbria	Penrith	Indigo	Unit 15 Devonshire Arcade	carolyn@indigoknits.co.uk	CA11 7SX	01768899917	www.indigoknits.co.uk
Cumbria	Whitehaven	The Knitting & Sewing Centre	28 Duke Street		CA28 7EU	01946 63091	
Derbyshire	Buxton	Sew-In of Buxton	1 Spring Gardens		SK17 6BJ	01298 26636	www.myknittingyarnandwool.co.uk
Derbyshire	Derby	Threads of Life	67 Borough St, Castle Donington	info@threadsoflife.co.uk	DE74 2LB	01332 811597	www.threadsoflife.co.uk
Derbyshire	Glossop	The Smithy Studios	1 Smithy Fold		SK13 8DD	01457 853196	
Derbyshire	Matlock	The Compleat Knit	22 Firs Parade	ann@patchworkdirect.com	DE4 3AS	01629 593700	www.patchworkdirect.com
Devon	Bovey Tracy	Spin A Yarn	26 Fore Street	info@spinayarndevon.co.uk	TQ13 9AD	01626 836203	www.spinayarndevon.co.uk
Devon	Exeter	Inspirations	5 Central Station Buildings, Queen Street		EX4 3SB	01392 435115	
Devon	Modbury	Hulu	Sentinel House, Poundwell	sales@hulucraft.co.uk	PL21 0XX	01548 831911	www.hulucrafts.co.uk
Devon	Modbury	Wild Goose Antiques	34 Church Street	wildgooseantiques@tiscali.co.uk	PL21 0QR	01548 830715	
Devon	Plymouth	House Of Fraser	40 Royal Parade		PL1 1DY	07725 214 802	
Devon	Plymouth	The Pin Tin	36/38 molesworth road, C/O C&R Lampshades, Millbridge	andie.thepintin@yahoo.co.uk	PL1 5NA	01752 313931	www.thepintin.com
Devon	Shaldon	Lana Pura	49 Fore Street	enquiries@lanapura.com	TQ14 0EA	01626 873615	www.lanapura.com
Devon	Tavistock	Knitting Korner	9 Pepper Street		PH9 0BD	01822 617410	
Devon	Tiverton	The Wool Merchant	3 Fore Street		EX16 6LN	01884 243569	
Devon	Totnes	Creative Crafts & Needlework	18 High Street		TQ9 5RY	01803 866002	www.creative-crafts-needlework.co.uk
Dorset	Bournemouth	Carlyís Crafts	Shop 1, 1a Cardigan Road, Winton	michelek1964@hotmail.com	BH9 1BJ	01202 512106	
Dorset	Bridport	Bridport Yarn	76 South Street	info@bridportyarn.co.uk	DT6 3NN	01308 455669	
Dorset	Christchurch	Honora	69 High Street, Christchurch	support@knittingyarns.co.uk	BH23 1AS	01202 486000	www.knittingyarns.co.uk
Dorset	Sturminster Newton	Hansons Fabrics,	Station Road		DT10 1BD	01258 472698	
Dorset	Swanage	The Wool & Craft Shop	17 Station Road	sales@craftywoolshop.co.uk	BH19 1AB	01929 422814	www.craftywoolshop.co.uk
Dumfries & Galloway	Newton Stewart	Inspirations	19 Victoria Street, Newton Stewart	rose.lawther@btconnect.com	DG8 6NH	01671 402627	
East Lothian	Haddington	The Bead Shop Scotland	29 Court St	info@beadshopscotland.co.uk	EH41 3AL	01620 822882	
East Sussex	Brighton	C & H Fabrics	179 Western Road,		BN1 2BA	01273 321959	www.candh.co.uk
East Sussex	Brighton	Purl	16 Upper Hamilton Road	purl.brighton@gmail.com	BN1 5DF	01273 248642	
East Sussex	Brighton	Brighton Sewing Centre	68 North Road		BN1 1YD	01273 621653	
East Sussex	Eastbourne	C & H Fabrics	82/86 Terminus Road		BN21 3LX	01323 410428	www.candh.co.uk
East Sussex	Eastbourne	Owl and Sewing Cat	5 Grand Hotel Bulidings, Compton Street	info@owlandsewingcat.com	BN21 4EJ	01323 410077	
East Sussex	Hastings	Knit Connections	10 claremont	knitconnections@hotmail.com	TN34 1HA	01424 444038	www.knitconnections.co.uk
East sussex	Lewes	The Stitchery	12/14 Riverside Cliffe Bridge, High Street	info@the-stitchery.co.uk	BN7 2RE	01273 473577	www.the-stitchery.co.uk
East Yorkshire	Goole	Hejhog	60 Pasture Road	shaun@hejhog-uk.com	DN14 6HD	08448757474	
Essex	Brentwood	We Three	16 Crown Street		CM14 4BA	01277 221709	
Essex	Colchester	Franklins	13/15 St Botolphs St		CO2 7DU	01206 563955	
Essex	Tiptree	The Cheap Shop	108 Church Street	info@thecheapshoptiptree.co.uk	CO5 0AB	01621 815576	www.thecheapshoptiptree.co.uk
Greater London	Herne Hill	Sharp Designs	226 Croxted Road		SE24 9DJ	020 8674 4382	
Greater Manchester	Manchester	John Lewis	Peel Avenue, The Trafford Centre		M17 8JL	0161 491 4040	
Greater Manchester	Manchester	Sew-In of Didsbury	741 Wilmslow Road, Didsbury		M20 6RN	0161 445 5861	www.myknittingyarnandwool.co.uk
Hampshire	Basingstoke	Pack Lane Wool Shop	171 Pack Lane, Kempshott	enquiries@packlanewool.co.uk	RG22 5HN	01256 462590	www.packlanewool.co.uk
Hampshire	Southampton	John Lewis	West Quay Shopping Centre		SO15 1GY	0238 021 6400	
Hampshire	Winchester	C & H Fabrics	8 High St		SO23 9JX	01962 843355	www.candh.co.uk
Hants	Andover	Love Yarns Ltd	305 The Commercial Centre, Picket piece	fiona@loveyarn.com	SP11 6RY	01264 357333	www.loveyarn.com
Herefordshire	Hay-on-Wye	Bedecked.co.uk	5 Castle Street	thegirls@bedecked.co.uk	HR3 5DF	01497 822769	www.bedecked.co.uk
Herefordshire	Hereford	Doughtyís	5 Capuchin Road, Church Street	sales@doughtysonline.co.uk	HR1 2LR	01432 267542	www.doughtysonline.co.uk
Hertfordshire	Boreham Wood	The Wool Shop	29 Shenley Road		WD6 1EB	0208 9052499	
Hertfordshire	Bushey	Mavis	44 High Street		WD23 3HL	0208 950 5445	www.mavis-crafts.com
Hertfordshire	Watford	John Lewis	The Harlequin, High St		WD2 8HL	01923 244266	
Hertfordshire	Welwyn Garden City	John Lewis,	Bridge Road		AL8 6TP	01707 323456	
Isle of Man	Onchan	Joanís Wools & Crafts	5B & 6B Village Walk	joans_wools_crafts@manx.net	IM3 4EA	01624 626009	
Isle of Skye	Portree	The Isle of Skye Baking Company Ltd t/a Skyeworks Gallery, Old Skye Wool Mill, Off Dunvegan Road		skyeworksgallery@gmail.com	IV51 9TR	01478 612669	www.skyeworksgallery.wordpress.com
Isle of Wight	Ryde	Crocus	41 Union St	jennings.crocusiw@tiscali.co.uk	PO33 2LF	01983 611144	
Kent	Broadstairs	C Wools	17 High Street	info@cwool.co.uk	CT10 1LP	01843 862848	
Kent	Canterbury	C & H Fabrics	2StGeorgeís Street		CT1 2SR	01227 459760	www.candh.co.uk
Kent	Greenhithe	John Lewis	Bluewater		DA9 9SA	01322 624123	
Kent	Tunbridge Wells	C & H Fabrics	113/115Mount Pleasant		TN1 1QS	01892 522618	www.candh.co.uk
Kent	Whitstable	Buzz 4 Wool and craft	5 Oxford Street		CT5 1DB	01227 282271	
Lancashire	Barnoldswick	Whichcrafts?	29 Church St	crafts@whichcrafts.co.uk	BB18 5UR	01282 851003	www.whichcrafts.co.uk
Lancashire	Chorley	& Sew What	247 Eaves Lane	info@sewwhat.gb.com	PR6 0AG	01257 267438	www.sewwhat.gb.com
Lancashire	Oldham	Yarn Barn	16 Milnrow Road, Shaw	info@yarnbarnshaw.co.uk	OL2 8EQ	01706 843538	www.yarnbarnshaw.co.uk
Lancashire	Thornton	Yarns of Lancashire Ltd	Unit 15, Marsh Mill Village, Fleetwood Road	yarns@tiscali.co.uk	FY5 4JZ	01253 822922	
Leicestershire	Leicester	John Lewis	2 Bath House Lane, Highcross		LE1 4SA	0116 242 5777	
Leicestershire	Loughborough	Quorn Country Crafts	18 Churchgate	quorncountrycrafts@hotmail.com	LE11 1UD	01509 211604	www.quorncountrycrafts.com
Lincolnshire	Cleethorpes	A Good Yarn	53 Cambridge Street		DN35 8HD	01472 508707	www.agoodyarn.co.uk
Lincolnshire	Lincoln	Spins and Needles	6 Clasketgate		LN2 1JS	01522 522865	http://www.spinsandneedles.co.uk
Lincolnshire	Louth	M&G Designs	14 Eastgate	mandgneedleworkdesigns@btconnect.com	LN11 9NE	01507604923	www.mandgdesignsneedlecraft.co.uk
London	Barnes	Creations	79 Church Road		SW13 9HH	020 8563 2970	
London	Central London	All the Fun of the Fair	Unit 2, 8 Kingly Court, Off Carnaby Street	buzzstokes@btinternet.com	W1B 5PW	0207 287 2303	www.allthefunofthefair.biz
London	Central London	John Lewis	300 Oxford Street		W1C 1DX	020 7629 7711	
London	Central London	Liberty	Regent St		W1B 5AH	020 7734 1234	
London	Central London	Peter Jones	Sloane Square		SW1W 8EL	0207 881 6364	
London	Chingford	JJ Wool & Crafts	89 Station Road	jjwoolandcrafts@yahoo.co.uk	E4 9RH	0208 523 7172	www.jjwoolandcrafts.co.uk
London	Chiswick	Creations	29 Turnham Green Terrace		W4 1RS	020 8747 9697	
London	Crouch End	Nest	102 Weston Park	info@handmadenest.co.uk	N8 9PP	02083408852	www.handmadenest.co.uk
London	Finsbury Park	Lenarow	169 Blackstock Road	michael@lenarow.co.uk	N4 2JS	020 7359 1274	www.lenarow.co.uk

London	Herne Hill	Sharp Works	220 Railton Road		SE24 0JD	02077387668	
London	Islington	Loop	15 Camden Passage	info@loop.gb.com	N1 8EA	0207 288 1160	www.loop.gb.com
London	London	Fringe	108 Alexandra Park Road		N10 2AE	0208 8839478	
London	London	Stitch Up Sewing Ltd	130 Arthur Road, Wimbledon	sandiebon@btinternet.com	SW19 5PN	0208 9446488	
London	London	Tricolette	93 Boundary Road		NW8 0RG	02073724944	www.tricoletteyarns.com
London	North London	John Lewis	Brent Cross Shopping Centre		NW4 3FL	0208202 6535	
London	Stratford	John Lewis	101 The Arcade, Montfichet Road		E20 1EL	020 8532 3500	
London		Moo Too Ltd	45 Lordship Lane	mootoo@btconnect.com	SE22 8EP	0208 299 6105	www.mootoo.com
London	Covent Garden	London Graphics Centre	16 Shelton Street		WC2H 9JJ	02077594500	
Merseyside	Liverpool	John Lewis	70 South John Street		L1 8BJ	0151 709 7070	
Merseyside	Liverpool	Purlesque	The Bluecoat, School Lane	purlesque@gmail.com	L1 3BX		
Merseyside	St Helens	The Knitting Centre	9 Westfield Street		WA10 1QA	0174423993	
Middlesex	Twickenham	Mrs Moon	41 Crown Road, St Margarets	info@mrsmoon.co.uk	TW1 3EJ	020 8744 1190	www.mrsmoon.co.uk
Norfolk	Dereham	Knitwits	1 Glencoe Court, Cherry Tree Car Park	knitwits.dereham@googlemail.com	NR19 2AX	01362 652961	www.knitwitsdereham.co.uk
Norfolk	Diss	Diss Wool & Craft Shop	2 Cobbs Yard, St Nicholas Street	sales@disswoolandcrafts.com	IP22 4LB	01379 650640	www.disswoolandcrafts.com
Norfolk	Norwich	John Lewis	All Saints Green		NR1 3LX	01603660021	
Norfolk	Sheringham	Creative Crafts	47 Station Road	info@creative-crafts.co.uk	NR26 8RG	01263823153	www.creative-crafts.co.uk
North Yorkshire	Bedale	New Jersey	38 Market Place		DL8 1EQ	01677 427 746	
North Yorkshire	Clapham	Beckside Yarn & Needlecraft	Church Avenue	info@becksideyarns.co.uk	LA2 8EA	01524 251122	www.becksideyarns.co.uk
North Yorkshire	Embsay	Embsay Crafts	Embsay Mills	enquiries@embsaycrafts.com	BD23 6QF	01756 700946	www.embsaycrafts.com
North Yorkshire	Filey	Beachcomber	35 Belle Vue St		YO14 9HU	01723 514434	
North Yorkshire	Northallerton	CB Furnishings	28 standard Way	sales@cbfurnishings.co.uk	DL6 1EQ	01609 772 916	www.cbfurnishing.co.uk
North Yorkshire	Whitby	Bobbins	Wesley Hall, Church Street	bobbins@globalnet.co.uk	YO22 4DE	01947 600585	www.bobbins.co.uk
North Yorkshire	York	Craft Basics	9 Gillygate		YO31 7EA	01904652840	
North Yorkshire	York	Knit and Stitch	11 Colliergate	york@knitandstitchonline.com	YO1 8BP	01904 270927	
Northamptonshire	Northampton	House of Fraser	37 Newland Walk, Grosvenor Centre		NN1 2EP	07730 456695	
Northamptonshire	Rushden	Manfield Crafts	24 Griffiths Street	enquiries@manfieldcrafts.com	NN10 0RL	01933 314920	www.manfieldcrafts.com
Northamptonshire	Weedon	Crafts & Quilts	Unit 5 The Barn, Heart of the Shires Shop Village	tintindowton@aol.com	NN7 4LB	01327 349276	
Northern Ireland	craigavon	Coolwoolz.co.uk	46 mill hill		BT66 7QP	028 38820202	www.coolwoolz.co.uk
Northern Ireland	Cullybackey	The Glen Gallery	48 Fenagh Road		BT43 5PH	02825880354	
Northern Ireland	Newry	Stitch 'n' Knit	102 Hill Street		BT34 1BT	028 3083 3900	
Northumberland	Berwick upon Tweed	The Needleworks Ltd,	54 Hide Hill	kp1612@btinternet.com	TD15 1AB	01289 330503	
Nottinghamshire	Beeston	Yarn	55 Chilwell Road	info@yarn-in-notts.co.uk	NG9 1EN	0115 925 3606	www.yarn-in-notts.co.uk
Nottinghamshire	Mansfield	Beales	Queen Street	coop.mansfield@coats.com	NG18 1JR	0784 1007491	
Nottinghamshire	Nottingham	John Lewis	Victoria Centre		NG1 3QA	0115941 8282	
Nottinghamshire	Southwell	The Little Wool Shop	18 Queen Street	mac8142@aol.com	NG25 0AA	01636 814198	www.thelittlewoolshop.co.uk
Oxfordshire	Bicester	Bicester Wools	86 Sheep Street	info@bicesterwools.com	OX26 6LP	01869 322966	www.bicesterwools.com
Oxfordshire	Burford	Burford Needlecraft	150 High Street	info@needlework.co.uk	OX18 4QU	01993 822136	www.needlework.co.uk
Perth & Kinross	Perthshire	Karelia House Ltd	Kenmore Road, Comrie Bridge		PH15 2LS	01887 822999	
Scotland	Aberdeen	John Lewis	George Street		AB9 1BT	01224 625000	
Scotland	Aberdeen	The Wool Shed	Ryehill, Oyne	info@thewoolshed.co.uk	AB52 6QS	01464 851539	www.thewoolshed.co.uk
Scotland	Aberdeen	Wool for Ewe	83-85 Rosemount Place	info@woolforewe.co.uk	AB25 2YE	01224 643738	
Scotland	Castle Douglas	Outback Yarns (Art 2 Go)	130-132 King Street	sarahmckie@btinternet.com	DG7 1LU	01556 504900	www.outbackyarns.com
Scotland	Edinburgh	Jenners	48 Princes Street		EH2 2YJ	07703 750974	
Scotland	Edinburgh	John Lewis	St James Centre		EH1 3SP	0131556 9121	
Scotland	Edinburgh	McAree Bros	19 Howe Street	sales@mcadirect.com	EH3 6TE	0131 558 1747	www.mcadirect.com
Scotland	Fife	Twist Fibre Craft Studio	88 High Street, Newburgh	enquiries@twistfibrecraft.co.uk	KY14 6AQ	01337 842843	www.twistfibrecraft.co.uk
Scotland	Glasgow	John Lewis	Buchanan Galleries		G4 0BZ	01413536677	
Scotland	Glasgow	Mandors	13 Renfrew Street	fabric@mandors.co.uk	G3 6ST	0141 332 7716	www.mandors.co.uk
Scotland	Gourock	Once A Sheep	60 Kempock Street	info@onceasheep.co.uk	PA19 1ND	01475 648089	www.onceasheep.co.uk
Scotland	Stirling	McAree Bros	55-59 King Street	sales@mcadirect.com	FK8 1DR	01786 465646	www.mcadirect.com
Shropshire	Ludlow	The Wool Shop	13 Broad Street		SY8 1NG	01584 872988	
Shropshire	Much Wenlock	Ippikin	59 The High Street	info@ippikin.com	TF13 6AE	01952 728371	www.ippikin.com
Shropshire	Shewsbury	Anca	Unit 10, The Mall, Bank Farm Road	anne@anca-wools.co.uk	SY3 6DU	01743 249504	www.anca-wool.co.uk
Somerset	Bath	Wool LTD	19 Old Orchard Street		BA1 1JU	01225 469144	www.woolbath.co.uk
Somerset	Clevedon	The Spinning Weal	63 Hill Road	mail@spinningweal.com	BS21 7NZ	01275 876000	www.spinningweal.com
Somerset	Frome	Marmalade Yarns	11 Catherine Hill	CatrionaandMaxine@marmaladeyarns.co.uk	BA11 1BZ	01373 473557	www.marmaladeyarns.co.uk
Somerset	Minehead	Jana Henrie	High Street, Porlock	info@janahenrie.com	TA24 8SP	01643 862058	www.janahenrie.com
South Lanarkshire	Hamilton	Stitching Time	7 Haddow Street	getit@stitchingtime.co.uk	ML3 7HX	01698 424025	
South Yorkshire	Doncaster	Knit and Stitch	26 Market Place	info@knitandstitchonline.com	DN1 1NE	01302 366022	www.knitandstitchonline.com
South Yorkshire	Rotherham	Knit and Stitch	92 High Street, Maltby	info@knitandstitchonline.com	S66 7BN		www.knitandstitchonline.com
South Yorkshire	Sheffield	John Lewis	Barkers Pool		S1 1EP	01142768511	
Staffordshire	Lichfield	The Knitting Corner	Unit 3, Curborough Hall Farm, Watery Lane	theknittingcorner@btinternet.com	WS13 8ES	01543 415837	
Staffordshire	Newcastle U Lyme	K2Tog	63 High Street, Wolstanton	sales@cucumberpatch.com	ST5 0ER	01782 862332	www.cucumberpatch.co.uk
Suffolk	Bungay	Knit and Yarn	3 Upper Olland Street	gillybell@knitandyarn.co.uk	NR35 1BD	01986 895400	www.shopknitandyarn.co.uk
Suffolk	Bury St Edmunds	Wibbling Wools,	24b Angel Hill	lynz@wibblingwools.co.uk	IP33 1UZ	01284 749555	www.wibblingwools.co.uk
Surrey	Carshalton Beeches	Maxime Wools,	68 Banstead Road	enquires@maximewools.co.uk	SM5 3NL	0208 66105625	
Surrey	Caterham	The Knit Club	27 High Street	louise@theknitclub.co.uk	CR3 5UE	01883 345220	
Surrey	Dorking	Gillian Gladrags	20 West street	gill@gilliangladrag.co.uk	RH4 1BL	01306 898144	www.gilliangladrag.co.uk
Surrey	Guildford	C & H Fabrics	6 Tunsgate Square		GU1 3QZ	01483 301380	www.candh.co.uk
Surrey	Guildford	Pandora	196 High Street	sales@craft-supplies-store.co.uk	GU1 3HZ	01483 572558	www.stitch1knit1.com
Surrey	Kingston	John Lewis	Wood Street		KT1 1TE	02085473000	
Teeside	Guisborough	Leven Crafts	7-9 Chaloner Mews, Chaloner Street	info@levencrafts.co.uk	TS14 6SA	01287 610207	www.levencrafts.co.uk
Tyne & Wear	Newcastle U Tyne	John Lewis,	Eldon Square		NE99 1AB	0191 232 5000	
Tyne & Wear	Newcastle upon Tyne	The Knit Studio,	Blackfriars	annemakepeace@btopenworld.com	NE1 4XN	07540 277764	
Tyne & Wear	Whitley Bay	Ring a Rosie	272 Whitley Road	loweringarosie@aol.com	NE26 2TG	0191 252 8874	www.ringarosie.co.uk
Wales	Abergavenny	The Wool Croft	9 Cross Street		NP7 5EH	01873 851551	
Wales	Aberystwyth	Clare's Wools	13 Great Darkgate Street	webenquiries@clarewools.co.uk	SA23 1DE	01970 617786	www.clarewools.co.uk
Wales	Anglesey	Copperfield, Four Mile	Bridge Road Valley		LL65 4HB	01407 740982	
Wales	Cardiff	John Lewis	The Hayes		CF10 1EG	029 2053 6000	
Wales	Dolgellau	Knit One	Maes Gwyn	malcolm.murgatroyd@btinternet.com	LL40 1RB	01341 422194	
Wales	Fishguard	Janeís of Fishguard	14 High Street		SA65 9AR	01348874443	www.janes-fishguard.co.uk
Wales	Mostyn	Abakhan	Coast Road		CH8 9DX	01745 562 100	
Wales	Penarth	Yarn & Yarns	22 Cornerswell Road		CF64 2UZ	02920 712097	
Wales	Swansea	Red House Quilting	Mumbles, 4 Cornwall Place		SA3 4DP	01792 368 080	www.redhousequilting.co.uk
Wales	Torfaen	Go Knit	35 Broad Street, Blaenavon	jenny@goknit.co.uk	NP4 9NF	07711616948	www.goknit.co.uk
Warwickshire	Nuneaton	Wool Mountain	Abbeygate Shopping Centre, Newdegate Street	info@woolmountain.co.uk	CV11 4EL	02476 346222	www.woolmountain.co.uk
Warwickshire	Shipston on Stour	Shipston on Stour Needlecraft	24/26 Sheep Street	info@needlework.co.uk	CV36 4AF	01608 661616	www.needlework.co.uk
Warwickshire	Warwick	Warwick Wools	17 Market Place		CV34 4SA	01926 492853	www.warwickwools.co.uk
West Midlands	Birmingham	House of Fraser	Corporation Street	hof.birmingham@coats.com	B2 5JS	07921 495736	
West Midlands	Solihull	House of Fraser	Warwick Road		B91 3DU	07703 750970	
West Midlands	Solihull	John Lewis	Touchwood		B90 4SH	0121 704 1121	
West Midlands	Sutton Coldfield	House of Fraser	132-138 The Parade, Gracechurch Centre		B72 1PB	07703 750973	
West Midlands	Wolverhampton	House of Fraser	71-78 Victoria Street		WV1 3PQ	07703 750972	
West Sussex	Chichester	C & H Fabrics	33/34 North Street		PO19 1LX.	01243783300	www.candh.co.uk
West Sussex	Shoreham by Sea	Shoreham Knitting	19EastStreet	sales@englishyarns.co.uk	BN43 5ZE	01273 461029	www.englishyarns.co.uk
West sussex	The fabric Store	Medway Cottages	Blisham Road Arundel	claire@thefabricandwoolstore.co.uk	BN18 0JW	01243 555312	
West Yorkshire	Haworth	Daisy Days	56 Main Street	info@daisy-days.co.uk	BD22 8DP	01535 644 653	www.daisy-days.co.uk
West Yorkshire	Holmfirth	Up Country	58 Huddersfield Road	root@rowan-upcountry.com	HD9 3AZ	01484 687803	www.upcountry.co.uk
West Yorkshire	Huddersfield	Woolly Minded Beady Eyed	130 Westbourne Road	woollyminded@sky.com	HD1 4LF	01484 424 703	
West Yorkshire	Ilkley	Create	Victorian Arcade, South Hawkworth Street	info@createcafe.co.uk	LS29 9DY	01943 817788	www.createcafe.co.uk
West Yorkshire	Leeds	Baa Ram Ewe	87 Otley Road, Headingley	info@baaramewe.co.uk	LS6 3PS	0113 278 1788	www.baaramewe.co.uk
West Yorkshire	Nr Hebden Bridge	Attica,	Unit 2, Brier Hey Business Park, Mytholmroyd	info@attica-yarns.co.uk	HX7 5PF	01422 884885	www.attica-yarns.co.uk
West Yorkshire	Shipley	Saltaire yarns LTD	3 Oastler Road, Saltaire	mail@saltaireyarns.co.uk	BD18 45E	01274 270142	www.saltaireyarns.co.uk
West Yorkshire	Wakefield	Wool 'N' Stuff	Unit 2, Wilson House, Charlotte Street		WF1 1UL	01924 565740	www.woolnstuff.co.uk
Wiltshire	Calne	Handi Wools	3 Oxford Road		SN11 8AA	01249 812081	
Wiltshire	Cricklade	Cricklade Needlecrafts	89a High Street	info@crickladecrafts.co.uk	SN6 6DF	01793 750604	www.crickladecrafts.co.uk
Wiltshire	Salisbury	Born To Knit	Studio 4, Fisherton Mill, Fisherton Street		SP2 7QY	07557 985935	
Wiltshire	Trowbridge	Fabric Magic	14 Silver Street		BA14 8JS	01225 768833	
Worcestershire	Broadway	Wool in Broadway	2 Cotswold Court, The Green	pat.davies2@ntlworld.com	WR12 7AA	01386 853779	www.woolinbroadway.com
Worcestershire	Evesham	Cotswold Needlecraft	Evesham Country Park	info@cotswoldneedlecraft.co.uk	WR11 4TP	01386 761217	www.cotswoldneedlecraft.co.uk
Worcestershire	Malvern	The Knitting Parlour	12 Graham Road	info@theknittingparlour.co.uk	WR14 2HN	01684 892079	www.theknittingparlour.co.uk
Worcestershire	Worcester	House of Fraser	Crowngate		WR1 3LD	07703 750975	

UNITED KINGDOM - Fabric Stockists

Avon	Bristol	Fabric Plus	6 The Centre, Keynsham	enquiries@fabricsplus.co.uk	BS31 1ED		www.fabricplus.co.uk
Avon	Bristol	John Lewis	Cribbs Causeway		BS12 5TP	0117 959 1100	
Berkshire	Reading	John Lewis	Broad Street		RG7 4AH	01189 575955	
Buckinghamshire	Milton Keynes	John Lewis	Central Milton Keynes		MK1 1NN	01908 679171	
Cambridgeshire	Cambridge	John Lewis	10 Downing Street		CB2 3DS	01223 361292	
Cambridgeshire	Ely	City Cycle	7 Market Street	craft@citycyclecentre.com	CB7 4PB	01353 663131	
Cambridgeshire	Peterborough	John Lewis	Queensgate Centre		PE1 1NL	01733 344644	
Cheshire	Cheadle	John Lewis	Wilmslow Road		SK9 3RN	0161 491 4914	
Cheshire	Chester	Stash	Unit 48, Evan's Business Park, Minerva Ave	stash@celticove.com	CH1 4QL	01244 389310	www.celticove.com
Cheshire	Northwich	Thimble Town	Unit 1, Blakemeret Centre	thimbletown@hotmail.co.uk	CW8 2EB	01606883232	
Conwy	Llanrwst	Ar-y-Gweill	24 Station Road	arygweill@aol.com	LL26 0EP	01492 641149	
Cornwall	Launceston	Cowslip Workshop	Newhouse Farm, St Stephens	info@cowslipworkshops.co.uk	PL15 8JX	01566 772654	www.cowslipworkshops.co.uk
Cornwall	Redruth	The Sewing Studio	5 Green Lane	sales@thesewingstudio.co.uk	TR15 1JY	01209 216942	www.thesewingstudio.co.uk
Cornwall	St Agnes	Linterior Design	Unit 4, Great Western Railway Yard	enquiry@linteriordesign.com	TR5 0PD	01208 814023	www.linteriordesign.net
Cornwall	Truro	Truro Fabrics	Lemon Quay	info@trurofabrics.co.uk	TR1 2LW	01872 222130	www.trurofabrics.com
Denbighshire	Ruthin	Threads	40 Clwyd Street	clwydfryn@btinternet.com	LL15 1HW	01824 703543	
Derbyshire	Glossop	The Smithy Studios	1 Smithy Fold		SK13 8DD	01457 853196	
Derbyshire	Matlock	Quiltessential	Arkwrights Mill, Mill Road, Cromford	annmayner@quiltessential.co.uk	DE4 3RQ	01629 825936	www.quiltessential.co.uk
Devon	Axminster	The Fabric Shop	West Street		EX13 5NU	01297 32973	
Devon	Exeter	Inspirations	5 Central Station Buildings, Queen Street		EX4 3SB	01392 435115	
Devon	Plymouth	House Of Fraser	40 Royal Parade		PL1 1DY	07725 214 802	
Devon	Totnes	Stone Fabrics	97 High Street	stone_fabrics@mac.com	TQ9 5PB	01803 868608	www.stonefabrics.co.uk
East Lothian	Haddington	The Bead Shop Scotland	29 Court St	info@beadshopscotland.co.uk	EH41 3AL	01620 822882	
East Sussex	Brighton	C & H Fabrics	179 Western Road,		BN1 2BA	01273 321959	www.candh.co.uk
East Sussex	Brighton	Quilty Pleasures	1B Upper Hamilton Road	quiltypleasures@hotmail.co.uk	BN1 5DF	01273 321964	
East Sussex	Brighton	Brighton Sewing Centre	68 North Road		BN1 1YD	01273 621653	
East Sussex	Eastbourne	Owl and Sewing Cat	5 Grand Hotel Bulidings, Compton Street	info@owlandsewingcat.com	BN21 4EJ	01323 410077	
East Sussex	Hastings	Knit Connections	10 claremont	knitconnections@hotmail.com	TN34 1HA	01424 444038	www.knitconnections.co.uk
East Sussex	Lewes	Charleston Farmhouse	Near Firle	j.birch-leonard@charleston.org.uk	BN8 6LL	01323 815158	
East sussex	Lewes	The Stitchery	12/14 Riverside Cliffe Bridge, High Street	info@the-stitchery.co.uk	BN7 2RE	01273 473577	www.the-stitchery.co.uk
Essex	Tiptree	The Cheap Shop	108 Church Street	info@thecheapshoptiptree.co.uk	CO5 0AB	01621 815576	www.thecheapshoptiptree.co.uk
Fife	Kirkcaldy	Rejects Department Store	Rejects Dept Store, 123 St. Clair St.		KY12BS	01592 655955	
Gloucestershire	Cirencester	Lexi Loves	19 Gloucester Road	info@originalsbyalexia.co.uk	GL7 2LB	07702 555015	
Hampshire	Basingstoke	Pack Lane Wool Shop	171 Pack Lane, Kempshott	enquiries@packlanewool.co.uk	RG22 5HN	01256 462590	www.packlanewool.co.uk
Hampshire	Southampton	John Lewis	West Quay Shopping Centre		SO15 1GY	0238 021 6400	
Hampshire	Winchester	C & H Fabrics	8 High St		SO23 9JX	01962 843355	www.candh.co.uk
Herefordshire	Hereford	Doughty's	5 Capuchin Road, Church Street	sales@doughtysonline.co.uk	HR1 2LR	01432 267542	www.doughtysonline.co.uk
Hertfordshire	Welwyn Garden City	John Lewis,	Bridge Road		AL8 6TP	01707 323456	
Isle of Skye	Portree	The Isle of Skye Baking Company Ltd t/a Skyeworks Gallery	Old Skye Wool Mill, Off Dunvegan Road	skyeworksgallery@gmail.com	IV51 9TR	01478 612669	www.skyeworksgallery.wordpress.com
Isle of Wight	Ryde	Crocus	41 Union St	jennings.crocusiw@tiscali.co.uk	PO33 2LF	01983 611144	

Kent	Canterbury	C & H Fabrics	2 St George's Street		CT1 2SR	01227 459760	www.candh.co.uk
Kent	Greenhithe	John Lewis	Bluewater		DA9 9SA	01322 624123	
Kent	Herne Bay	Through the Loop	169 High Street	julie_crump@yahoo.co.uk	CT6 5AQ	01227 742224	
Kent	Rochester	Hometown	74 High Street	hometownquilts@hotmail.co.uk	ME1 1JY	01634 838880	
Kent	Royal Tunbridge Wells	World of Sewing,	56-64 Camden Road		TN1 2QP	01892 533188	
Kent	Sandwich	Rose N Tony's	26 King Street	rosentonys@googlemail.com	CT13 9BT	01304 612131	
Kent	Sevenoaks	Puddleducks	116 St John's Hill		TN13 3PD	01732 743642	
Kent	Tunbridge Wells	C & H Fabrics	113/115 Mount Pleasant		TN1 1QS	01892 522618	www.candh.co.uk
Kent	Upper Belvedere	Yarnia Ltd,	18 Nuxley Road	yarnia@hotmail.co.uk	DA15 5JF	01322 440611	
Leicestershire	Leicester	John Lewis	2 Bath House Lane, Highcross		LE1 4SA	0116 242 5777	
Leicestershire	Loughborough	Quorn Country Crafts	18 Churchgate	quorncountrycrafts@hotmail.com	LE11 1UD	01509 211604	www.quorncountrycrafts.com
Lincolnshire	Louth	M&G Designs	14 Eastgate	mandgneedleworkdesigns@btconnect.com	LN11 9NE	01507604923	www.mandgdesignsneedlecraft.co.uk
London	Central London	John Lewis	300 Oxford Street		W1C 1DX	020 7629 7711	
London	London	Ray Stitch	99 Essex Road	rachel@raystitch.co.uk	N1 2SJ	02077041060	www.raystitch.co.uk
London	London	Sew Over It Ltd	78 Landor Road, Clapham	lisa@sewoverit.co.uk	SW9 9PH	0207 3260376	www.sewoverit.co.uk
London	London	The Village Haberdashery	8 Cavendish Mansions, Mill Lane	annie@thevillagehaberdashery.co.uk	NW6 1TE		
London	London	Tricolette	93 Boundary Road		NW8 0RG	02073724944	www.tricoletteyarns.com
London	Stratford	John Lewis	101 The Arcade, Montfichet Road		E20 1EL	020 8532 3500	
London		Liberty Plc	Regent Street		W1B 5AH	0207 734 1234	
London		Moo Too Ltd	45 Lordship Lane	mootoo@btconnect.com	SE22 8EP	0208 299 6105	www.mootoo.com
London		Sew Much Fun	46 Chalcot Road	sewmuchfun@btinternet.com	NW1 8LS	0207 722 9889	
London		The Make Lounge	49-51 Barnsbury Street		N1 1TP	02076090275	
London		Tikki Limited	293 Sandycombe Road	info@tikkilondon.com	TW9 3LU	0208 948 8462	www.tikkilondon.com
Merseyside	Liverpool	John Lewis	70 South John Street		L1 8BJ	0151 709 7070	
Norfolk	Hoveton	Sew Creative	Wroxham Barnes Ltd, Tunstead Road	sewcreative@sylvia79.fsbusiness.co.uk	NR12 8QU	01603 781665	
Norfolk	Norwich	John Lewis	All Saints Green		NR1 3LX	01603 660021	
North Yorkshire	Embsay	Embsay Crafts	Embsay Mills	enquiries@embsaycrafts.com	BD23 6QF	01756 700946	www.embsaycrafts.com
North Yorkshire	York	Grace and Jacob	7 Barley Corn Yard, Walmgate	mail@graceandjacob.co.uk	YO1 9TX	01904 627583	www.graceandjacob.co.uk
North Yorkshire	York	Knit and Stitch	11 Colliergate	york@knitandstitchonline.com	YO1 8BP	01904 270927	
Northern Ireland	Londonderry	Mission Hall Quilts	7 Lower Fountain Street	info@crescotrust.com	BT48 6QX	028 7136 2500	www.missionhallquilts.com
Nottinghamshire	Beeston	Yarn	55 Chilwell Road	info@yarn-in-notts.co.uk	NG9 1EN	0115 925 3606	www.yarn-in-notts.co.uk
Nottinghamshire	Nottingham	John Lewis	Victoria Centre		NG1 3QA	0115 941 8282	
Nottinghamshire	Southwell	The Little Wool Shop	18 Queen Street	mac8142@aol.com	NG25 0AA	01636 814198	www.thelittlewoolshop.co.uk
Oxfordshire	Bicester	Bicester Wools	86 Sheep Street	info@bicesterwools.com	OX26 6LP	01869 322966	www.bicesterwools.com
Scotland	Aberdeen	John Lewis	George Street		AB9 1BT	01224 625000	
Scotland	Castle Douglas	Outback Yarns (Art 2 Go)	130-132 King Street	sarahmckie@btinternet.com	DG7 1LU	01556 504900	www.outbackyarns.com
Scotland	Edinburgh	Avery Homestore Ltd	7-9 Church Hill Place	joave@btconnect.com	EH10 4BE	0131 4471000	
Scotland	Edinburgh	John Lewis	St James Centre		EH1 3SP	0131 556 9121	
Scotland	Glasgow	John Lewis	Buchanan Galleries		G4 0BZ	0141 353 6677	
Scotland	Glasgow	Mandors	13 Renfrew Street	fabric@mandors.co.uk	G3 6ST	0141 332 7716	www.mandors.co.uk
Shropshire	Newport	Zig Zags	24 St Mary's Street	zigzags@hotmail.co.uk	TF10 7AB	01952 814962	
Shropshire	Shewsbury	Anca	Unit 10, The Mall, Bank Farm Road	anne@anca-wools.co.uk	SY3 6DU	01743 249504	www.anca-wool.co.uk
Shropshire	Whitchurch	Quilters Trading Post	63 Green End	emma@quilterstradingpost.com	SY13 1AJ	01948 666313	
Somerset	Bath	Country Threads	2 Pierrepoint Place		BA1 1JX		
Somerset	Clevedon	The Spinning Weal	63 Hill Road	mail@spinningweal.com	BS21 7NZ	01275 876000	www.spinningweal.com
Somerset	Frome	Millie Moon	20 Paul Street, Catherine Hill	info@milliemoonshop.co.uk	BA11 1DT	01373 464650	www.milliemoon.co.uk
Somerset	Midsomer Norton	Rose Crafts,	123 High Street		BA3 2DA	01761 414390	
South Yorkshire	Doncaster	Knit and Stitch	26 Market Place	info@knitandstitchonline.com	DN1 1NE	01302 366022	www.knitandstitchonline.com
South Yorkshire	Rotherham	Knit and Stitch	92 High Street, Maltby	info@knitandstitchonline.com	S66 7BN		www.knitandstitchonline.com
South Yorkshire	Sheffield	John Lewis	Barkers Pool		S1 1EP	0114 2768511	
Suffolk		Quilters Haven Ltd	68 High Street, Wickham Market	quilters.haven@btinternet.com	IP13 0QU	01728 746275	www.quilters-haven.co.uk
Surrey	Dorking	The Quilt Room	37-39 High Street	info@quiltroom.co.uk	RH4 1AR	01306 740739	www.quiltroom.co.uk
Surrey	Guildford	C & H Fabrics	6 Tunsgate Square		GU1 3QZ	01483 301380	www.candh.co.uk
Surrey	Guildford	Pandora	196 High Street	sales@craft-supplies-store.co.uk	GU1 3HZ	01483 572558	www.stitch1knit1.com
Surrey	Kingston	John Lewis	Wood Street		KT1 1TE	020 8547 3000	
Tyne & Wear	Newcastle upon Tyne	John Lewis,	Eldon Square		NE99 1AB	0191 232 5000	
Tyne & Wear	Newcastle Upon Tyne	The Fat Quarters,	5 Chopwell Road, Blackhall Mill	sales@thefatquarters.co.uk	NE17 7TN	01207 565728	www.thefatquarters.co.uk
Wales	Cardiff	John Lewis	The Hayes		CF10 1EG	029 2053 6000	
Wales	Llanelli	Isabeau Inspirations	Cross Hands Sqaure Shopping Centre		SA14 6NT	01269 844 969	
Wales	Monmouth	The Cotton Angel	2 Church Street	info@thecottonangel.com	NP25 3BU	01600 713548	www.thecottonangel.com
Wales	Mostyn	Abakhan	Coast Road		CH8 9DX	01745 562 100	
Wales	Powys	The Deco Shop	37 Heol Maen Gwyn , Machynlleth	machdeco@btinternet.com	SY20 8EB	01654 700001	
West Midlands	Birmingham	The Cotton Patch	1285 Stratford Road, Hall Green	mailorder@cottonpatch.co.uk	B28 9AJ	0121 702 2840	www.cottonpatch.co.uk
West Midlands	Solihull	John Lewis	Touchwood		B90 4SH	0121 704 1121	
West Sussex	Angmering	Angmering Framing & Stitches	The Square	angmeringpat@aol.com	BN16 4EA	01903 782202	
West Sussex	Chichester	C & H Fabrics	33/34 North Street		PO19 1LX.	01243 783300	www.candh.co.uk
Wiltshire	Warminster	Think outside the box	10 Chinns Court, Market Place		BA12 9AN		
Worcestershire	Bewdley	Totally Patched	24 Load Street	contact@totallypatched.com	DY12 2AE	01299 409390	www.totallypatched.com
Worcestershire	Malvern	The Knitting Parlour	12 Graham Road	info@theknittingparlour.co.uk	WR14 2HN	01684 892079	www.theknittingparlour.co.uk

EUROPEAN - Fabric Stockists

Austria	Mödling	Krawany GmbH	Hauptstrasse 83	handarbeit@krawany.com	2340	0043/2236 41500 15	
Belgium	Chênée	Rêve de quilts	Rue d'Embourg 29	quiltsdream@skynet.be	4032	0475 66 76 61	www.revedequilts.be
Belgium	Oostende	Paulette	Torhoutsesteenweg 479		8400	059 43 04 95	
Belgium	Ronse	Creasis VOF	Zonnestraat 24	creasis@telenet.be	9600	0495 70 81 90	www.creasis.be
France	La Varenne St. Hilaire	Lili Coquelicot	124 avenue Pierre Semart	contact@lilicoquelicot.fr	94210	01 47 06 71 63	
Germany	Chemnitz	Zwilllingsnadel	Neumarkt 2	info@zwillingsnadel.de	9111	0371-3331866	www.zwillingsnadel.de
Germany	Stadtlohn	Wolle und Design	Görkeskamp 6	info@wolleunddesign.de	48703	02563/98208	www.wolleunddesign.de
Holland	Amersfoort	H.W. Mur	Langestraat 13	info@hwmur.nl	3811 AA	033 461 7837	www.hwmur.nl
Holland	Nieuwpoort	De Schapekop	Hoogstraat 30	info@deschapekop.nl	2965 AL	0184-602678	www.deschapekop.nl

ROWAN INTERNET ONLY STOCKIST

All Rowan Internet stockists offer secure online shopping facilities of a wide selection of Rowan products.

AUSTRALIA

Wool Shack	www.woolshack.com

CANADA

The Needle Emporium	www.needleemporium.com

FRANCE

Bleu de Toile	www.bleudetoiles.com
Pretty Laine	www.prettylaine.com

GERMANY

umGarnt	www.umgarnt.de
Wolle Design	www.wolleunddesign.de

ITALY

Hobby Donna	www.hobbydonna.it

JAPAN

Rowan-Jaeger	www.rowan-jaeger.com

NEW ZEALAND

Knit World Mail Order	www.knitworldstudio.co.nz

UK

A Bit Woolly	www.abitwoolly.co.uk
Art of Yarn	www.artofyarn.co.uk
Colourway	www.colourway.co.uk
Craft Supplies Store	www.knitting-supplies-store.co.uk
Deramores	www.deramores.com
Get Knitted	www.getknitted.com
Irene J Noad	www.jannettesrareyarns.co.uk
Knits in the City	www.knitsinthecity.co.uk
Knitters Needs	www.knittersneeds.co.uk
Laughing Hens	www.laughinghens.com
Peachey Ethknits	www.ethknits.co.uk
Rucraft @ The hobby Warehouse	www.rucraft.co.uk
Sandcastle Yarns	www.sandcastleyarns.co.uk
Serenity Knitting	www.serenityknitting.co.uk
The Knitting Shop	www.theknittingshop.co.uk
The London Wool Company	www.londonwools.com
Twist	www.twistshop.co.uk
Wee County Yarns	www.wee-county-yarns.co.uk
Wight Yarns	www.wightyarns.webeden.co.uk
Wool and Buttons	www.woolandbutton.co.uk
Wool Warehouse direct Ltd	www.woolwarehouse.co.uk

USA

Fabric.com	www.fabric.com
Colorful Stitches	www.colorful-stitches.com
Webs	www.yarn.com
Royal Yarns	www.royalyarns.com
Jimmy Beans Wool	www.jimmybeanswool.com
Hampton Knitting Yarn	www.hamptonknittingyarn.com
Yarnmarket	www.yarnmarket.com
The Web-sters	www.yarnwebsters.com
Skein Scene	www.skeinscene.com
Got Yarn	www.gotyarn.com

FABRICS UK

Antique Angel Ltd	www.antiqueangel.co.uk
Backstitch	www.backstitch.co.uk
Brenda Higgs LTD	
Celtic Fusion Crafts	www.celticfusionfabrics.com
Crafsty	www.crafsty.com
Dragonfly Fabrics	www.dragonflyfabrics.co.uk
Eclectic Maker	www.eclecticmaker.co.uk
Fiber Wild	www.fiberwild.com
Gone To Earth	www.gonetoearth.co.uk
Great British Yarns	www.greatbritishyarns.co.uk
Keepsake Quilting	www.keepsakequiliting.com
M is for Make	www.misformake.co.uk
Miss Gingers	missgingermakes.blogspot.com
Nerybeth Crafts	www.nerybethcrafts.co.uk
Quilters Cloth	www.quilterscloth.co.uk
Rucraft @ The hobby Warehouse	www.rucraft.co.uk
Saints and Pinners	www.saintsandpinners.co.uk
Seamstar	www.seamstar.co.uk
Twist	www.twistshop.co.uk

ROWAN YARNS, GREEN LANE MILL, HOLMFIRTH, WEST YORKSHIRE, ENGLAND TEL: +44 (0)1484 681881

THE DESIGN GALLERY

GLORIOUS

SANTORINI
Purelife Revive & Wool Cotton
Marie Wallin
Pattern page 104
Main image page 4, 6 & 7

SYMI WRAP
Fine Lace & Kidsilk Haze
Vibe Ulrik
Pattern page 89
Main image page 8, 9, 10 & 11

HYDRA
Siena 4ply
Martin Storey
Pattern page 92
Main image page 12 &13

KOS
Siena 4ply
Marie Wallin
Pattern page 98
Main image page 14 & 15

CRETE
Wool Cotton 4ply
Martin Storey
Pattern page 106
Main image page 16 & 17

CORFU
Purelife Revive, Wool Cotton & Wool Cotton 4ply
Kaffe Fassett
Pattern page 107
Main image page 18 & 19

ARTEMIS
Purelife Revive & Kidsilk Haze
Lisa Richardson
Pattern page 90
Main image page 20 & 21

RHODES
Fine Lace & Kidsilk Haze
Lisa Richardson
Pattern page 100
Main image page 22 & 23

IKON

CARNABY
Siena 4ply
Martin Storey
Pattern page 118
Main image page 34, 36 & 37

HIP
Panama, Siena 4ply & Kidsilk Haze
Lisa Richardson
Pattern page 110
Main image page 38 & 39

VIDAL
Creative Linen
Josh Bennett
Pattern page 141
Main image page 40 & 41

PIERRE
Handknit Cotton
Marie Wallin
Pattern page 125
Main image page 42 & 43

MOD
Handknit Cotton
Ruth Green
Pattern page 126
Main image page 42 & 43

BONNIE
Creative Linen
Marie Wallin
Pattern page 94
Main image page 44 & 45

PIXIE
Kidsilk Haze & Siena 4ply
Kaffe Fassett
Pattern page 122
Main image page 46 & 47

LAMBRETTA
Summerspun & Wool Cotton
Brandon Mably
Pattern page 120
Main image page 48 & 49

ESSENTIALS

MARSHMALLOW
Kidsilk Haze & Handknit Cotton
Julia Frank
Pattern page 140
Main image page 65 & 66

AMARETTO
Panama
Lisa Richardson
Pattern page 130
Main image page 67

BANOFFI
Panama & Siena 4ply
Lisa Richardson
Pattern page 134
Main image page 68

PRALINE
Summerspun
Lisa Richardson
Pattern page 139
Main image page 69

RUM & RAISIN
Panama
Amanda Crawford
Pattern page 131
Main image page 70

BUBBLEGUM
Panama
Marie Wallin
Pattern page 135
Main image page 71

COOKIES & CREAM
Creative Linen
Ruth Green
Pattern page 137
Main image page 72

HONEYCOMB
Handknit Cotton
Ruth Green
Pattern page 132
Main image page 73